SOUTHERN SCOUNDRELS

SOUTHERN SCOUNDRELS

Grifters and Graft in the Nineteenth Century

EDITED BY

Jeff Forret and Bruce E. Baker

LOUISIANA STATE UNIVERSITY PRESS

BATON ROUGE

Published by Louisiana State University Press
www.lsupress.org

Manufactured in the United States of America
First printing

DESIGNER: Michelle A. Neustrom
TYPEFACE: Whitman

Cover illustration courtesy *Harper's Weekly*.

Jeff Forret's essay "'How Deeply They *Weed* into the Pockets':
Slave Traders, Bank Speculators, and the Anatomy of a Chesapeake
Wildcat, 1840–1843" first appeared in *Journal of the Early Republic* 39
(Winter 2019): 709–736, and is reprinted here with permission.

LIBRARY OF CONGRESS CATALOGING-IN-PUBLICATION DATA

Names: Forret, Jeff, 1972– editor. | Baker, Bruce E., 1971– editor.
Title: Southern scoundrels : grifters and graft in the nineteenth century / edited by
    Jeff Forret and Bruce E. Baker.
Description: Baton Rouge : Louisiana State University Press, [2021] | Includes
    bibliographical references and index.
Identifiers: LCCN 2020034798 (print) | LCCN 2020034799 (ebook) | ISBN 978-
    0-8071-7219-3 (cloth) | ISBN 978-0-8071-7533-0 (pdf) | ISBN 978-0-8071-7534-7
    (epub)
Subjects: LCSH: Swindlers and swindling—Southern States—History—19th century.
    | Capitalism—Southern States—History—19th century. | Southern States—
    Economic conditions—19th century.
Classification: LCC HV6698.S67 S68 2021 (print) | LCC HV6698.S67 (ebook) |
    DDC 364.16/3097509034—dc23
LC record available at https://lccn.loc.gov/2020034798
LC ebook record available at https://lccn.loc.gov/2020034799

CONTENTS

SOUTHERN SCOUNDRELS

Introduction

JEFF FORRET AND BRUCE E. BAKER

I n 1821, two brothers slunk into Knoxville, Tennessee, where their luck ran out. George and James Welch, alias Goforth, alias Loyd, had arrived from Georgia, where each had reportedly "*borrowed* . . . a horse with saddle and bridle, which they forgot . . . to return." But the siblings were not merely horse thieves. Their criminality also extended to rudimentary counterfeiting operations. Unfortunately for them, their specious notes "were not quite well enough executed . . . to pass . . . *without suspicion*." One brother, upon his arrest "for attempting to pass counterfeit money," was found to have "[a] number of the most base counterfeits on different banks . . . in his possession." A local magistrate committed the "scoundrel" to jail to await trial. Just days later, when two gentlemen from Georgia arrived in Knoxville in pursuit of their purloined horses, town constables rooted out the other brother, still lurking in the vicinity. Upon his apprehension, he, too, was confined to jail, to share a cell with his sibling. As soon as the first brother's trial concluded on the counterfeiting charge, a local newspaper reported, "One or both of them will be taken to Georgia to be tried for horse stealing."[1]

The Knoxville paper declared the Welch/Goforth/Loyd brothers "scoundrels," although unlike this pair of horse thieves and counterfeiters, not all scoundrels in the nineteenth-century South were necessarily criminals. The region was brimming with clever individuals who pursued the main chance, took risks, wheeled and dealed, shifted identities, ran cons, and exploited cracks in the constantly evolving capitalist system. Economically, some were well-heeled, others poor, but all were ambitious. Some swooped in from the North; others were native. Whatever their origins, these were the men—and they were usually men—whose day-to-day economic activities proved crucial to capitalism's transactions and transformations. Capitalism incentivizes innovation, but this positive structural feature is also among its greatest faults. In unregulated, lightly regulated, or underregulated capitalist systems like those of the nineteenth century, opportunities abounded for shady, unscrupulous characters to devise various stratagems to sabotage the economy for selfish purposes while defrauding the masses. Their behaviors in these circumstances were not necessarily illegal but nonetheless unethical. This anthology sets off on a quest to resurrect these scoundrels and grifters who manipulated for personal gain the peculiarly southern capitalist economy of the nineteenth century.[2]

One of capitalism's distinctive features in the region was its connection to slavery, which figures prominently in the essays by Alexandra J. Finley, Jeff Forret, and Maria R. Montalvo. Each of their contributions focuses less on the quantifiable effects of enslaved people as laborers and property and more on the ways that slavery as a social and political system shaped the daily interactions at the heart of what capitalism looked like in practice. Whereas Montalvo examines the subject of fraud and deception in the slave market, Finley and Forret study slave traders' relationship to the antebellum southern banking industry. Despite proslavery apologists' ubiquitous proclamations of slave dealers as disreputable and peripheral to business enterprise in the Old South, they were in fact financially savvy experts in currency and important conveyors of the multifarious bank notes circulating in antebellum America. The wide distribution of some southern institutions' notes propped them up for longer periods of time than if their issue had circulated closer to home, where it could be more readily redeemed. Taken together, these three essays point out the important role of the slave trader in guiding the development of southern capitalism.

The violence that lay at the heart of slavery was itself another recognizable characteristic of southern capitalism. This is not to say that violence was not important to capitalist development elsewhere, as the bloody history of labor clashes reminds us, but that the distinctive character of violence in the South pervades the form that capitalism took there. How could it not? To the extent that we conceive of capitalism as defined by the market and the market as involving actors entering into contracts freely, then violence has no explanatory power. It is an aberration that distorts the market, and in a state that has a monopoly on the legitimate use of force, it is only economically effective around the margins of the economy until it is rooted out. This model might work well enough in some times and places, particularly the United States in the middle of the twentieth century. For the American South in the nineteenth century, however, it is thoroughly inadequate. Slavery was a system predicated on violence, and as scholars such as Jeff Forret, Keri Leigh Merritt, and others have reminded us, this violence was directed at poor whites as well as enslaved people. It follows naturally that violence was one among many tools used to advance people's economic interests and must be considered an integral part of how capitalism functioned in the South.[3]

Some individuals in the nineteenth-century South made a viable career of violence. Elaine S. Frantz usefully describes these figures as "violence workers," and in her essay here, William Faucett can be considered in that category. For him, violence that was explicitly economic, rooted in property disputes, the bootlegging trade, control over women's domestic and sexual labor, or over African American labor, existed on a broader continuum of violence. A more clear-cut example is Alfred W. Burnett and the men he employed to work for corporations in Appalachia, as discussed by T. R. C. Hutton. The "rough men bred in the violent, depredated postbellum years who rejected yeomanry and regular wage labor in favor of a mercenary career" were crucial to the smooth running of the extractive industry that dominated this part of the South in the late nineteenth and early twentieth centuries, and these men were workers, integrated tightly into the economic order, every bit as much as the men who worked underground to bring the coal out.

If slavery and violence laid a foundation for the forms of capitalism under development in the studies here, questions of identity and presentation of self also run through the essays in this collection. In an era with fairly limited state or institutional capacities to settle these sorts of questions decisively, the field was open to men to present themselves however they liked to whomever they could convince. As Karen Halttunen explained, "In what was believed to be a fluid social world where no one occupied a fixed social position, the question, 'Who am I?' loomed large."[4] It was a question that people asked themselves in the nineteenth-century South, but they also asked others, "Are you who you say you are?" Several of the essays presented here, including those by John Lindbeck and Jimmy L. Bryan, Jr., feature individuals whose masquerades allowed them to con people who lacked sufficient knowledge to assess them accurately. Controlling the flow of information and, conversely, what remained hidden facilitated the work of the scoundrel, a point that Maria R. Montalvo makes clear in her examination of slave trader Bernard Kendig.[5]

In the context of the Civil War, the fraudulent presentation of self was tied to the fraught and fluid question of loyalty, and the question, "Are you who you say you are?" morphed into, "Are you who we say you are supposed to be?" Jeff Strickland and Rodney J. Steward confront this dynamic in their respective essays on confiscation and sequestration in the wartime South. Over the course of the nineteenth century, institutions and practices arose to determine and fix the identities of people and businesses—at least the ones that operated within the more stable parts of the economy. The Mercantile Agency, later R. G. Dun and Company, used a vast network of correspondents and field agents to compile and circulate information on merchants as a means of determining their creditworthiness.[6] At the other end of the economy, police increasingly used photography to compile rogues galleries for the purpose of identifying habitual criminals.[7] By the early twentieth century, state governments would begin to build systems of records of individuals.[8] But until then, fraudsters could circulate freely, making and remaking themselves as circumstances warranted.

Our emphasis on scoundrels and grifters reflects a conscious choice about the best approach to take when studying nineteenth-century southern capitalism. We could have taken one of two directions. What we might call the purist approach assumes that there is some sort of ideal form of capitalism and that by starting with a clear idea of what that is, from a theoretical perspective, we can catch sight of how it worked in particular cases, drawing examples of this pure capitalism out of the muddy reality of experience. In such an approach, the false starts, the errors, and the corruptions are secondary to the shining thing itself. We prefer to view southern capitalism more broadly, less tied to an ideology about perfectible and pure markets, if we are to truly understand it. As rank empiricists, we prefer to look at the cases and find a way of discussing them that keeps as much of the specificity as possible, in the belief that the devil, and quite possibly a more interesting sort of truth, is in the detail. With such an approach, scoundrels and grifters of the sort the authors in this volume consider are excellent guides, showing the many ways that capitalism actually worked in real life and not just in theory. As the great poet (and, perhaps, nascent social historian) Leonard Cohen almost wrote, "There is a crack in everything, that is how the historians get in." The scoundrels placed under the microscope here managed to find the many cracks in the jury-rigged structures of capitalism as it existed in the nineteenth-century South, and they squeezed through, often widening those cracks into crevasses, permitting light to shine in.[9]

They oftentimes maneuvered outside the formal markets vital to neoclassical economics. Alongside the more traditional economic channels present in the nineteenth-century United States lurked an underground economy, one that, in the Old South, often involved enslaved people who sold or bartered stolen goods in clandestine networks of exchange that included fellow blacks as well as poor whites who lacked scruples against participating in unlawful market activity. Although many of the scoundrels described in this volume navigated the legitimate economy and were crucial to its operation, they equally flourished in this vigorous underground economy. Despite not always following capitalism's central rule to respect private property, they still distributed goods, drove investment, and set prices, as Bruce E. Baker's essay on pilfered goods in New Orleans demonstrates. Whether through the licit or illicit economy, the historical actors featured in this volume were shrewd enough to comprehend the opportunities available to them and savvy enough to seize the main chance and manipulate the system to work in their favor.[10]

Some historians have examined similar kinds of scoundrels as outliers within systems that were fundamentally sound. Even in so high-minded an organization as the Noble and Holy Order of the Knights of Labor, "'swindlers' and 'mercenaries' abounded."[11] Ian Klaus, in *Forging Capitalism*, argues that trust underpinned capitalism, and fraud tended to provoke the creation of new mechanisms of trust since "free enterprise works, some economists argue, because most people obey the rules."[12] We are not entirely convinced, at least with regard to the South in the nineteenth century, that Klaus has things the right way around. What we suggest here takes a bolder position: These scoundrels were not bad apples in a good barrel. The stories we recount here were not outside the true nature of capitalism in the nineteenth-century South but, to the contrary, wholly integral to it.[13]

Historians concerned with the development of capitalism in the United States have long suggested that there was no such thing as capitalism in the South until long after slavery ended, at which time the region embraced, in a lethargic, southern sort of way, the same form of capitalism found in the rest of the country. The vigorous debate among historians in the 1970s and 1980s over the rural transition to capitalism almost wholly neglected the South. Scholars instead concentrated their energies on New England or the mid-Atlantic as they struggled to determine if early Americans became capitalists over time or if they possessed capitalist impulses from the beginnings of settlement. Similarly, starting in the 1990s, research on the "market revolution" privileged developments in the North. The South boasted too little industry and enthusiastically embraced too much slavery to merit much attention in these conversations. And scholars such as Charles Sellers, writing from a Marxist perspective, would argue that a wage labor market is a precondition for capitalism. Since slavery instead operated on the basis of force, violence, and the lash, capitalist labor relations could not with propriety be said to have predominated in the region.[14]

Yet the development of capitalism in the United States was not something that occurred elsewhere, entirely outside of the South, and unless one adheres to strictly Marxist definitions of the term, there is nothing demonstrably antithetical about the relationship between capitalism and slavery. Countering Eugene Genovese's understanding of slaveholders' paternalistic ethos laid out in the mammoth *Roll, Jordan, Roll,* James Oakes argued decades ago that slave owners were acquisitive capitalists striving to get ahead. More recently, ample scholarship within the past several years has not only revealed slavery's compatibility with capitalism but has gone further still to assert the centrality of slavery to the rise of capitalism in the United States. In these studies, the persistent, nagging presence of slavery in the South after 1800 stood not as an impediment but as the very engine of southern—and national—economic growth. Nineteenth-century slavery thrived as an institution in the South, but its economic benefits accrued to the country as a whole in ways that American society is only now beginning to fully comprehend and acknowledge.[15]

The new history of capitalism positions nineteenth-century southern slavery in global context. Enslaved people produced the cotton and other commodities that fueled transatlantic trade and American economic growth. But while this set of scholarship has traced the broad macroeconomic outlines of U.S. capitalist development, it has been less useful in chronicling the advance of capitalism on the ground, from a more microeconomic perspective. What is needed now are bottom-up social histories of the obscure actors who enabled "capitalist transformation" at the local level. One such volume already succeeds admirably in chronicling how "ordinary people, through their varied struggles to survive and succeed, created capitalism as much as captains of commerce and industry did," but it focuses overwhelmingly on the North.[16]

Given its unique history, the South deserves a separate anthology unto itself. The region's much longer and deeper commitment to slavery, its intense struggles on the home front during the Civil War, and the turmoil it witnessed during Reconstruction and its aftermath all supplied opportunities for economically shrewd and calculating individuals to shape the course of capitalist development. After the Civil War swept away slavery as a lawful institution except as a punishment for crime, it became clear that the South's agricultural economy was becoming bound up by lines of credit reaching through the crossroads store back to Wall Street. With the sudden expansion of industry, moreover, the New South decisively entered the capitalist mainstream of the nation. That transition generated a wealth of historiography in the 1970s and 1980s, largely focused on the effects of emancipation on the reconfiguration of labor and the plantation as a productive unit.[17] Around the same time, a more limited body of scholarship discussed how the Civil War and emancipation affected commerce and finance across the region.[18] For all this, though, we lack an account of how capitalism developed in the South to match the works we have on the North.[19] Chronologically, then, this volume spans the duration of the nineteenth century, as it traverses a geographical circuit around the South, from the Chesapeake, to South Carolina, to the Lower Mississippi River Valley, to Texas, north to Missouri, and ending in Appalachia. Across the region, a panoply of charlatans and unseemly characters, perhaps masquerading under the guise of respectability, engaged in sketchy business practices that probed capitalism's dark underside.

Just as we suggest that slavery and violence shaped a peculiarly southern form of capitalism, the same factors, and others, shaped a distinctively southern form of swindling. If the archetypal figure pushing the boundaries of northern capitalism was either the shrewd Yankee peddler or the Wall Street banker of the "moneyed metropolis" of New York, the South was heir to a long tradition of tricksters, coming out of both African and backcountry folk traditions.[20] The African American tricksters emerging from animal tales such as those featuring Br'er Rabbit were "weak, relatively powerless creatures who attain their ends through the application of native wit and guile rather than power and authority," though their victims were as likely to include the weak as the strong.[21] In a place and time when the mechanisms of capitalism were developing in the form of banks and large-scale corporations such as railroads, the southern scoundrels we describe in this volume should be seen in this context: as the functionaries of an emerging capitalist order rather than its masters; as scrappers who used their wits and ruthlessness to make their way from a position of weakness, all too ready to exploit the vulnerable as well as the powerful. Yet for all their potential to cause damage and loss, they should also be considered within the "outlaw folk heroic traditions [that] represent the expressive embodiment of a conception of behavior that members of the affected group might adapt to equalize social, economic, or even political conditions in their society."[22]

The scoundrels and grifters under examination here often operated at the margins—even well beyond the margins—of legality, but by exploiting the inexorable march of a powerful new economic order, they were not universally reviled, even by those whom they hoodwinked. In that way, we might consider how they compare to the modern-day heroes of the financial world, whose decisions have wreaked havoc upon millions of lives but who still serve as role models for some.

Notes

1. *Knoxville (Tenn.) Register,* February 13, 1821, italics in original.

2. Economists, economic historians, and others are often critical of scholars who either neglect to define or carelessly articulate precisely what constitutes "capitalism." Certainly the term is a malleable one, devoid of any single, unifying definition agreeable to all, and we do not presume to advance anything so concise or authoritative in this volume. An admittedly incomplete list of capitalism's tendencies might include a number of factors: the production of goods or services for market, where consumers pay to purchase them; acquisitiveness, the pursuit of self-interest, and the accumulation of maximal profit; an emphasis on individual ownership, enterprise, and entrepreneurship; and a willingness to invest capital and resources and to take risks in the quest for economic reward. None of these factors, in isolation, offers *prima facie* evidence or satisfactory proof of capitalism's presence, however. The essays included here are more interested in how the scoundrels and grifters of the nineteenth-century South could make the economy work for them.

3. Jeff Forret, *Race Relations at the Margins: Slaves and Poor Whites in the Antebellum Southern Countryside* (Baton Rouge: Louisiana State University Press, 2006); Keri Leigh Merritt, *Masterless*

Men: Poor Whites and Slavery in the Antebellum South (New York: Cambridge University Press, 2017).

4. Karen Halttunen, *Confidence Men and Painted Women: A Study of Middle-Class Culture in America, 1830–1870* (New Haven, Conn.: Yale University Press, 1982), xv.

5. Richard White, "Information, Markets, and Corruption: Transcontinental Railroads in the Gilded Age," *Journal of American History* 90, no. 1 (June 2003): 19–43.

6. James D. Norris, *R. G. Dun & Co., 1841–1900: The Development of Credit-Reporting in the Nineteenth Century* (Westport, Conn.: Greenwood, 1978).

7. Simon A. Cole, *Suspect Identities: A History of Fingerprinting and Criminal Identification* (Cambridge, Mass.: Harvard University Press, 2001).

8. Susan J. Pearson, "'Age Ought to Be a Fact': The Campaign against Child Labor and the Rise of the Birth Certificate," *Journal of American History* 101, no. 4 (March 2015): 1144–65. This is part of a larger project of states figuring out ways of seeing their populations not simply as undifferentiated masses but as aggregations of distinct, and knowable, individuals, as described in James C. Scott, *Seeing Like a State: How Certain Schemes to Improve the Human Condition Have Failed* (New Haven, Conn.: Yale University Press, 1998).

9. This point underpins Scott Reynolds Nelson, *A Nation of Deadbeats: An Uncommon History of America's Financial Disasters* (New York: Vintage, 2013).

10. Brian P. Luskey and Wendy A. Woloson, eds., *Capitalism by Gaslight: Illuminating the Economy of Nineteenth-Century America* (Philadelphia: University of Pennsylvania Press, 2015); Forret, *Race Relations at the Margins,* chap. 2; Kathleen M. Hilliard, *Masters, Slaves, and Exchange: Power's Purchase in the Old South* (New York: Cambridge University Press, 2014), chap. 4; Merritt, *Masterless Men.*

11. Gregory S. Kealey and Bryan D. Palmer, *Dreaming of What Might Be: The Knights of Labor in Ontario, 1880–1900* (New York: Cambridge University Press, 1982), 176.

12. Ian Klaus, *Forging Capitalism: Rogues, Swindlers, Frauds and the Rise of Modern Finance* (New Haven, Conn.: Yale University Press, 2014), 1–5 (quotation 1–2).

13. Bruce E. Baker has argued that "Capitalists need criminals" because "corruption and crime were diagnostic, finding cracks and weak spots in systems and exploiting them for gain, inspiring those with more power to control and shape those systems to fix the problems, to find more efficient and effective ways to do things" (see Baker, "Fires on Shipboard: Sandbars, Salvage Fraud, and the Cotton Trade in New Orleans in the 1870s," *Journal of Southern History* 86, no. 4 (August 2020): 601–624.

14. Important works that helped launch the extensive scholarship on the rural transition to capitalism debate included James T. Lemon, *The Best Poor Man's Country: A Geographical Study of Early Southeastern Pennsylvania* (Baltimore: Johns Hopkins University Press, 1972); Michael Merrill, "'Cash Is Good to Eat': Self-Sufficiency and Exchange in the Rural Economy of the United States," *Radical History Review* 4 (Winter 1977): 42–71; and James A. Henretta, "Families and Farms: Mentalité in Pre-Industrial America," *William & Mary Quarterly,* 3d ser., 35, no. 1 (January 1978): 3–32. Charles Sellers, *The Market Revolution: Jacksonian America, 1815–1846* (New York: Oxford University Press, 1991) carried the debate forward into a new decade in grand, sweeping

strokes. Sven Beckert and Christine Desan, introduction to *American Capitalism: New Histories,* ed. Beckert and Desan (New York: Columbia University Press, 2018), 4–5.

15. Eugene D. Genovese, *Roll, Jordan, Roll: The World the Slaves Made* (New York: Vintage, 1976); James Oakes, *The Ruling Race: A History of American Slaveholders* (New York: Norton, 1982); Walter Johnson, *River of Dark Dreams: Slavery and Empire in the Cotton Kingdom* (Cambridge: Belknap Press of Harvard University Press, 2013); Edward E. Baptist, *The Half Has Never Been Told: Slavery and the Making of American Capitalism* (New York: Basic, 2014); Sven Beckert, *Empire of Cotton: A Global History* (New York: Vintage, 2015); Calvin Schermerhorn, *The Business of Slavery and the Rise of American Capitalism, 1815–1860* (New Haven, Conn.: Yale University Press, 2015); Sven Beckert and Seth Rockman, eds., *Slavery's Capitalism* (Philadelphia: University of Pennsylvania Press, 2016).

On the importance of slavery to the insurance and banking industries and in the continuing racial wealth gap, see, for example, Sharon Ann Murphy, "Securing Human Property: Slavery, Life Insurance, and Industrialization in the Upper South," *Journal of the Early Republic* 25 (Winter 2005): 615–52; Bonnie Martin, "Slavery's Invisible Engine: Mortgaging Human Property," *Journal of Southern History* 76 (November 2010): 817–66; and Thomas M. Shapiro, *Toxic Inequality: How America's Wealth Gap Destroys Mobility, Deepens the Racial Divide, & Threatens Our Future* (New York: Basic, 2017). On slavery's significance to American educational, religious, and other institutions, see Craig Steven Wilder, *Ebony and Ivy: Race, Slavery, and the Troubled History of America's Universities* (New York: Bloomsbury, 2013); Jennifer Oast, *Institutional Slavery: Slaveholding Churches, Schools, Colleges, and Businesses in Virginia, 1680–1860* (New York: Cambridge University Press, 2016); and Alfred L. Brophy, *University, Court, and Slave: Pro-Slavery Thought in Southern Colleges and Courts and the Coming of Civil War* (New York: Oxford University Press, 2016). On the history of slave reparations, see Mary Frances Berry, *My Face Is Black Is True: Callie House and the Struggle for Ex-Slave Reparations* (New York: Vintage, 2006); and Ana Lucia Araujo, *Reparations for Slavery and the Slave Trade: A Transnational and Comparative History* (New York: Bloomsbury, 2017).

16. Beckert and Rockman, eds., *Slavery's Capitalism,* 1–2, 5, 12, 27; Luskey and Woloson, eds., *Capitalism by Gaslight,* 2 (quotations), 3.

17. A couple of starting points for this historiography would be Peter A. Coclanis's reflections in "In Retrospect: Ransom and Sutch's 'One Kind of Freedom,'" *Reviews in American History* 28, no. 3 (September 2000): 478–89; the forum around Jonathan M. Wiener, "Class Structure and Economic Development in the American South, 1865–1955," *American Historical Review* 84, no. 4 (October 1979): 970–1006, including the response by Harold D. Woodman; and Joseph P. Reidy, *From Slavery to Agrarian Capitalism in the Cotton Plantation South: Central Georgia, 1800–1880* (Chapel Hill: University of North Carolina Press, 1992).

18. Harold D. Woodman, "Postbellum Social Change and Its Effects on Marketing the South's Cotton Crop," *Agricultural History* 56, no. 1 (January 1982): 215–30; Larry Schweikart, *Banking in the American South from the Age of Jackson to Reconstruction* (Baton Rouge: Louisiana State University Press, 1987).

19. Sven Beckert, *The Monied Metropolis: New York City and the Consolidation of the American Bourgeoisie, 1850–1896* (New York: Cambridge University Press, 2001).

20. Johannes Dietrich Bergmann, "The Original Confidence Man," *American Quarterly* 21, no. 3 (Autumn 1969): 560–77; Lawrence W. Levine, *Black Culture and Black Consciousness: Afro-American Folk Thought from Slavery to Freedom* (New York: Oxford University Press, 1977), 101–33; Winifred Morgan, *The Trickster Figure in American Literature* (New York: Palgrave Macmillan, 2013), 73–101.

21. Levine, *Black Culture and Black Consciousness,* 103 (quotation), 108.

22. John W. Roberts, *From Trickster to Badman: The Black Folk Hero in Slavery and Freedom* (Philadelphia: University of Pennsylvania Press, 1989), 6.

Preachers and Peddlers

CREDIT AND BELIEF IN THE FLUSH TIMES

JOHN LINDBECK

Sometime in the early 1830s, a tall and garrulous young man, dressed in a plain black cloak and a broad black hat, rode across the Elk River in Middle Tennessee to keep an appointment he had made. He was an itinerant minister, visiting "Brother Nobs," whom he had met a year earlier while preaching in the neighborhood. When Nobs and his family offered the clergyman supper, he was "lengthy in his supplications at table," and his sermons made "all around" think "he was just going to open the windows of heaven, and select its richest blessings for brother Nobs." He also discussed with Nobs his farm and slaves in south Alabama and his struggle to find a humane overseer. Nobs "drank it all down." When morning came, Nobs refused the minister's payment for the night's lodging, but the itinerant asked if he would at least make change for his twenty-dollar bill. Additionally, he decided he would buy a mule from Nobs for $250 and pay him at the next camp meeting. Brother Nobs did not know as he watched this eloquent minister ride away on his circuit that he would never see him again. No doubt he must have been upset to find out that the twenty-dollar bill the preacher gave him was a counterfeit note. The itinerant proceeded in a long circuit throughout the South; made connections with men he called "speculators," with whom he "scattered some United States' paper"; robbed a few men; and "preached some d——d fine sermons." He stole horses and slaves with his wide-reaching band of confederates, dubbed the "mystic clan." While plotting a mass slave insurrection in 1834, he was finally captured and arrested by Virgil Stewart and became infamous throughout the country as John Murrell, the "Western Land Pirate."[1]

Though Stewart's account of Murrell is factually dubious in parts, the religious element that recurs throughout it sheds light on the significant connections between religion and the Lower Mississippi River Valley's anxiety-filled flush times. Joshua Rothman has discussed the Murrell story as part of a larger analysis of slavery and capitalism in the antebellum Southwest, and although Rothman mentions Murrell's disguise as a Methodist minister in passing, he minimizes the importance of religion and preachers in the 1830s Southwest. By claiming there were no "permanent ministers" in Vicksburg, Mississippi, in the early 1830s, he dismisses the long history of Methodist and Baptist preachers in the area and misunderstands how evangelical denominations functioned in antebellum society. Just among Methodists in Vicksburg at the time of Murrell's arrest, for instance, there was a presiding elder of Yazoo District in Vicksburg, Rev. John Lane, with Rev. Robert D. Smith preaching in Vicksburg, and Rev. Charles Kimball Marshall in the Warren County circuit outside of town. This is beyond the fact that Vicksburg was settled by Methodist minister Newit Vick and the extended Vick and Cook families of Methodists.[2]

But even more important than Rothman's omission of religion from his Murrell analysis is his misunderstanding—shared by other recent historians of slavery and capitalism—of the centrality of ministers and churches for the commercial success of the antebellum Lower Mississippi Valley. As Jimmy L. Bryan, Jr., points out later in this volume, credit networks in antebellum America relied primarily on personal relationships with trusted business partners. And while other contributors show that wildcat bankers and slave traders were instrumental in the development of antebellum southern capitalism, the system could only work if those planters, wholesale merchants, bankers, and slave traders could trust the individuals with whom they did business. Churches and preachers filled the need for that trust. Ministers—especially itinerant preachers who made personal contacts around the South—facilitated financial transactions, ensured the reliability of faraway planters and businessmen, and provided an overarching belief in the economic system of the South under God's providence. But if ministers were instrumental for economic success, then the prospect of frauds such as Murrell, who posed as preachers for their own nefarious reasons, had the potential to terrify the region.[3]

The commercial boom in 1830s Mississippi, which evangelical ministers helped create, depended on overlapping webs of credit. The white population of Mississippi doubled from 1830 to 1836, and capital-intensive plantations in which enslaved African Americans outnumbered whites by a substantial margin dominated many of the newly settled areas in central Mississippi. There, the cotton frontier filled with fortune seekers eager to borrow on credit to acquire land and slaves. But the fortunes of these speculators were tied to unknown white neighbors, distant merchants, newly bought and mortgaged enslaved people, and, of course, roving peddlers and preachers who attempted to "civilize" the countryside by selling products and belief. Quite suddenly the region had become a society built on credit.[4]

But credit was not just—or even predominantly—about the actual lending of money; instead, antebellum Americans tied credit to faith and religion in a more holistic web than twentieth- and twenty-first-century Americans have done. If Noah Webster's 1828 American dictionary is to be taken as an accurate reflection of American English at the time, Webster's primary definition of credit was "belief; faith." As an example, Webster wrote, "We give *credit* to a man's declaration, when the mind rests on the truth of it, without doubt or suspicion, which is attended with wavering." For its etymology, "See Creed," Webster wrote. After other definitions of credit revolving around "reputation," "honor," "confidence," and "character," Webster finally reached the topic of business with his sixth definition: "In *commerce,* trust; transfer of goods in confidence of future payment."[5] For Americans of the period, the credit on which planters, shopkeepers, and merchants depended was intimately bound to faith, trustworthiness, honor, confidence, and character—values that they associated with religion and respectability.

Under the surface of this belief-fueled boom period, however, was the pervasive fear of counterfeit preachers. The Cotton Kingdom relied on a culture of credit—a network of beliefs that the price of cotton would not plummet, that paper money and stock in railroad banks would retain its value, that enslaved people were docile and would not rebel, and ultimately that God bound the entire system together. The many links in this economic chain had the potential to cause intense anxiety, so evangelical ministers in the Lower Mississippi Valley were welcome symbols of trustworthiness. Additionally, without a modern credit reporting system, ministers were frequently the informal credit reporting agents, men who knew the reliable and creditworthy planters and businessmen of the cities and countryside alike. Methodist ministers, in particular, proved the most instrumental of all evangelicals in facilitating the expansion of the Cotton Kingdom's credit networks. Their peculiar system of itinerant ministers allowed them to link distant planters and merchants more effectively than the more immobile Presbyterians and Baptists. Methodists also tended to be in more frequent contact with the middling slaveholders and farmers who fueled the cotton boom.

Yet because of their assumed position of respectability and authority, itinerant ministers—especially Methodists—often stoked the underlying anxieties of such a new and precarious society. Although there is only a handful of actual reports of counterfeit preachers, the trope of the swindler itinerant was a potent symbol for a society with no roots and paper money with no specie. If the only symbol of stability, respectability, and divine providence was a fraud, too, then nobody could be believed, and the whole system of credit would collapse. Lurking under the frenzied optimism of white newcomers to the Cotton Kingdom was a sense that they were building a house on a foundation of sand. When the rain finally descended and the winds blew, it might all crumble at once. In this tumultuous environment, with its wild swings between bullish excitement and desperation, a few ministers could capitalize on the need for faith and respectable authorities and in the process become minor religious celebrities. One such minister was John Maffitt, a famous revivalist of the 1830s Southwest, who was also frequently condemned as a fraud and an impostor. Historians of southern evangelism have mostly ignored Maffitt, only occasionally placing him in the context of the Methodist Church's growing respectability and acceptance of wealth. But Maffitt's true significance lies in the intense confidence he inspired among southern Christians, in both God and himself, as well as in the anxiety and suspicion he aroused. Although Maffitt and other preachers like him were often under the microscope of an anxious public, they proved that belief in God's providence, which sanctified the social and economic system of the South, might run into periods of doubt, but faith in Christ and his evangelists would ultimately prevail.

Credit and the Economics of the Cotton Kingdom

The cultural concepts of credit in the Lower Mississippi Valley, whether of faith or reputation, coincided with a perfect storm of material economic factors. First among these factors was the cheap and abundant land offered for sale with the removal of Choctaw and Chickasaw claims to sovereignty. The Land

Office in Washington, D.C., sent surveyors out to "civilize" the wilderness, crisscrossing the varied landscape with imaginary lines forming 640-acre sections and quarter-sections of 160-acre plots.[6] Newly surveyed land could then be sold to white farmers and planters. Hinds County, Mississippi, sprouted from the lands seized from the Choctaw Nation to count 8,645 inhabitants in 1830, among whom 3,212 were enslaved. By 1836 the central and northern portions of Mississippi had filled up so much that the total state population had doubled since 1830.[7] Initially the surveyed plots were sold at $1.25 per acre, but the demand for more fertile land to produce cotton pushed the price much higher. Speculators bought up whole swaths of land during the cotton boom of the 1830s, making it feasible for investors to make quick 100 percent returns on land they had never seen.[8]

The second economic factor in the southwestern boom was the price of cotton. From 1830 to 1834, New Orleans cotton prices increased by more than 80 percent, from 8.4 cents per pound to 15.5 cents per pound, as foreign manufacturers craved more of the crop that was increasingly monopolized by American planters. With soaring cotton prices and newly opened fertile land, a frenzy of speculators and more modest men-on-the-make swooped into the land offices. The federal government sold more than one million acres of land in 1833 and nearly three million acres in 1835. Land booms had occurred in America before, but never on this scale, and never at such a fever pitch.[9]

To purchase this land, however, buyers needed capital, and the lack of hard specie—gold and silver—in the Southwest made this a difficult task. The pre-1830 banking infrastructure was not capable of lending sufficient funds for these purchases, so state legislatures stepped in to fill the need. The State of Louisiana led the way with some of the more innovative financial tools of the era, building from an older concept of land banks but allowing planters to put up not just land but personal property, including enslaved people, as collateral to buy bank stock and secure loans. The State of Louisiana then issued bonds, sold them to investors in New York and England, and used the revenue from the bond sales to capitalize the bank. The plan began small in 1827 with the Consolidated Association of the Planters of Louisiana, a bank with $2 million of capital reserves. Quickly the demand for land and cotton set off a frenzy of bank chartering, note issuing, and lending as Louisiana chartered the Union Bank in 1832 with $7 million in capital and the Citizens' Bank the following year with $12 million in capital. But Mississippi, late to the banking game, upped the ante with the most highly capitalized bank in the region, the Union Bank of Mississippi, chartered in 1838 for $15.5 million in stock, with the State of Mississippi underwriting the loans. Within a period of eight years, the total value of loans issued in Mississippi jumped from about $1 million to more than $15 million.[10]

Planters' banks based on securities in slaves and property were one method of obtaining capital, but another was the creation of infrastructure projects and what were known as "railroad banks." Mississippians and Louisianans proposed a flurry of new railroads in the 1830s, hoping to connect the interior of their states to river and sea ports. To raise the capital, agents for these nascent corporations collected subscriptions from investors throughout the region. But many of the railroad corporations that arose in this period, such as the Vicksburg and Jackson Railroad, were not designed primarily to improve the region's infrastructure but to serve as banks. Using the capital raised from investors, they issued paper currency, some of which could then be used with the Planters' Bank and later the Union Banks, which could then issue greater loans based on the value of railroad banknotes.[11] One planter noted in 1835 that "for once, Mississippians have ceased to talk of land, negroes and cotton bales, and have turned their attention *in good earnest*, to the Railroad enterprize."[12]

The largest corporation with the highest hopes was the New Orleans and Nashville Railroad, a grand project designed not only to cut through the heart of Mississippi's cotton frontier but also to link with a proposed railroad from Boston to Nashville via Lynchburg, Virginia.[13] Newspapers reported on the enormous demand for the company's stock that could only be bought for "extravagant rates." The president of the New Orleans and Nashville Railroad gleefully wrote, "Conceive, if you can, of those locomotives, all puffing and snorting, bearing in their train 2360 cars, laden with 10,000 passengers; 40,000 bales cotton." "Is this fiction, is it romance?" he asked rhetorically. No, of course it was "the all-powerful eye of faith, turning aside the impenetrable veil that's suspended at the vestibule of futurity," where dreamers would find that all this was "fully personified by actual fact."[14] With the combined powers of credit and technology, Mississippians confidently asserted that the New Orleans and Nashville Railroad would increase the value of surrounding property and double the region's population, further shoring up the competitiveness of Mississippi planters and removing their dependence on merchants in Natchez.[15]

Dreams of the Lower Mississippi Valley as "the vestibule of futurity" were common in the 1830s, but under the surface lurked unprecedented anxiety. Cotton production in Mississippi had increased enormously from ten million pounds in 1820 to eighty-five million pounds in 1834.[16] Credit from speculators and foreign investors financed this boom in production, but they did so with the calculation that cotton prices would not fall back down to their late-1820s levels. Additionally, residents of the Lower Mississippi Valley realized that the economic system from which they profited was fragile and depended on a series of links in an economic chain. They relied on paper currencies from start-up banks without an established reputation.

Even beyond the value of genuine banknotes, the fear of counterfeit notes was omnipresent. In August 1834, residents of Holmes County, Mississippi, arrested between thirty and forty men suspected of being part of a counterfeiting company from Black Creek, with two operations for manufacturing counterfeit notes in Shawnee Point, Arkansas Territory, and upon the Osage River in Missouri.[17] Just five months later, residents of Woodville, Mississippi, caught a counterfeiter named Jeremiah Terry, who was carrying twenty-one counterfeit notes of one hundred dollars each for the Bank of the United States. He claimed to be an agent for a larger counterfeit company headquartered "somewhere in Arkansas," and he passed counterfeit bills from Florida to Columbus, Mississippi.[18]

But perhaps an even greater anxiety in the Cotton Kingdom concerned the large population of enslaved black men and women. With the memory of Nat Turner's recent rebellion in Virginia, and even before the suspected slave insurrection plot in Madison County, Mississippi, in 1835, planters in newly settled areas were fearful of the enslaved people they had recently bought. In 1834, for instance, two enslaved women and one enslaved man were accused of murder and held in the Benton jail in Madison County after their master and mistress became suddenly sick. When the mistress died, and the master's fate was still unknown, enslaved witnesses purportedly claimed that the cooks had steeped the heads of a rattlesnake and a scorpion in their master and mistress's coffee, which caused the fatal illness. Incidences and rumors of incidences like these fostered a hypervigilant environment among white citizens against any suspicious characters.[19]

Itinerant Preachers and Peddlers

To alleviate the economic worries of white Mississippians in the 1830s, evangelical ministers served as central symbols of respectability and faith. If planters had difficulty trusting their cotton factors, a pair of Methodist ministers, John Lane and William Curtiss, stepped in to occupy that role. Curtiss served for many years as a factor and wholesale merchant in New Orleans with members of the prominent Methodist Wailes family in the late 1830s and into the 1840s. Ministers were reliable judges of fellow churchgoers, and some might write letters vouching for a potential business partner's reputation. They also might stand in to mediate slave sales, such as when the prominent minister William Winans connected two fellow Methodists looking to sell and buy a slave. The Cotton Kingdom required the cooperation of numerous people along a vast economic chain, and although these might be faceless individuals for ordinary Mississippians, the trusted authority of ministers served as a common facilitator for these transactions.[20]

But because of their central role in binding together the Cotton Kingdom, preachers, especially the traveling circuit riders who often resembled peddlers, inspired some of the greatest anxieties. Peddlers of various kinds were well known characters in frontier communities, supplying new products for curious residents across the countryside, but their reliability was often suspect. In addition to selling products, peddlers could also be steam doctors (itinerant physicians of a new, untested medicine), book sellers, or gamblers. Such services were a boon to rural communities, providing them with medical help in the absence of a professionally trained doctor or with the latest popular books far from any bookstore. But the combination of their mobility and shifting identities placed them in a liminal space of society. One physician and wealthy slaveholder in Natchez complained in 1836 of the "*heap* of trouble in this country" caused by "freebooters," and especially "landjobbers and slavedealers" who traveled back and forth between the Lower Mississippi Valley and the newly independent Texas.[21] The Methodist circuit riders and Baptist preachers who scattered into the newly settled portions of Mississippi often inspired faith in white settlers and planters, but the fear that they could be counterfeits like Murrell often rose to the surface.

Elijah Skaggs was one of those traveling chameleons who both mirrored and frightened white southerners. Skaggs learned to be a professional gambling cheat—popularly known as a "sharper"—in the backwoods of Kentucky. He traveled to Nashville and toured throughout the Southwest to profit from the faro and monte games he set up. As card games of chance, faro and monte fit well into the cultural milieu of the Lower Mississippi Valley that sought to make a quick fortune. But Skaggs was not an ordinary faro banker. He arrived in towns on horseback, "dressed in a frock-coat and pants of black broadcloth . . . a white shirt with standing collar, and around his neck was wound a white choker, while, resting on his cranium, was a black stove-pipe hat." The combination of his attire and "solemn young face" earned him the nickname the "preaching faro dealer." Dressed as an itinerant minister, Skaggs represented the trickster character type of peripatetic peddlers selling what the people wanted, consciously mixing their belief in God with their belief in economic fortune. He tapped into the popular association between itinerant gamblers, peddlers, and preachers, all potentially helpful but dangerous figures. Skaggs eventually created a large, nationwide criminal enterprise stretching from New York through New Orleans to California, in which "artists"—always "men of genteel appearance"—did the dirty work of conning suckers out of their money, while Skaggs raked in 75 percent of the profits.[22]

While figures like Skaggs, whether gamblers or peddlers, advanced on the Lower Mississippi Valley looking for consumers, regular licensed ministers did the same in search of converts. Particularly in the new territories opened up for white settlement by Choctaw removal, Methodists were among the first to pour into interior cotton-producing areas such as Madison County, Mississippi. Prior to 1828, the Methodist minister John G. Jones described Madison County as having "only a scattered population," but among them was "a fair proportion of Methodist families and local preachers."[23] Baptists also expanded into the region, establishing in Choctaw County, Mississippi, thirty-four churches with one thousand members in just four years between 1830 and 1834.[24] "They had taken possession of the field," the Methodist John G. Jones wrote, which was "already white unto the harvest."[25] Although Jones's biblical reference to fields

"white unto the harvest" was not about cotton, the most apt image for opportunity in the Southwest was indeed a sprawling field of cotton. The minister
William Winans made the same analogy in an 1835 letter to another minister,
describing prospective converts as a "vast field, so white to the harvest."[26] The
southwestern frontier was a land to gain fast wealth through cotton, and circuit
riders could not help but see this particular metaphor as illustrative of their own
intentions of raising up revivals and profiting with "net gains" by saving souls.[27]

But the understanding of fields "already white unto the harvest" was not
merely metaphorical for these religious men, for they invested a great deal of
their own economic interests in the Cotton Kingdom. In his famous narrative
of the Southwest composed after living in Natchez for a few years, Joseph Holt
Ingraham wrote that, like all white Mississippians, ministers participated in
"the universal mania" for cotton planting. He noted that, without the restraints
of stricter customs regarding lavish dress to which northern ministers generally adhered, Mississippi Methodists in particular attracted "many of the afflu-
ent and a majority of the merely independent planters, throughout the state."[28]

The Methodist practice of "locating" became increasingly popular in the
early 1830s as a way for former circuit riders to become permanent residents in
a particular location while remaining a licensed minister who often preached
at a nearby church. The practice of locating allowed ministers to concentrate
more of their efforts on the actual profits of the Cotton Kingdom rather than
on ministering to those who profited. As one example, the minister Orsamus
Nash, who decided to preach locally in Columbus, Mississippi, did so because
he had accumulated a few hundred dollars in debt in 1835 but desired to join
the planter class in east Mississippi. He found opportunity with a land agency
owned by wealthy speculators, but all the while he continued to preach locally.
William Winans was sad to hear that Nash was leaving the itinerancy, but he
believed that if the agency were profitable, and if Nash had "a conscience void
of offense both towards God and towards men," then there could be "nothing objectionable in it."[29] Another Methodist, John Shrock, moved to Madison County being "sanguine of success in worldly matters," but, according to
a contemporary, he became "deeply involved in debt."[30] Every year, as more
ministers joined the regular circuit riders, others left the itinerancy, a lifestyle
that usually kept them from becoming large planters. Instead they preached
locally and tried their hand in the secular affairs of speculating, planting, and

shopkeeping, with seven leaving at the 1835 Mississippi Conference, and four, including Nash, in 1836.[31]

Ministers who located often did so to profit from the cotton mania, but white southerners often regarded local ministers as symbols of stability compared to itinerant ministers, who, like peddlers or gamblers, prompted anxiety about the fragile social order. Foremost among those anxieties was the fear of "counterfeit" preachers. While counterfeiters of banknotes proliferated across the South with operations based in Arkansas Territory, counterfeiters of respectable reverends also were common. Evangelicals had spread throughout the region and gained the confidence of settlers since the early decades of the nineteenth century, so those who posed as itinerants to hide their identity were the worst nightmares for southern whites in frontier counties.

One prominent example was a traveling antimission Baptist preacher who went by the name of William Biddle. Biddle styled himself the nephew of the famous naval commodore James Biddle and roamed throughout much of the country preaching, collecting money, and apparently promising marriage to a variety of young women along the way. A local Baptist minister in Franklin, Louisiana, recalled that, at his church in 1826, Biddle had preached scathing sermons against the greed of large-scale missionary societies for three months, while collecting $300 for his own support. When Biddle departed with a stolen mule, leaving "a poor deluded young woman" still in Franklin, he continued to preach throughout the Lower Mississippi Valley. He reappeared on the radar of religious publications in Copiah County, Mississippi, in early 1837, was exposed for who he was, and next headed for the Pearl River farther in the interior with a $300 bounty on his head.[32]

Due to the prevalence of traveling Methodist circuit riders, southwestern Methodists had problems detecting impostor preachers. In 1833, it came to the attention of the Mississippi Methodist leadership that a preacher in Natchez named Andrew Adams had left a wife in New York without a justifiable cause. To put his former life behind him, he had changed his name from Amos Adams. Even with Adams's prompt dismissal, the fears of impostor preachers who profited from gullible followers plagued the region, especially around Natchez, following Adams's removal.[33]

The story of a fraudulent missionary at an Arkansas tavern on the Mississippi River makes plain the common sentiment of the period. After expressing interest in learning how to play cards, the missionary of "genteel and dignified appearance and manner" gradually won $3,000 from a naïve clerk, showing that all along "he was a thorough-bred gambler on a special mission" to defraud the clerk. "But that sanctimonious face," the clerk wondered, "under the mask of a missionary was a counterfeit." Like counterfeit notes, preachers traveled from town to town under the public's assumption that they were licensed, that their character could be credited as trustworthy. In the flush times of the 1830s, residents of the Lower Mississippi Valley wanted to believe that their preachers were legitimate and that their money was backed by sound currency, but underneath their confidence were the lurking doubts that all around them were frauds.[34]

The story of highly leveraged planters, counterfeit notes, untrustworthy peddlers, and impostor preachers brings us back to the far-reaching phenomenon of John Murrell and his mystic clan. Although Stewart's account of Murrell was probably exaggerated, if not mostly untrue, the pervasiveness of this problem of counterfeit preachers in a bustling frontier society shows why the story took such firm root in the southern white imagination. Impostor preachers were a problem throughout antebellum America, especially in frontier societies in both the North and South, but the additional factors of an enormous cotton bubble and a newly settled society with a majority enslaved population heightened white settlers' anxieties about any unknown traveling men looking to make a buck or raise money for the cause of evangelization. The story of Murrell duping innocent settlers had such powerful purchase in the Southwest, and even across the rest of the South, because the story seemed so plausible and because it played on those fears that were at a fever pitch. The religious element of Murrell's gang was not incidental to the story but a central component in a society searching for stability and a source of firm, unshakeable confidence.

After the arrest of Murrell, the suspected slave insurrection of Madison County in the summer of 1835 set off a firestorm of paranoia throughout the Southwest. When rumors of a slave rebellion began, white residents of this wealthy interior county began pressing slaves for answers, asking for names, and whipping them to elicit information. Not only were slaves suspected, but white residents of the county were also named as co-conspirators. The inquisition began holding sham trials, hanging suspected slave stealers whom they believed to be in league with the Murrell gang, and torturing each suspect to extract more names. By the end of the ordeal, some twenty slaves had been executed, along with a handful of white men.[35]

Although the fears of a slave rebellion were foremost in many white Mississippians' minds in 1835, the southwestern clergy immediately saw the Murrell story and the Madison County slave conspiracy as a threat to themselves. The *Woodville Republican* reported that the two white Madison County men they knew to have been executed, Joshua Cotton and William Saunders, were "both steam doctors and occasionally preachers." The newspaper added that those who were most suspected were roving itinerants of various kinds, including "gamblers, itenerant [sic] preachers, steam doctors, and clock pedlars."[36] These reports threw the Methodist minister William Winans into a frenzy. He wrote his fellow minister in Columbus, Orsamus Nash, to ask if Cotton "was a Methodist Preacher, as the Franklin Republican represents him." Winans believed that these accusations were "to involve the *body* of *Methodist Itinerant* Preachers in suspicion of belonging to the Murrell gang." One local man even "endeavored to fix that suspicion on [fellow Methodist preacher] Brother Cooper personally!" Even as far away as the town of Franklin in the southern Louisiana bayou it had "been attempted to implicate the preachers of the Gospel, and, especially, *Itinerant Methodist Preachers,* in the plots of Murrell and in the mad and mischievous machinations of the Abolitionists."[37]

Only a couple years after the frenzy died down, the South Carolina novelist William Gilmore Simms wrote a fictionalized version of the events that contained many of the central concerns of the 1830s Southwest. Religion was important to the story he told. In Simms's 1838 novel *Richard Hurdis: A Tale of Alabama,* set in the borderlands between Mississippi and Alabama, the primary antagonist leads the "Mystic Brotherhood," a vast conspiracy of criminals and rogues clearly inspired by the Murrell gang. Richard Hurdis, the hero of this particular "border romance" by Simms, receives the same kind of offer to join the Brotherhood that Virgil Stewart received when traveling with Murrell. Importantly, *Richard Hurdis*'s antagonist—who goes by Clement Foster, though Hurdis later finds out he "had twenty other names"—poses as an itinerant minister in all of his journeys. "With the cassock of a sanctified profession, which we no more dare assail now than we did four hundred years ago, he made his way not only at little or no expense, but with great profit." Much like Murrell's preaching to Brother Nobs, Foster prayed at a tavern in Columbus, Mississippi, paying "for his bacon and greens with his eloquence," as no other form of payment was desired.[38]

Simms's ties between itinerant preachers and the Murrell gang played on the common anxieties about preachers in the 1830s, but his descriptions of the Mystic Brotherhood's relationship with the rest of southern society revealed the fragile economic bonds of the cotton frontier. Foster gathered 1,500 men to join his gang, "not professing roguery," but "professing religion, law, physic, planting, shopkeeping." In short, his men were of respectable character. This "fellowship of risk and profits" was "a nice system of cobwebs . . . as snares to catch and enslave the feeble and confiding" whom outsiders could not see. With the vast networks of the Mystic Brotherhood, "crime of all sorts and complexions, seemed reduced to a perfect system, and the hands which ministered seemed to move rather like those of automata than of thinking and resolving men." This system of crime terrified white settlers, but just as pervasive fears of Murrell and slave stealers reflected the anxious underbelly of the Cotton Kingdom's flush times, so, too, did Hurdis's description of the Mystic Brotherhood reflect southern anxieties about their social system. Planters, local merchants, and cotton factors all could seem much more like the hands of "automata" in a vast unseen system than "thinking and resolving men" who had control over their economic destiny. The fields full of enslaved people were reduced to mindless "hands which ministered" on the cotton frontier. Yet white southerners depended on this vast economic network of capital, credit, and news of current prices to propel themselves into unprecedented prosperity. They grasped desperately for something they trusted—a minister or their local church—or they desired to believe in a divine Providence that controlled such a system, but even these institutions, they feared, had become overrun by confidence men looking to turn a quick profit.[39]

"Like Omnipotence on Earth": John Newland Maffitt, the Preaching Entrepreneur

In this fraught environment, some of the more enterprising preachers could hit it big as mass revivalists, instruments of God, and celebrities, but the stakes were high since even the best of preachers came under the suspicious gaze of an anxious public. One individual exemplified this tension between celebrity and anxiety. John Newland Maffitt, an Irish newcomer to the Lower Mississippi Valley in the midst of its antebellum economic boom, created a large following through his published sermons, books, and a memoir, but most of all through his dramatic oratory on the revival circuit. Maffitt reflected the culture of the Lower Mississippi Valley by self-consciously crafting a god he could preach to large audiences, and he received widespread suspicion and resistance as a fraud. Although he does not seem to have defrauded anyone in a strict legal sense, southern evangelicals often saw Maffitt as a silver-tongued swindler, who preached fine-sounding sermons for lucre while living a lecherous private life. From the beginning of his career until his death, accusations of infidelity and impropriety dogged him, and he always seemed to be in the midst of a libel suit against his opponents. But despite all of these obstacles, his popular appeal throughout the country never seemed to falter from controversy. In a culture that thrived on different forms of credit, men like Maffitt who successfully spread belief in God were naturally at the center of these conflicting forces.

Maffitt was an Irishman raised as a Methodist in Dublin, but his career as a preacher began in New England soon after moving to the United States with his young wife in 1819. Within the first few years of his connection with the New York Methodist Conference, Maffitt created a stir as he traveled and preached through New England. At the age of twenty-seven he had already published a memoir of his life titled *Tears of Contrition*. The next year, 1822, accusations swirled that he had told other ministers that he doubted the fundamental doctrines of Christianity, that he secretly mocked those penitents who were converted at his New England revivals, and that he displayed "loose, light and lascivious behaviour" with "certain young ladies."[40] When these accusations were published in the *New England Galaxy*, Maffitt sued the editor for libel but lost in court.[41] Already in the 1820s, pamphlets supporting and opposing Maffitt circulated widely. One anonymous writer called him a "theological swindler," "a notorious impostor" who did not believe what he preached, and a licentious hypocrite, preaching for monetary gain and his own vanity.[42] In 1831, he decided that he would pursue "worldly matters" and left his connection with the New York Conference.[43]

Maffitt's choice for where to pursue such "worldly matters" was telling. In the 1830s, the frontier for gaining easy money and new evangelical converts was in the Southwest. His reputation there began with glowing reports. Sometime early in 1833 he arrived in Louisville, Kentucky, as an anonymous Methodist preacher, but he began a six-week-long revival that resulted in hundreds of conversions. The local minister found that Maffitt was "a splendid man, highly imaginative, rich in metaphor . . . and always eloquent and very theatrical." Even compared to the famous Methodist revivalist Henry Bascom of Kentucky, Maffitt exceeded him as the most "official, and able conductors of revivals."[44] Over the next couple of years, Maffitt toured mostly in the Southwest, making lively appearances in New Orleans, Natchez, and the surrounding areas that had been settled for at least a decade or so. In New Orleans, where the Methodist clergy felt they were "weak handed," Maffitt was described as "a Host of himself" with "the power through God . . . to slay the Soldier in the field of Battle."[45] After a revival in Natchez, Maffitt moved to the small town of Woodville, Mississippi, south of Natchez. Woodville was the county seat of Wilkinson County, home of more than eleven thousand inhabitants, nearly eight thousand of whom were enslaved.[46] Maffitt's enthusiastic preaching made a particular impact on the most respectable of Woodville's sizeable planter class. "The Judge and many Gentlemen of the Bar," Woodville minister William Winans bragged, "were among those who openly bore testimony to the power with which [Maffitt] preached the Cross of Christ."[47]

As Maffitt scorched the earth with his revivalist enthusiasm, he extracted money from those respectable converts, both for local Methodist churches and himself. His preaching in New Orleans helped to raise $3,000 in subscriptions for the erection of a church on Poydras Street. The remaining $10,000 needed for the church was put up as a loan by the wealthy Methodist benefactor Edward McGehee, placing confidence in Maffitt as the new preacher at the Poydras Street church.[48] The *Times-Picayune* called on the rest of the city of New Orleans to be generous to Maffitt and the local Methodist church. "When a spirit of enterprize and adventure is animating every class of citizen," the newspaper wrote, "when the wings of commerce are waxing with every breeze the treasures of our native soil to be exchanged for the luxuries of foreign regions . . . shall the voice of religion be paralyzed and silent?"[49] For himself, various local churches generally allowed Maffitt to give extra lectures on particular topics, such as education, which admitted only paying attendees. Although some expressed concern that Maffitt's converts were prone to backsliding once the excitement calmed down, most reveled in the rapid growth of both converts and money.[50]

To strengthen his presence in the region, Maffitt became co-editor, alongside Lewis Garrett, of a new Nashville-based Methodist newspaper in 1833, the *Western Methodist*. Subscribed to by both the Tennessee and Mississippi Methodist Conferences, the *Western Methodist* gave Maffitt a platform for his sermons, writings, and poems that would become essential to increasing the popularity of his preaching. While he was nominally co-editor of the journal with Garrett, Maffitt was rarely in Nashville for the actual work of editing the paper. Instead, he continued touring through the Southwest, raising money for the *Western Methodist*, acting as official agent for collecting funds to support LaGrange College in northwestern Alabama, and contributing a few articles here and there. In summer 1834, he held a months-long revival in Huntsville, Alabama, reportedly attracting thousands from the likes of drunkards, gamblers, and swearers, in addition to planters and professionals. It was also at that point that Maffitt began to style himself "the Stranger."[51] As Maffitt toured, he often encountered resistance, presumably from people who either had suspicions of a "stranger" for a preacher or who had heard of his dubious past in New England. In one town, he was "calumniated, pelted with rotten eggs and hung in effigy," but he was still apparently able to convert even some of the most hard-hearted who previously had slandered him.[52]

In addition to raising funds and gaining converts, however, Maffitt was able to use the *Western Methodist* as a platform from which he could launch his literary career. In June 1834, articles appeared advertising Maffitt's future publications. Subscriptions were raised for the publication of his *Oratorical Dictionary*, a handbook for "the practical business of public speaking," containing words for the "higher English scholar or the professional gentleman."[53] The paper also published advertisements for Maffitt's future book of poems to be titled *Man*, which later appeared in 1839 under the title *Poems*, alongside a separate book of sermons.[54] After officially separating from Garrett and the *Western Methodist*, Maffitt even began to make a temporary home in Natchez in 1836 to try his hand at his own journal, the *Mississippi Christian Herald*, supported by the Mississippi Methodist Conference. And still Maffitt traveled and preached, giving lectures along the way on various topics, from mechanics, education, and money, to global revolutions. With his reputation for eloquence, revivalist energy, and expertise on a range of subjects, he reached the pinnacle of his public career with a position as chairman of the Department of Elocution and Belles Lettres at LaGrange College in 1837 and finally as chaplain for the U.S. Congress in 1841.[55]

In his sermons, but especially in his more far-reaching lectures, Maffitt touched on subjects that resonated with the southwestern public. At the heart of Maffitt's appeal was his admiration of American—and especially southwestern—society and his elevation of mankind to something like divinity. Maffitt identified the people of the "South West" as "pious specimens of the true American character," "never satisfied with the past—in religion—sentiment—pathos—affection," virtue, and other glowing traits.[56]

In particular, Maffitt was enamored with the region's push for commercial progress through technological innovation. As the spree for chartering banks and railroad corporations was near its peak in 1836, Maffitt spoke in Vicksburg on "The Glory of Mechanism." Mechanism, which Maffitt understood as the material advancements that distinguished different civilizations, was the defining feature of national identity. Yet even more important than perfecting the mechanical arts of society was imitating "the Most High, the mechanist whose work should stand forever." As white Mississippians chartered railroad banks and began to build the infrastructure of the Cotton Kingdom, they were not only manifesting their own peculiar national identity. According to Maffitt, they were building up their collective minds into the divine image.[57]

Maffitt also claimed that the path to divinity was not solely through building up the mind but also through conveying ideas to the masses and transforming public opinion. Maffitt sold his *Oratorical Dictionary* on the basis that "expression in eloquence is . . . an approximation to spirituality." "Man becomes like God," he wrote, "when he can by a word unchain the impulses" of goodness "which ever throbbed in the bosom of humanity."[58] Using the American Revolution as an example, Maffitt wrote that "opinion influences the will of community, and the public will, when aroused to decisive measures is like Omnipotence on earth." To study the leaders of the American Revolution, the Irishman argued, was to see "the great sum or aggregate of human actions" as well as "God behind the smoke of conflict," who "moved the machinery of independence." Maffitt preached a gospel of the innate goodness of mankind, and publicly admired white Americans of the Southwest, comparing their spread of civilization, Christianity, and knowledge to godlike acts. Although the processes of mortgaging land and slaves, selling cotton, buying stock, and trading banknotes constantly tested the boundaries of belief in the Southwest, Maffitt assured listeners that the risks were underwritten by God, who moved the machinery of modern capitalism in the Cotton Kingdom.[59]

As he gained fame and wealth, however, Maffitt encountered resistance by both the clergy and the secular press. Some regarded him as doing more harm than good for the state of Christianity. He might burn a town to the ground with revivals, but critics charged that, afterward, converts went back to their former ways more stubbornly than they did before.[60] Others charged him with deception, that his adjective-laden sermons were a fancy veneer to cover a lack of theological or intellectual knowledge. "You think at one moment that you discover a substance," wrote one critic, "grasp at it, and lo! 'tis moonshine."[61] One newspaper editor witnessed a Maffitt lecture in Louisville and remarked that, "save in the way of hyperbole and awkward, mixed metaphors, festooned with no small amount of floridity," the speech "was quite common-place."[62]

Beyond theological vacuity, Maffitt also confronted consistent allegations of sexual impropriety with women throughout his career. He married Ann Carnie in Ireland while just twenty years old, a few years before they moved to the United States. Together they had seven children, but rumors of Maffitt's "excessive gallantry" with other young women began to circulate in his early years of itinerancy, and Ann left with the children in 1830.[63] Beyond "excessive gallantry," one early critic noticed that, of all his followers, "there is but *one male* in the whole number."[64] While he and his wife slowly worked out a divorce by the late 1830s, Maffitt toured through the Southwest as a freelance revivalist, making a reputation as particularly popular with young women along the way.[65] He paid undue attention to one, for example, in Nashville. Observers noted that his "peculiar *proclivity*" was apparent one night at the Tennessee revival, when "his sole attentions were paid, the entire night, to a beautiful lady of fashion, the elegant and accomplished Miss H. of Nashville." Such a scene caused "a mild reproof" from the presiding elder of the local Methodist district.[66] By 1847, Maffitt had run into trouble yet again, this time with allegations of indecent exposure to a woman who was a servant at the house in which he was temporarily staying. Although Maffitt insisted it was a mistake, the Methodist clergy seemed to think this was not the first time such an accident had occurred with the preacher.[67]

In many respects Maffitt's story does not sound particularly southern. He was a national celebrity after all, and his most famous scandal occurred in the 1840s in New York. Evangelical preachers in both the North and South could become extraordinarily popular and financially successful through eloquent preaching. They also increasingly profited from publications directed toward a growing evangelical audience. And charges of preachers being impostors were common to both regions. These similarities suggest that the economic and social dislocations occurring throughout the antebellum North were also common to the South, especially along their western frontiers. Yet the distinction between the Northwest and Southwest was in the degree of anxiety caused by the more volatile export economy of the Southwest, along with the extreme paranoia that an untrustworthy roving preacher might spark a mass slave insurrection.

Beyond just vague spiritual platitudes, Maffitt's message of a mechanical society governed by God through the popular will struck a comforting chord in the Lower Mississippi Valley. In the machinelike society Maffitt described to his listeners, enslaved people would not rebel, and the fluctuations of prices and railroad bank stocks were directed by God through the vehicle of the market's demands. As southern planters and merchants were still constructing this society through the lives and labor of enslaved African Americans, the demand for belief in a providential God who guided their actions was supplied by evangelicals like Maffitt. With speculators hyping new bank stocks and Maffitt encouraging their optimism, it seemed that nobody could lose on an investment, and the price of cotton and land would continue to rise inexorably.

But underneath the surface of loose credit and revivalist belief was the fear of another Murrell—a sham preacher who sold them a worthless god, stole their enslaved property, and took their money in exchange. Preachers like Maffitt might be successful if they could read the religious market better than their competitors and if they had the oratorical skills to sell the right belief. But even the best could not solve the problem of doubt—and debt—that lurked beneath a society built on credit between planter and factor and between preacher and layperson. As long as ministers were needed as cornerstones of trust and respectability, they were simultaneously the most feared members of society, especially those itinerants who mirrored the traveling peddlers of the rural South.

In 1837 those fears were realized. Investors in New York and London lost confidence in highly leveraged planters. Once-valuable railroad banknotes turned into worthless shinplasters. The Panic of 1837 revealed that itinerants of all sorts could not be trusted and that the whole system was not bound together by a providential invisible hand. The economic system had indeed been built on a flimsy foundation of paper and extraordinary debt, and perhaps those suspected preachers had been frauds and swindlers after all.

Notes

1. Augustus Q. Walton, *A History of the Detection, Conviction, Life and Designs of John A. Murel, the Great Western Land Pirate; Together with the System of Villainy, and Plan of Exciting a Negro Rebellion* (Cincinnati: U. P. James, 1835), 29–31. For descriptions of itinerant Methodists, see Charity R. Carney, *Ministers and Masters: Methodism, Manhood, and Honor in the Old South* (Baton Rouge: Louisiana State University Press, 2011), 35; and John G. Jones, *A Complete History of Methodism as Connected with the Mississippi Conference of the Methodist Episcopal Church, South*, vol. 2 (Nashville: Methodist Episcopal Church, South, 1908), 191.

2. For a list of Methodist appointments, see *Minutes of the Annual Conferences of the Methodist Episcopal Church, for the Years 1829–1839*, vol. 2 (New York: T. Mason and G. Lane, 1840), 184. For his mentions of ministers, see Joshua D. Rothman, *Flush Times and Fever Dreams: A Story of Capitalism and Slavery in the Age of Jackson* (Athens: University of Georgia Press, 2012), 55, 76, 256 (quotation on 181).

3. Walter Johnson, *River of Dark Dreams: Slavery and Empire in the Cotton Kingdom* (Cambridge, Mass.: Belknap Press of Harvard University Press, 2013); Edward E. Baptist, *The Half Has Never Been Told: Slavery and the Making of American Capitalism* (New York: Basic, 2014); Sven Beckert, *Empire of Cotton: A Global History* (New York: Knopf, 2014); Adam Rothman, *Slave Country: American Expansion and the Origins of the Deep South* (Cambridge, Mass.: Harvard University Press, 2007); Sven Beckert and Seth Rockman, eds., *Slavery's Capitalism: A New History of American Economic Development* (Philadelphia: University of Pennsylvania Press, 2016).

4. For population increase, see Rothman, *Flush Times*, 4.

5. *An American Dictionary of the English Language (1828)*, s.v. "credit."

6. Johnson, *River of Dark Dreams*, 35.

7. *Abstract of the Returns of the Fifth Census* (Washington, D.C.: Duff Green, 1832), 36; Rothman, *Flush Times*, 4.

8. For a more detailed discussion of the Land Office and land speculation in the Lower Mississippi Valley, see Johnson, *River of Dark Dreams*, chap. 1; and Rothman, *Slave Country*, chap. 2.

9. Lewis Cecil Gray, *History of Agriculture in the Southern United States to 1860*, vol. 2 (Washington, D.C.: Carnegie Institution, 1933), 1027; Rothman, *Flush Times*, 4.

10. Willis Levi Meadows, Jr., "The Union Bank of Mississippi" (master's thesis, University of Mississippi, 1949), 23–35; Rothman, *Flush Times*, 4. See also Baptist, *The Half Has Never Been Told*, 243–59.

11. "Vicksburg Rail Road," *The Mississippian* (Jackson), October 24, 1834; Clifford Thies, "Repudiation in Antebellum Mississippi," *Independent Review* 19 (Fall 2014): 193; Dennis J. Mitchell, *A New History of Mississippi* (Jackson: University Press of Mississippi, 2014), 104–5. For other railroad plans in the 1830s, see *The American Almanac and Repository of Useful Knowledge, for the Year 1837* (Boston: Charles Bowen, 1836), 250; John MacGregor, *The Progress of America, from the Discovery by Columbus to the Year 1846*, vol. 2 (London: Whitaker and Co., 1847), 743–44; and "Rail Roads," *Woodville (Miss.) Republican*, October 3, 1835.

12. A Baker's Creek Planter, "Vicksburg and Jackson Rail Road," *The Mississippian*, June 15, 1835.

13. "Grand Project" and "The New Orleans and Nashville Rail Road," *The Mississippian*, December 11, 1835.

14. Joshua Baldwin, "New Orleans and Nashville Rail Road," *The Mississippian*, October 2, 1835.

15. "To the Citizens of Mississippi, Alabama and Tennessee," *Woodville Republican*, May 9, 1835.

16. *Writings of Levi Woodbury, LL.D., Political, Judicial, and Literary*, vol. 3 (Boston: Little, Brown and Company, 1852), 260.

17. Cives [pseud.], "Black Creek Counterfeiters Routed," *The Mississippian*, August 8, 1834.

18. "A Counterfeiter Detected," *Woodville Republican*, January 31, 1835.

19. "Murder by Poison," *The Mississippian*, September 5, 1834.

20. For Curtiss, see J. B. Cain, *Methodism in the Mississippi Conference, 1846–1870* (Jackson, Miss.: Hawkins Foundation, 1939), 340–43. For letters by Curtiss as factor, see William Curtiss to Benjamin Drake, March 11, 1839, Box 3, Folder 18, Benjamin M. Drake and Family Papers, Mississippi Department of Archives and History, Jackson (hereinafter cited as MDAH); Curtiss to Drake, May 19, 1843, Drake Papers, Box 3, Folder 21, MDAH. For Lane, see Jones, *History of Methodism*, 2:389. On vouching for a business partner, see William Winans vouching for James Fugua in Winans to Lane, October 29, 1841, Box 17, Folder 10, William Winans Papers, J. B. Cain Archives of Mississippi Methodism, Millsaps-Wilson Library, Millsaps College, Jackson, Miss. (hereinafter cited as CA). For the slave sale, see Winans to Francis D. Richardson, April 15, 1847, William Winans Papers, Box 17, Folder 12, CA, as well as Ray Holder, *William Winans: Methodist Leader in Antebellum Mississippi* (Jackson: University Press of Mississippi, 1977), 182–83; and Cain, *Methodism in the Mississippi Conference*, 184.

21. A. P. Merrill to Thomas Kinnicutt, June 18, 1836, Box 2, Folder 3, Thomas Kinnicutt Papers, American Antiquarian Society, Worcester, Massachusetts (hereinafter cited as AAS). See also Rothman, *Flush Times*, 121–24; and Stephen Mihm, *A Nation of Counterfeiters: Capitalists, Con Men, and the Making of the United States* (Cambridge, Mass.: Harvard University Press, 2007), 88, 226.

22. John Morris, *Wanderings of a Vagabond: An Autobiography* (New York: John Morris, 1873), 242–46; Jackson Lears, *Something for Nothing: Luck in America* (New York: Viking, 2003), 119; Herbert Asbury, *Sucker's Progress: An Informal History of Gambling in America* (1938; repr., New York: Thunder's Mouth, 2003), 149–54.

23. Jones, *History of Methodism*, 2:215.

24. Randy J. Sparks, *On Jordan's Stormy Banks: Evangelicalism in Mississippi, 1773–1876* (Athens: University of Georgia Press, 2012), 79.

25. Jones, *History of Methodism*, 2:370.

26. William Winans to Orsamus L. Nash, August 29, 1835, Box 17, Folder 8, William Winans Papers, CA.

27. Jones, *History of Methodism*, 2:64.

28. Joseph Holt Ingraham, *The South-West by a Yankee*, vol. 2 (New York: Harper and Brothers, 1835), 86, 12, 72.

29. William Winans to Orsamus L. Nash, August 29, 1835, Box 17, Folder 8, William Winans Papers, CA.

30. Jones, *History of Methodism*, 2:215.

31. *Minutes of the Annual Conferences of the Methodist Episcopal Church, 1829–1839*, 2: 398, 435. For another minister who located in Madison County but pursued wealth in other ways, see George W. Stewart, the "talented young physician," in Jones, *History of Methodism*, 3:61–63.

32. *Southwestern Religious Luminary* (Natchez, Miss.), April 1837, 57, 60; *Southwestern Religious Luminary*, May 1837, 69–71.

33. Jones, *History of Methodism*, 2:302–3, 308.

34. Autobiography of Benjamin Chase, vol. 2, 135–38, Benjamin Dorrance Chase Papers, MDAH. For another example of a widely traveled impostor preacher, see "A Base Impostor!!" *Spirit of Kosciusko* (Miss.), July 7, 1838.

35. Rothman, *Flush Times*, 118–53; Johnson, *River of Dark Dreams*, 46–72.

36. "Postscript: More News from Madison, Hinds, and Warren," *Woodville Republican*, July 18, 1835.

37. William Winans to Orsamus L. Nash, August 29, 1835; Winans to E. N. Talley, September 4, 1835, Box 17, Folder 8, William Winans Papers, CA.

38. William Gilmore Simms, *Richard Hurdis: A Tale of Alabama* (1838; repr., Fayetteville: University of Arkansas Press, 1995), 282.

39. Simms, *Richard Hurdis*, 276, 280, 291.

40. *Report of the Trial of Mr. John N. Maffitt, before a Council of Ministers, of the Methodist Episcopal Church* (Boston: True and Greene, 1823), 12–13.

41. Joseph T. Buckingham, *Personal Memoirs and Recollections of Editorial Life*, vol. 1 (Boston: Ticknor, Reed, and Fields, 1852), 105–10.

42. Candour [pseud.], *Theological Pretenders, or, an Analysis of the Character and Conduct of the Rev. J. N. Maffit, Preacher in the Methodist Episcopal Society* (New York, 1830), 7, 23–24, 31.

43. Robert E. Cray, Jr., "High Style and Low Morals: John Newland Maffitt and the Methodist Church, 1794–1850," *Methodist History* 45 (October 2006): 36.

44. S. Luckett to John C. Burruss, February 6, 1833, Box 1, Folder 5, John C. Burruss Papers, Louisiana and Lower Mississippi Valley Collection, Hill Memorial Library, Louisiana State University, Baton Rouge.

45. W. Nools to Charles Kimball Marshall, February 27, 1835, Folder 2, Charles Kimball Marshall Papers, MDAH.

46. *Abstract of the Returns of the Fifth Census*, 36.

47. William Winans to Rev. Lewis Garrett, May 8, 1835, Box 17, Folder 8, William Winans Papers, CA.

48. Jones, *History of Methodism*, 2:348–49.

49. "New Methodist Church," *New Orleans Times-Picayune*, March 18, 1838.

50. W. H. Richardson to William Winans, April 7, 1835, Box 2, Folder 17, William Winans Papers, CA.

51. "Lagrange College," *Western Methodist* (Nashville), November 8, 1833; "Revival in Huntsville," *Western Methodist*, August 1, 1834. For identity as "the Stranger," see "Huntsville, Alabama," *Western Methodist*, August 22, 1834.

52. William Winans to Lewis Garrett, May 8, 1835, Box 17, Folder 8, William Winans Papers, CA.

53. John Newland Maffitt, *The Oratorical Dictionary* (Nashville: Western Methodist Office, 1835), iii–iv. Promotional ads for Maffitt's publications in *Western Methodist*, June 13, June 20, and July 25, 1834.

54. John Newland Maffitt, *Poems* (Louisville, Ky.: Prentice and Weissenger, 1839); John Newland Maffitt, *Pulpit Sketches* (Louisville, Ky.: W. Harrison Johnston, 1839).

55. Jones, *History of Methodism*, 2:345; Anna G. Taylor to William Winans, December 29, 1836, Box 2, Folder 18, William Winans Papers, CA; W. H. Richardson to William Winans, April 7, 1835, Box 2, Folder 17, William Winans Papers, CA; Cray, "High Style," 37. As one example of his lectures, see John Newland Maffitt, "Era of Revolution: An Oration," *Western Methodist*, March 21 and March 28, 1834.

56. "An Editor's Letter to Himself," *Western Methodist*, May 2, 1834.

57. Anna G. Taylor to William Winans, December 29, 1836, Box 2, Folder 18, William Winans Papers, CA.

58. Maffitt, *Oratorical Dictionary*, xvi, xviii.

59. Maffitt, "Era of Revolution: An Oration," *Western Methodist*, March 21, 1834.

60. William Winans to Charles K. Marshall, October 18, 1852, Box 18, Folder 14, William Winans Papers, CA.

61. W. Nools to Charles Kimball Marshall, February 27, 1835, Folder 2, Charles Kimball Marshall Papers, MDAH.

62. *Times-Picayune*, November 10, 1847.

63. Cray, "High Style," 32–36.

64. Candour, *Theological Pretenders*, 24, 8.

65. *American National Biography*, s.v. "John Newland Maffitt"; Richard Carwardine, *Transatlantic Revivalism: Popular Evangelicalism in Britain and America, 1790–1865* (Westport, Conn.: Greenwood, 1978), 21–22.

66. Moses Elsemore, *An Impartial Account of the Life of the Rev. John N. Maffitt, with a Narrative of the Difficulties Attending His First Marriage, and a Circumstantial and Correct History of All the Facts of His Late Marriage to Miss Smith, of Brooklyn, and the Causes of Her Death, with Many Particulars Never Before Published* (New York: John F. Feeks, 1848), 11.

67. Cray, "High Style," 39. For more contemporary accounts of suspicion regarding Maffitt and women, see "Johnny Maffitt and the Ladies," *Times-Picayune*, March 23, 1842.

A Gentleman and a Scoundrel?

ALEXANDER MCDONALD, FINANCIAL REPUTATION, AND SLAVERY'S CAPITALISM

ALEXANDRA J. FINLEY

It is not surprising to find slave traders featured in a collection about the scoundrels of nineteenth-century capitalism. Any twenty-first-century humanitarian readily identifies the slave trade as a heinous traffic in which to engage. On the surface, many nineteenth-century commentators seemed to agree. Abolitionists in the northern United States, for instance, targeted the slave trade in their campaigns, believing it the epitome of all the wrongs of slavery and the most likely to invoke outrage from those otherwise indifferent to the fate of enslaved peoples. Once placed under abolitionists' scrutiny, southern proslavery writers also appeared to critique the trade and particularly the men who made it their profession to buy and sell human beings. Authors who defended the "southern way of life" portrayed all slave traders as akin to Mr. Haley in *Uncle Tom's Cabin*: uncouth, vagrant, and shunned from polite society. Daniel R. Hundley, for instance, described the typical trader as "outwardly a coarse, ill-bred person, provincial in speech and manners"—the exact opposite of how Hundley envisioned the better residents of the South. Historians have at times taken proslavery authors' words too seriously, echoing their claims that slave traders were outside of respectable society.[1]

An examination of the business networks and account books of antebellum southerners reveals, however, the emptiness of their contemporaries' protests against the slave trade and its practitioners. One New Orleans city councilman, a Mr. Peters, while defending the location of slave jails in the heart of the city, allowed that "the business of slave dealing is considered highly discreditable, but still as one of our institutions, this species of traffic [is] necessary. . . . Slaves being in requisition—they must be bought and sold—some place, where they could be offered to view." Public sales within the city were "indispensable." To force slave traders to operate outside the municipality, Peters argued, was "unjust" and "positively illegal." Peters recognized the centrality of the slave trade to the continuation of slavery as an institution. While arguing with abolitionists, southern whites might have attempted to distance themselves from the slave market, but in practice they could not avoid its centrality to their economy. As Peters pointed out, enslaved laborers "must be bought and sold" for the "Cotton Kingdom" to expand and thrive. Planters' booming international trade in cotton, the adoption of slavery by new states such as Mississippi and Arkansas, and slaveholders' access to loans and mortgages based on enslaved property were all inextricably tied to the slave trade. Far from uncouth outsiders, slave traders were southern businessmen par excellence, at the helm of a multimillion-dollar industry.[2]

In everyday life, white southerners were less concerned with the moral shortcomings of slave traders than with their business acumen and economic status. While a few likely had genuine misgivings about the morality of the trade, most southern whites had no trouble rubbing elbows with these alleged social outcasts when a slave trader was financially successful. If southerners did feel disdain for traders, it was usually for a particular trader's class, not the nature of his work. There was a hierarchy within the business world of the slave market, and traders' agents occupied the bottom rung. Agents were generally younger traders, oftentimes men just starting in the business, who performed the work of going from one courthouse sale or farm to the next, inspecting potential purchases and bargaining with enslavers over the sale price. These men were wage laborers who dirtied their hands in day-to-day tasks, not that different from men who worked on the docks or in factories. Even elite traders looked down on this lower class of speculators. One Kentucky trader, Silas Marshal, claimed that his agent's role in his business was like that of a "domestic servant waiting upon his house." Abolitionist Theodore Dwight Weld perceptively captured this attitude when he noted the role of a Kentucky senator in the slave trade "not as the driver, for that would be vulgar drudgery, beneath a gentleman, but as a nabob in the state, ordering his understrappers."[3]

For those slave traders who had proven themselves in business and distanced themselves from wage labor, there were no bars to entering polite society. They could marry into the planter class, be elected to public office, or sit on the board of a bank. It was often the very business in which they engaged that connected traders with well-to-do southerners. Men involved in the slave trade had to be in contact with the banking elite in the South's urban centers. Without an immediate influx of cash from sales, slave traders had to borrow substantial sums from bankers—or write a substantial number of notes—to purchase enslaved people at the beginning of each trading season. Slave traders thus proved profitable clients to bankers, who welcomed their applications for loans and happily discounted their notes. One bank president, Dr. Kemp Battle, later claimed: "The borrowers who were of most value to the bank were negro-traders and horse-traders. They scattered our bills throughout the South from the Potomac to the Rio Grande . . . and these bills [only] very slowly came back for redemption." Any objection that banks had to slave traders as customers came not from questions of morality but from questions of individual business acumen.[4]

While historians have documented slave traders' reliance on national and international financial networks to sustain the antebellum slave trade, as well as slavery's ties to global finance, less attention has been paid to slave traders as not just beneficiaries but orchestrators of antebellum financial infrastructure. After all, their profession, as Jeff Forret illustrates in the next essay in this volume, "inherently demanded expertise in local money markets." This knowledge meant that traders' involvement with banks could easily extend beyond that of a customer to playing a role in the establishment and running of financial intermediaries. Slave traders who sat on the boards of directors of banks, provided initial capital outlays, or served as bank presidents helped establish policy, influenced investments, and decided which customers would receive loans and under what conditions. Their position within the banking elite was a clear reflection of slave traders' position at the heart of the southern—and by extension, national—economy.[5]

To further explore the centrality of slave traders to southern society through the lens of antebellum finance, this essay looks at the business networks of five related antebellum slave traders to tease out the ways in which slave trading and banking interests aligned. Brothers Hugh and Alexander McDonald and their nephews, the Hagan brothers, were members of a wealthy slave-trading class that emerged in the second quarter of the nineteenth century. Men like the McDonalds and Hagans were no rough itinerant traders but, rather, established figures in the urban markets of the South, where they possessed clear financial and, importantly, social capital. A case study of these men allows a glimpse into the fabric of daily economic life in the antebellum South that centers on-the-ground interactions rather than politicians' rhetoric. Such a focus shows that, far from reviled anomalies, slave traders were at the heart of nineteenth-century southern capitalism.

Hugh and Alexander McDonald immigrated to the fledgling nation of the United States in the early nineteenth century from County Monaghan, Ireland, becoming citizens in 1813 and 1819, respectively. They settled in Charleston, South Carolina, where Alexander operated a grocery and liquor store but was "principally engaged in the negro trade," as was Hugh. Hugh married a wealthy widow, Leonora G. Colclough, in 1833. Colclough, who apparently had no qualms about marrying a slave trader, brought to the marriage a plantation in the state, Sand Hill, which included "eight thousand five hundred acres more or less." This added to the "plantation on Taw Caw" of 1,750 acres and "summer residence at Bradford Springs" that McDonald already owned. Together, Leonora and Hugh enslaved at least 197 individuals.[6]

Hugh and Alexander McDonald's engagement in the interstate slave trade predated Hugh's marriage, beginning in 1830 at the latest. Surviving manifests from the 1830s show the brothers trading primarily from Charleston, South Carolina, to Savannah and Augusta, Georgia, and New Orleans, Louisiana. In 1832 Hugh McDonald signed the paperwork for sending fourteen enslaved people from Charleston to Augusta via the steamboat *John Honey,* and in January 1839 Alexander McDonald forced thirty enslaved men, women, and children onto the steamboat *Almena* in the port of Charleston, bound for New Orleans. The McDonalds participated in the trade for at least a decade, through the Panic of 1837 that retired many slave traders and into the 1840s.[7]

Alexander McDonald's additional financial interests may have helped keep the brothers afloat. At the same time they were profiting from the slave trade, Alexander was also making a name for himself in the world of banking. Known as a "man of good credit and character" by Charleston's banking insiders, McDonald was elected thirteen times to the board of directors of the Bank of the State of South Carolina. Alexander's first election came in 1827, from which time he served consecutively until 1831, and then again consecutively from 1838 to 1845.[8]

The South Carolina legislature had chartered the bank in 1812 with the idea that the institution could provide long-term credit more favorable for planters. It was not a private bank but a state bank in the antebellum sense, meaning that the bank had to apply for and receive a charter from the state legislature to operate. In the case of the Bank of the State of South Carolina, the state also supplied the initial capital, pledged its support of the bank, and deposited all public funds to the institution. The bank charter specified that a president and twelve directors manage the daily operations of the bank, with the state legislators to elect the directors through an annual vote.[9]

Alexander McDonald's selection as bank director thus reflected lawmakers' high regard for him. One of the presidents of the Bank of the State of South Carolina during McDonald's tenure on the board, F. H. Elmore, described the influence of the directors, saying, "The power to direct the management and control the whole business of the Bank, is in the Directors." According to another contemporary commentator on banking, "Bank directors are chosen for their wealth, commercial experience, and influence in attracting to the institution a good class of dealers." Nothing about McDonald's or his brother's involvement in the slave trade precluded their entrance into elite financial circles.[10]

McDonald's position on the board of directors was not an anomaly. Charleston's banks had plenty of connections with slave traders, or, as they often called themselves, brokers. The label "broker" is simultaneously revealing and misleading. In some cases, it has led historians to discount these men's role in the slave trade, since they did not always refer to their profession as "negro trader" or even "trader" as their counterparts in other cities often did. While the term "broker" does not, for modern readers, immediately bring to mind the slave trade, it perfectly captures these men's view of their professional place in the world. Men like Alexander and Hugh McDonald engaged heavily in the buying and selling of human beings but did not consider themselves solely as slave traders. Rather, trading in enslaved people fell under the scope of "brokerage," the buying and selling of assets for clients, whether those assets were stocks, bonds, tracts of land, or living, breathing people. Calling themselves "brokers" allowed them to signal to customers that they would handle investments of any sort.[11]

Occasionally, men who traded in slaves, securities, and real estate also advertised themselves as "commission merchants and auctioneers." Like "broker," these terms encompassed many different kinds of sales. For example, one such commission merchant, L. T. Levin, paid for a large advertisement in the Columbia city directory in which he labeled himself an "Auctioneer and Commission Merchant" and promised to pay "strict attention" to selling and purchasing "real estate, stocks, [and] negroes." By calling himself a commission merchant and auctioneer, Levin was not trying to hide his slave-trading activities; he included "negroes" in his advertisement. Rather, Levin was signaling that buying and selling enslaved people was part of a larger commission business. Slave trading was not an isolated economic activity, separated from other forms of business or the broader economy. Even professional slave traders had other economic interests.[12]

The "auctioneer" Thomas N. Gadsden is another example of the central role slave traders played in South Carolina banking. Gadsden was involved in no fewer than three banking institutions and sat beside McDonald on the board of the Bank of the State. Abolitionist author Theodore Weld described Gadsden as "the principal slave auctioneer in Charleston, South Carolina," who was "from one of the first families in the state and moves in the very highest class of society there." Besides operating an auction house on the corner of Chalmers and State Streets, Gadsden served in the 1830s as a director of the State Bank of South Carolina. He then helped form the People's Bank of Charleston in 1853, of which he became a substantial shareholder and director from 1853 to 1855. Gadsden also owned significant stock in the Bank of Charleston.[13]

Another major slave trader, Thomas Ryan, original owner of the slave jail known as Ryan's Mart, which still stands on Chalmers Street, followed Thomas N. Gadsden on the board of the State Bank of South Carolina, serving as a director from 1857 to 1865. Unlike Gadsden, genealogical connections can't explain away Ryan's position at the bank. An Irish immigrant, Ryan did not come from an elite family. Like the McDonalds, he earned his position through his business reputation alone, a clear illustration of how slave traders could rise in society with economic success. His connections to the city's financial elite did not stop at the State Bank. Ryan additionally sat on the board of directors of the Bank of the State of South Carolina from 1857 to 1860 and helped found the Palmetto Savings Institution in 1857. Ryan lent money as an individual as well; in 1847 he lent prominent commission merchant Ker Boyce, former president of the Bank of Charleston, $5,000.[14]

Close ties between financial institutions and slave traders existed outside of South Carolina as well. Banks and traders formed a mutually beneficial relationship. Banks valued that slave traders' profession often required them to disperse their banknotes far and wide, thus slowing the notes' return for redemption. In turn, slave traders were favored customers across the slaveholding states, investing widely and receiving favorable terms for loans and renewals. As Jeff Forret shows, bankers "understood their importance to slave traders' livelihood" and even "sometimes appealed directly to the purveyors of human chattel to capitalize their institutions." Slave traders purchased bank stock, served on bank boards, and occasionally even served as bank presidents.[15]

The epitome of this connection came to fruition in late 1850s Richmond, Virginia, where prominent slave traders chartered a financial institution, the appropriately named Traders' Bank of Richmond, by and for men of their particular business. The men involved did not charter the bank because they could not access credit elsewhere, as they continued to engage with other banks in the city. Rather, they took their prior involvement in finance, whether as directors or simply as customers, and attempted to create an institution from which they could more directly profit.[16]

Trader Hector Davis spearheaded the chartering of the bank. Davis, as his clerk R. H. Elmore later recalled, "was an active business man and kept his money constantly moving, turning it over in trade of some sort." Speculating in the rising or falling value of human bodies was for him not altogether different than assessing the relative value of stocks and bonds. Alongside assessments of profit and loss on human flesh in Davis's account books were returns on his investments in bank stock and government bonds. At his death, Davis owned 103 shares of stock in the Farmers' Bank of Virginia, ten shares of Exchange Bank stock, seventy-five shares of Bank of the Commonwealth stock, twenty-five shares of stock from the Bank of the City of Petersburg, and three shares of the Virginia Life Insurance Company's stock, as well as investments in the Roanoke Valley Railroad and the Richmond City Railway. He also held bonds from the City of Richmond, the Commonwealth of Virginia, and, eventually, the Confederate States of America. Davis's total financial instruments were valued at $75,840.[17]

Acting alongside Davis were thirteen other men who signed on as commissioners for the Traders' Bank. Of the eleven identifiable commissioners, nine were slave traders, while one operated a livery stable next to a slave jail. Even if the remaining three were not directly involved in the slave trade, slave traders made up 70 percent of the bank's commissioners.[18] They opened the books of subscription for the bank on March 22, 1860. Newspaper advertisements instructed interested investors to visit one of five businesses to purchase stock: four slave-trading firms and one private banking house, that of Isaacs & Taylor.[19]

Once the necessary subscriptions had been collected and the minimum capitalization reached, the stockholders came together to elect the bank's president and board of directors. The meeting was held in April 1860 at the St. Charles, the fashionable hotel across from Davis's auction house that he and other slave traders frequented. The *Richmond Daily Dispatch* approvingly reported of the meeting that "every member is well known for his business capacities, and each has a large moneyed acquaintance[;] there seems to be no doubt that the new Bank will do well."[20]

The elected board of directors was no less a who's who of the city's slave-trading elite than the bank's commissioners had been. In a reflection of Davis's position at the center of Richmond's banking and trading networks, the stockholders of the Traders' Bank elected him president, a post that he held until his death in 1863. Of the commissioners, slave traders S. R. Fondron, Thomas Jones, and John B. Davis were elected to the board. Other identifiable directors included C. E. Whitlock, a lumber merchant, and Joseph Brummel, who owned a flour mill in the city and was involved in the private banking firm of Isaacs & Taylor until 1861. Brummel's business associate in private banking, Isaacs, was appointed the board's secretary. The composition of the Traders' Bank directorate exemplifies the confidence and mutual interest that Richmond businessmen had with one another. Merchants in what twenty-first-century society would deem morally acceptable markets did not differentiate between themselves and slave traders when it came to making a profit.[21]

As members of a board of directors, slave traders such as McDonald played a managerial role in the operations of the bank. Ideally, the board of directors met at least once a week, and the majority of the meetings were taken up with "the discounting of promissory notes, and the loaning of money or securities." When deciding what notes to discount and what loans to approve, the directors carefully assessed potential clients, considering "their standing in the community, the character of the trade in which they are engaged, the credit of persons whose notes they offer for discount, the state of the market, the value of securities, and whatever concerns the safety of the bank dealings." In practice, the directors, who were generally merchants themselves, were not always able to attend such regular meetings. Day-to-day supervision usually fell to the president and cashier of the bank, reserving for the directors decisions about "large loans or other exceptional trans actions" and the institution of new policies.[22]

Serving on the board of directors of a bank thus came with certain benefits. Directors could speak on behalf of friends and associates, encouraging the board to approve discounts or extend loans. They also had an advantage in accessing personal loans. While the practice was discouraged by many bank officers, directors often asked the president for loans outside of the formally designated times for such requests. Critics of these behind-the-scenes favors noted that they "not infrequently led to the most serious results," but "tacit consent to the practice might easily grow up from the direct personal confidence established between" the president and directors. Such practices certainly existed at the Bank of the State of South Carolina, and President F. H. Elmore defended them by arguing: "Borrowing by the Director is not in itself objectionable. If it is confined to aid him in operations fairly undertaken and within the proper scope of his own actual capital, he does no more than every capitalist is compelled to do at times, and what it is the appropriate function of a Bank to sustain." Whatever outside commentators may have argued, proponents of the practice framed it as an integral part of both business and banking.[23]

Alexander McDonald used his connections with the Bank of the State of South Carolina to further his and his family's interests in the slave trade. The bank's books do not survive, so it is not possible to trace all of McDonald's financial activity; however, a series of large transactions in the late 1830s and 1840s fell under public scrutiny, allowing for a closer look into some elements of ties between the city's banks and the slave trade. These transactions involved McDonald's brother Hugh before his death in 1841 and three other slave traders—his nephews John, Alexander, and Hugh Hagan.[24]

The three Hagans were all born between 1800 and 1812 in North or South Carolina to John Hagan and Rosanna McDonald Hagan, the sister of Hugh and Alexander McDonald. Rosanna McDonald had immigrated to the United States shortly after her elder brothers did, and she named two of her sons in their honor. According to his brother Alexander, John Hagan was the first to engage in the slave trade in Hamburg, South Carolina, in 1832. Though the Hagans later denied that their uncles had ever "aided or befriended" them, Alexander clerked for and lived with Alexander McDonald for at least a year, and evidence of their cooperation in the slave trade dates to 1833 at the latest.[25]

The Hagans, operating under the name of John Hagan & Co., did business on behalf of the McDonalds as well as independently. An 1833 ship manifest from the port of Charleston, for example, lists Hugh McDonald as the "owner or shipper" of twenty-nine enslaved men and women, but with the note that they were under the supervision of "J. Hagan, on board." John and Alexander Hagan continued to oversee the movement of enslaved people from South Carolina to New Orleans on behalf of their uncles for several years.[26]

Like many successful slave traders of the era, the Hagan brothers used geographically dispersed kin networks and connections to financial institutions to further their slave-trading interests across the South. Though originally based out of South Carolina, the Hagans expanded their geographic reach in the later 1830s, strategically basing themselves in the three major markets of the slave trade at that time: Richmond, Virginia; Charleston, South Carolina; and New Orleans, Louisiana. Using letters, telegraphs, banknotes, and bills of exchange, the Hagans and the McDonalds transferred information and finances across the southern states.

Youngest brother Hugh Hagan relocated to Richmond, where he oversaw the purchasing of enslaved people to be sold in the New Orleans market. At least initially, Hugh conducted his business out of Robert Lumpkin's jail in Richmond's slave-trading district. Lumpkin was one of the commissioners of the Traders' Bank of Richmond. Hugh was the only brother to legally marry, wedding a Pennsylvania-born woman named Sarah sometime after 1850. By the time of his marriage, Hugh had a great deal of money—$75,000 worth of personal property and $13,000 in real estate, according to the 1860 census—and lived in the fashionable Court End neighborhood, one house down from fellow trader (and another commissioner of the Traders' Bank) Solomon Davis. Both men gave their occupation to census takers as "Gentleman." Hugh Hagan was also active in local politics. In the 1850s, for instance, Hugh sat on the Democratic Vigilance Committee with a variety of businessmen, ranging from fellow traders N. B. and C. B. Hill to the owner of the Gallego Mills, Richard O.

Haskins, and Dr. T. P. Mayo. Like them, Hagan was a wealthy man, and the source of his wealth did not seem to trouble the Richmond Democrats.[27]

John Hagan, meanwhile, moved to New Orleans around 1838, though he spent his summers traveling to work with his brothers, buying enslaved people. He likely rented before eventually purchasing a lot on the corner of Esplanade and Moreau Streets that was previously the property of Hope H. Slatter, a member of another slave-trading family business. The lot included a slave jail as well as a residence for Hagan. After 1849, Hagan shared this space with a woman he enslaved, Lucy Ann Cheatham. With Cheatham, Hagan had two surviving children, Frederika Bremer Hagan and William Hagan. While he bought and sold people, invested in railroad companies and banks, and exchanged drafts and promissory notes, Hagan relied on Cheatham to care for their children, manage their household, and provide him with the necessities of life.[28]

The eldest brother, Alexander, spent several years in New Orleans prior to John's residence, before returning to Charleston, South Carolina, where he remained into the 1850s. Alexander's relationship with his brothers and uncles was volatile; he moved between partner, employee, and unofficial assistant based on his allegedly "intemperate" and "troublesome" behavior. Nonetheless, Alexander accumulated a considerable profit. He lived for many years in Charleston "about a hundred yards" from the Bank of Charleston, where he was "daily in the habit of seeing and conversing with the officers and several directors of the Bank." His deposits there ranged in the 1840s from $6,572.64 to $118,682.92.[29]

The men's mother, Rosanna, also stayed in Charleston into the 1850s before moving to Richmond to live near her youngest son, Hugh. Rosanna, too, was an important player in the family business. John made use of his mother's residence in Charleston, staying with her during his annual visits to purchase slaves and occasionally asking her to witness documents. Alexander reported that John "always leaves [New Orleans] in summer to purchase slaves at the north [Charleston and Richmond] and he could not do without going." Rosanna facilitated these trips by providing lodging for her sons even after they had all left Charleston.[30]

Like other slave traders, the Hagans worked closely with banks to secure loans, draw bills of exchange, and discount acceptances and other financial paper. All of the brothers were in close proximity to well-capitalized banks that were ready to assist them. They could use their relationships with nearby banks to facilitate the transfer of money from one location to another, enabling the purchasing partner in Charleston or Richmond to receive profits from sales made in New Orleans. In 1845, for example, Alexander McDonald discounted a total of $15,000 in drafts or checks drawn in favor of John Hagan from the Mechanics and Traders Bank of New Orleans. Without national credit networks, it would have been difficult for Hugh and Alexander to have ready money with which to purchase enslaved people.[31]

Thanks to the McDonalds, the Hagans had strong connections to banks in Charleston, South Carolina. When Alexander Hagan was in Charleston, his contacts at the Bank of the State of South Carolina made conducting business easy. When Alexander was out of the city, particularly after his brothers moved away, he needed someone to manage his business affairs in Charleston as their legal power of attorney. Luckily for them, the Hagan kinship network provided them with the perfect candidate for such a representative.

John and Alexander Hagan must have felt confident in Alexander McDonald when, in October 1841, they signed over to him their power of attorney. The Hagan brothers gave McDonald the right to act on their behalf in financial matters with the Bank of the State of South Carolina and the Bank of Charleston. Besides having a relative and respected businessman to tend to business in their absence, giving McDonald power of attorney facilitated the quick purchase and sale of enslaved people. If McDonald wanted to purchase on the Hagans' behalf, as he often did, he now had easy access to their funds to do so. In granting McDonald power of attorney, one of the Hagan brothers authorized him, "for me and in my name[,] to draw, endorse or accept any bills of exchange, promissory notes, drafts, checks, for any sum or sums of money whatsoever; also to receive from the Bank of Charleston, South Carolina, all moneys that may from time to time be due me by the said bank, whether for dividends or otherwise." As Alexander Hagan explained, his initial impetus to give McDonald power of attorney "was to enable him to draw a note in my name in the event of his wanting money during my absence." Purchasing enslaved people meant paying large sums of money up front; having access to the Hagans' accounts in South Carolina enabled McDonald to do this.[32]

Alexander McDonald made good use of his power of attorney. From 1841 to

1846, McDonald regularly issued promissory notes to individuals on behalf of the Hagans, made payable at the Bank of Charleston or the Bank of the State of South Carolina. He also endorsed acceptances, checks, and bills of exchange in their names. On several instances, McDonald made out promissory notes to himself and then signed the notes as John Hagan's power of attorney. While the antebellum credit system was in some ways sophisticated, information exchange could be slow and haphazard. Traders tried to keep apprised of other markets, but any number of delays could keep them in the dark: lost letters, flooding, or storms, to name a few. Thus, the Hagans were apparently unaware of some of the financial actions their uncle was taking as their power of attorney, particularly McDonald's use of the power of attorney to "endorse his own notes."[33]

John Hagan must have had some suspicions, however, for he repeatedly asked McDonald whether or not he had used the power of attorney and then requested a settlement of accounts with his uncle on July 28, 1846. At the meeting, John again asked "whether [McDonald] owed any money in the bank and McDonald said positively that he had not used the power and did not owe anything to the Banks." With Alexander Hagan acting as witness, the two sorted out the finances of their trade in enslaved human beings. When this was done, Hagan announced his intention to cancel the power of attorney. Hagan still felt somewhat favorably toward his uncle, for he agreed to wait until the three could go to the banks together to revoke the power, "lest it should be supposed that McDonald had forfeited the confidence of John Hagan," which would have harmed his reputation. McDonald asked that they wait until the return of "Mendenhall," likely M. T. Mendenhall, a director at the Bank of the State, so the meeting was postponed until the following Monday.[34]

In the meantime, on July 31, Alexander McDonald "absconded." At first, the Hagans assumed he had only temporarily absented the city. Within a week, on August 8, 1846, one of the tellers from the Bank of Charleston sent for Alexander Hagan and informed him of McDonald's outstanding note with his endorsement as his brother's power of attorney. This signaled to the Hagans that McDonald's intentions were to leave them liable for his hidden debts, and on August 13 John Hagan revoked McDonald's power of attorney. Word of McDonald's escape and his fallout with the Hagans spread, and the Bank of the State and the Bank of Charleston acted quickly.[35]

Now aware of McDonald's true financial standing, the banks turned to John Hagan as their only hope of recovering their former director's debts. John Hagan had technically endorsed McDonald's notes, after all. In October, the Bank of the State of South Carolina filed a petition against Hagan in a district court of New Orleans, where Hagan resided, while the Bank of Charleston followed suit in February 1847. According to the Bank of the State and the Bank of Charleston, McDonald had, as power of attorney, contracted $46,000 and $6,150, respectively, in protested promissory notes in John Hagan's name. Legal representatives of both banks insisted that they were unaware McDonald and the Hagans were partners and that they believed McDonald had acted in accord with Hagan's wishes in regard to the protested promissory notes.[36]

John Hagan denied his liability for the debts vigorously. Hagan claimed that McDonald, with the full knowledge of the Bank of the State of South Carolina and the Bank of Charleston, who actively "connived and participated in this fraud," made out the notes to pay off his own long-standing debts to the banks. The banks, despite their knowledge of the situation, according to Hagan, accepted the notes as the only way to recover McDonald's mounting debts. Hagan specifically critiqued McDonald's insider standing with the Bank of the State, expressing surprise that, despite his debts, "still said McDonald continued to hold his seat at the Board of Directors of said institution in violation of its by-laws." Hagan also raised questions about McDonald's relationship with a director (and former president) of the Bank of Charleston, Ker Boyce. Boyce, who was one of the wealthiest men in the state as well as a former congressman, had endorsed personal notes of McDonald's. Hagan's legal counsel implied that Boyce had performed favors for McDonald that he would not have done for an ordinary customer of the bank.[37]

Whether or not the banks actively abetted his fraud, McDonald's fellow directors, the officers, and his other business associates bought into his public persona as a respectable financial success. Though he personally owed an estimated $90,000 to the Bank of Charleston alone, the bank's cashier claimed he "neither knew, nor had I reason to believe that Alexander McDonald was laboring under pecuniary embarrassment in the months of June or July last. I thought him wealthy and his resources most abundant." Similarly, fellow slave trader and bank director Thomas Ryan, a longtime friend of the McDonalds and the Hagans, testified that "McDonald passed as a rich man." McDonald's public reputation, as well as his personal connections to the banks, allowed him to operate for several years without repercussion for his considerable debts.[38]

As the litigation between the banks and John Hagan proceeded, McDonald's relationship with the Bank of South Carolina was about to receive attention from another outside source: the state Senate. The Bank of the State of South Carolina had long been the subject of intense debate between pro- and antibank factions in the state. In 1848, J. H. and M. C. Hammond had published a series of critiques of the bank, and the ensuing discussion in the state's newspapers meant that the institution was one of the issues debated in that year's election. When the legislature met in 1849, they clashed over whether or not the charter of the bank should be renewed.[39]

In the midst of these ongoing discussions, J. Foster Marshall, an antibank senator from Abbeville, made several accusations of corruption on the part of the bank's president, F. H. Elmore, as well as that of its directors, and decried the bank's general political influence. Marshall "charged the Bank of the State with having violated its charter, mismanaged its funds, and perverted its trust and powers from their proper and legitimate ends and uses." Among Marshall's charges were several benefits regularly granted to slave-trading customers: that the bank made individual loans of more than $2,000 at one time; that one-tenth of the loans had not been paid in annually; that the bank was negligent in collecting overdue debts; and that the bank lent funds outside of the state.[40]

Alexander McDonald was one of the individuals whose behavior troubled Senator Marshall and his supporters. Of the twelve accounts Marshall chose to submit to the legislative special committee assigned to investigate the bank, McDonald's was one, and John Hagan's was another. To the antibank faction, McDonald's actions served as a perfect example of the corruptibility of banking institutions. Marshall argued that both men's protested promissory notes were themselves discounted "as renewals of other notes of the same parties previously discounted." In other words, Marshall claimed that, due to McDonald's influence, the bank allowed him to extend the time of repayment indefinitely. Senator Marshall claimed at least one bank officer knew that McDonald "was the principal partner in a large trading company. One of the partners lived in Richmond, Va., and another traded in New Orleans," and because of this he allowed McDonald to abuse his privileges as director to assist his business partners.[41]

The president and directors of the Bank of the State of South Carolina, in an effort to refurbish their reputation, defended the institution's actions toward McDonald and Hagan. The bank's representatives retorted, in a published answer to Marshall's accusations, "Mr. McDonald was for years a very influential person with the members of the Legislature, and was repeatedly re-elected, with a full knowledge of his indebtedness to the Bank." In other words, McDonald was a well-connected and influential man whose behavior no one had viewed as unusual until Senator Marshall's outcry over the practices of the bank in general. The bank's spokesman also denied knowledge that the men for whom McDonald had power of attorney—the Hagans—were in fact his business partners (despite fervently arguing that they were in simultaneous legal proceedings in Louisiana). Rather, they stated only that the bank had "what they considered reliable information of the most satisfactory kind, as to the ability of John Hagan, who resided in New Orleans" as an endorser of McDonald's notes. Neither the initial report nor the bank's rebuttal, despite their acrimonious nature, questioned or critiqued McDonald's or Hagan's involvement in the slave trade. Engagement in that particular business did not tarnish their reputation in the eyes of the bank or its critics. Only their inability to repay their debts caused concern.[42]

By 1850, the investigation had turned its attention to the question of F. H. Elmore's involvement with the Nesbitt Manufacturing Company and that company's outstanding debt to the Bank of the State. With Alexander McDonald still missing and their focus elsewhere, the congressional investigative committee seemed satisfied with the bank's answer to concerns over John Hagan: They were pursuing the collection of the protested notes in court. The Bank of the State was ultimately successful in its suit against Hagan, as was the Bank of Charleston. The Bank of Charleston's case made its way to the Supreme Court of Louisiana, dragging on for several years before the court finally confirmed that John Hagan was liable for the notes signed by McDonald.[43]

Despite the substantial rulings against him, John Hagan was not in serious danger of losing the wealth he had accumulated in the slave trade. By the time of his death in 1856, Hagan's estate totaled $253,091.93, or almost $8 million in 2020 real wealth relative value. Nearly three-fourths of this was in financial instruments: forty-three drafts totaling $121,235.61, ten promissory notes worth $24,645.50, and four due bills valued at $47,720.84. The money due him came from a representative mixture of slave traders, financiers, and railroad companies, including a note from W. G. Hewes, president of the New Orleans & Opelousas Railroad, for $15,000.[44]

John Hagan, like McDonald, had also been an investor in banks, including 182 shares in the Citizens' Bank of Louisiana worth $28,210. Hagan additionally had bank accounts at three banks—the Citizens' Bank of Louisiana, the Union Bank of Louisiana, and the Bank of Louisiana—with varying balances in his favor. None of his bank accounts, however, totaled more than $1,000, suggesting that the majority of his wealth lay in financial paper and slaves. Hagan also owned several lots of ground in New Orleans, including the household on the corner of Esplanade and Moreau, worth an estimated $4,000, with the furniture valued at a little more than $300.[45]

It was this relatively small portion of his estate, along with $10,000, that John Hagan left to the formerly enslaved mother of his children, Lucy Ann Cheatham, and the children he had with her. To his white relatives, he left substantially more: $50,000 to his mother, by then living with Hugh Hagan in Richmond; $25,000 to Hugh; and a collective $20,000 to their sister, Eleanor Manson, and her two children. Alexander Hagan received nothing, presumably because he had previously borrowed and not repaid more than $25,000. All of John Hagan's white relatives already had substantial property or had ready means to earn an income. Cheatham, while emancipated prior to Hagan's death, was limited in what work she could find, and she had two young children to raise. Even for the biological heirs of slave traders, the profits of the trade were not evenly distributed.[46]

Hugh and Alexander Hagan continued in their brother's line of work. Alexander died shortly after John. Lucy Cheatham nursed him, too, during his last illness. Despite the end of the slave trade, in 1870 Hugh Hagan could describe himself as a "retired merchant" to census takers and afford to employ an African American cook and nurse. His children, too, benefited from their father's buying and selling of people, and perhaps from the large inheritance their uncle John had left them. The *Richmond Dispatch* reported in 1885 that the young "Mr. Hugh Hagan and his sister, Miss Stella Hagan, arrived in New York on Saturday last from Bremen, having been absent from this country for eighteen months visiting all the principal places of interest in the old country." For the second white generation, their parents' slave trading meant European tours and an entrance into high society.[47]

As for Alexander McDonald, he disappeared from surviving written records just as his alleged fortune disappeared from out of the Bank of the State's grasp. Once a man of "good character," McDonald had proved himself a confidence man gone too far into debt to recover. He vanished out of his creditors' clutches and started again in an unknown location without that crucially important established reputation but with, presumably, whatever cash, specie, and personal estate he managed to smuggle out of Charleston. As late as 1870, McDonald's former associates were still ignorant of his fate and still in "great surprise" that a man who "enjoyed the confidence of the public and was reputed to be a man of large means and responsible for all his engagements" could have "clandestinely left the state."[48]

Alexander McDonald was no different in his mind-set, his practices, or his ethos than many other of slavery's capitalists. He was different only because he was caught. The insider information, the preferential treatment based on family and business connections, and the importance of the performance of wealth were not unusual. Most significantly, McDonald's acceptance of the commodification and trade of human beings as the basis of his wealth underlay the commercial mind-set of most white Americans of the era. Whether mortgaging enslaved people to banks or neighbors, trading in slave-grown cotton, or manufacturing "plantation goods" to be sold in the slaveholding states, all of this wealth rested on slavery, and businessmen of the era were perhaps more aware of this connection than are twenty-first-century readers.[49]

While proslavery writers painted slave traders as scoundrels, and while they certainly meet that description when looking backward from the present, to their fellow nineteenth-century capitalists they were not scoundrels but fellow businessmen. Disdain for slave traders extended only as far as their economic failures. Judgment was reserved for one's bottom line, not the nature of the business in which one accumulated a profit. His peers did not see Alexander McDonald as a scoundrel because he was a slave trader; they saw him as a scoundrel because he failed to repay his debts and in so doing provided fodder for critics of banking. Slave traders in this sense were not outside of nineteenth-century southern society but the epitome of it, embodying the converging interests of slavery, racism, and capital accumulation. In their disregard for how that accumulation happened, they *sine qua non* represent the heart of the capitalistic ethos.

Notes

1. D. R. Hundley, *Social Relations in Our Southern* States (New York, 1860; repr., Baton Rouge: Louisiana State University Press, 1960), 139–49, quoted in Walter Johnson, *Soul by Soul: Life inside the Antebellum Slave Market* (Cambridge, Mass.: Harvard University Press, 1999), 24. For an example of historians taking antebellum critiques of slave traders too seriously, see Scott P. Marler's claim that traders in New Orleans were "nearly as shunned in polite society as free blacks" (Marler, *The Merchants' Capital: New Orleans and the Political Economy of the Nineteenth-Century South* [Cambridge: Cambridge University Press, 2013], 62). Walter Johnson alternatively argues that slave traders were a convenient scapegoat for slaveholders (Johnson, *Soul by Soul*, 24–25). Michael Tadman also points to slave traders who were "citizens of standing" (Tadman, *Speculators and Slaves: Masters, Traders, and Slaves in the Old South* [Madison: University of Wisconsin Press, 1989], chap. 7, esp. 192–200). For further discussions of slave traders' social standing, see Steven Deyle, *Carry Me Back: The Domestic Slave Trade in American Life* (New York: Oxford University Press, 2005); Robert H. Gudmestad, *A Troublesome Commerce: The Transformation of the Interstate Slave Trade* (Baton Rouge: Louisiana State University Press, 2003); Joshua D. Rothman, "The Contours of Cotton Capitalism: Speculation, Slavery, and the Economic Panic in Mississippi, 1832–1841," in *Slavery's Capitalism: A New History of American Economic Development*, ed. Sven Beckert and Seth Rockman (Philadelphia: University of Pennsylvania Press, 2016), 122–45; Calvin Schermerhorn, *Money over Mastery, Family over Freedom: Slavery in the Antebellum Upper South* (Baltimore: John Hopkins University Press, 2011); Kari J. Winter, *The American Dreams of John B. Prentis, Slave Trader* (Athens: University of Georgia Press, 2011); and Maurie D. McInnis, *Slaves Waiting for Sale: Abolitionist Art and the American Slave Trade* (Chicago: University of Chicago Press, 2011).

2. "Second Municipality Council," *Jeffersonian Republican* (New Orleans), May 14, 1854, 2; Johnson, *Soul by Soul*, 6. For calculations of the profit of the slave trade, see Johnson, *Soul by Soul*, 5–7; and Tadman, *Speculators and Slaves*, chap. 5.

3. Carpenter v. Robards, Fayette County Circuit Court 1024 (1859), Kentucky Department of Libraries and Archives, Frankfort; Theodore Dwight Weld, *American Slavery As It Is* (New York: American Anti-Slavery Society, 1839), 174.

4. Kemp quoted in Robert S. Neale, *The Bank of Cape Fear of Wilmington, North Carolina: A History of North Carolina's First Antebellum Bank and Its Paper Money, Branches, Key Personnel, and Local Impact* (Wilmington: Lower Cape Fear Historical Society Archives Division, 1999), 25; Calvin Schermerhorn, *The Business of Slavery and the Rise of American Capitalism, 1815–1860* (New Haven, Conn.: Yale University Press, 2015); Tadman, *Speculators and Slaves*.

5. Jeff Forret, "'How Deeply They Weed into the Pockets': Slave Traders, Bank Speculators, and the Anatomy of a Chesapeake Wildcat, 1840–1843," in this volume. For the rich history of slavery and nineteenth-century financial networks, see L. Diane Barnes, Brian Schoen, and Frank Towers, eds., *The Old South's Modern Worlds: Slavery, Region, and Nation in the Age of Progress* (New York: Oxford University Press, 2011); Edward E. Baptist, *The Half Has Never Been Told: Slavery and the Making of American Capitalism* (New York: Basic, 2014); Sven Beckert and Seth Rockman, eds., *Slavery's Capitalism: A New History of American Economic Development* (Philadelphia: University of Pennsylvania Press, 2016); Sven Beckert and Christine Desan, eds., *American Capitalism: New Histories* (New York: Columbia University Press, 2018); Sven Beckert, *Empire of Cotton: A Global History* (New York: Vintage, 2014); Deyle, *Carry Me Back;* Walter Johnson, *River of Dark Dreams: Slavery and Empire in the Cotton Kingdom* (Cambridge, Mass.: Harvard University Press, 2013); Richard Holcombe Kilbourne, Jr., *Debt, Investment, Slaves: Credit Relations in East Feliciana Parish, Louisiana 1825–1885* (Tuscaloosa: University of Alabama Press, 1995); Kilbourne, *Slave Agriculture and Financial Markets in Antebellum America: The Bank of the United States in Mississippi, 1831–1852* (London: Pickering and Chatto, 2006); Bonnie M. Martin, "Slavery's Invisible Engine: Mortgaging Human Property," *Journal of Southern History* 76, no. 4 (November 2010): 817–66; Scott Reynolds Nelson, *A Nation of Deadbeats: An Uncommon History of America's Financial Disasters* (New York: Knopf, 2012); Seth Rockman, *Scraping By: Wage Labor, Slavery, and Survival in Early Baltimore* (Baltimore: John Hopkins University Press, 2009); Seth Rockman, "Slavery and Capitalism," *Journal of the Civil War Era* 2, no. 1 (March 2012): 5; Caitlin Rosenthal, *Accounting for Slavery: Masters and Management* (Cambridge, Mass.: Harvard University Press, 2018); Joshua D. Rothman, *Flush Times and Fever Dreams: A Story of Capitalism and Slavery in the Age of Jackson* (Athens: University of Georgia Press, 2014); Schermerhorn, *Business of Slavery;* and Tadman, *Speculators and Slaves.*

6. "Hugh McDonald" and "Alexander McDonald," U.S. Naturalization Records, National Archives and Records Administration (NARA), Washington D.C.; Record of Admissions to Citizenship, District of South Carolina, 1790–1906, NARA Series M1183, Reference: (Roll 1) Vol. 1: Aliens Admitted as Citizens 1790–1860; Colclough v. Colclough, Bill 347 (1849) and Bill 348 (1852), Sumter District Equity Court, South Carolina Department of Archives and History, Columbia (hereinafter cited as SCDAH); Sumter District Equity Court, Green et al. v. McDonald et al., Bill 415 (1866), Sumter District Equity Court, SCDAH.

7. Testimony of A. Moise, Bank of Charleston v. John Hagan, Supreme Court of Louisiana Docket 464 (December 1847) 2 La. Ann 999; Southeast Coastwise Inward and Outward Slave Manifests, 1790–1860, Ports of Charleston, Savannah, and Augusta; New Orleans Slave Manifests 1807–1860. Alexander Hagan later claimed that he and his brothers predated the McDonalds' entrance into the slave trade, but port manifests clearly contradict this (Testimony of Alexander Hagan, Bank of Charleston v. John Hagan, Supreme Court of Louisiana).

8. J. Mauldin Lesesne, *The Bank of the State of South Carolina: A General and Political History* (Columbia: University of South Carolina Press, 1970), Appendix II, 187–93.

9. Howard Bodenhorn, *State Banking in Early America: A New Economic History* (New York: Oxford University Press, 2003), 5–6; Lesesne, *The Bank of the State,* 17–19.

10. James S. Gibbon, *The Banks of New-York, Their Dealers, The Clearing House, and the Panic of*

1857 (New York: D. Appleton, 1859), 21, 51–52; "Report of the President of the Bank," 1848, F. H. Elmore Papers #814, Southern Historical Collection, The Wilson Library, University of North Carolina at Chapel Hill (hereinafter cited as SHC). McDonald was also a Free Mason. His signature appeared on several petitions of the South Carolina lodge to the state legislature. See, for instance, "Committee of The Grand Lodge of Ancient Free Masons . . . Asking for Permission to Hold a Lottery . . ." (1827) Series S165015–00114, SCDAH; "Grand Lodge of Ancient Free Masons of S.C., Petition Asking for the Right to Hold a Lottery . . ." (1840) Series S165015–04703, SCDAH.

11. For known slave traders advertising as brokers, see, for example, "Thomas M Hume" and "Thomas Ryan," *Directory of the City of Charleston, for the Year 1852* (Charleston: Edward C. Councell, 1851), 62, 111; "Hugh McDonald" and "Thomas N. Gadsden," in *Charleston City Directories for the Years 1830–1841*, ed. James William Hagy (Baltimore: Clearfield Company, 1997), 80, 117; and Ziba Oakes Papers, Boston Public Library.

12. Advertisement in J. T. Hershman, comp., *Columbia City Directory* (Columbia, S.C.: R.W. Gibbes, 1859), n.p.

13. State v. Lehre, in J. S. G. Richardson, *Reports of Cases at Law Argued Determined in the Court of Appeals and Court of Errors South Carolina 1853–1854*, 234–326; Thomas N. Gadsden v. Francis Lance, 1 J. J. McMullan, *Equity Cases Argued and Determined Court of Appeals of South Carolina 1840–1842*, 87–93; Washington Augustus Clark, *The History of the Banking Institutions Organized in South Carolina Prior to 1860* (Columbia: The State Company, 1922), 173, 198.

In addition to the individuals listed above, several other slave traders were involved in banking in Charleston. The directors of the Southwest Railroad Bank included two successful slave traders, P. J. Porcher (1850–63) and Ziba Oakes (ca. 1860–65). The board of the People's Bank of Charleston included Thomas Savage Heyward of the firm Capers & Heyward. At least three slave traders were major investors in the Planters and Mechanics Bank of South Carolina, including I. S. K. Bennett, Thomas M. Hume, and Alonzo J. White. These men and their peers likely invested in multiple banks at once, but due to the scarcity of surviving records, it is impossible to know exact numbers. Lewis N. Shelton also served alongside McDonald on the board of the Bank of the State of South Carolina. Shelton started out as a commission merchant in Charleston with his brother Joseph. Joseph first served on the board in 1826, with Lewis serving from 1830 to 1832. Lewis Shelton later relocated to New Orleans, where he was active in overlapping circles of financiers and slave traders. Shelton was friendly with Theophilus Freeman and testified in court cases concerning Freeman's relationship with Sarah Conner. He was also very close with Joseph Barelli, a New Orleans-based commission merchant and freight charterer who at one time worked in conjunction with John Hagan in the coastwise slave trade (see Planters and Mechanics Bank of South Carolina Records, South Caroliniana Library, University of South Carolina, Columbia; Bank of Charleston Records, 1179.01, South Carolina Historical Society, Charleston [hereafter cited as SCHS]; Southwest Railroad Bank Papers, Bank of Charleston Records,1179.02.15, SCHS; and Clark, *History of the Banking Institutions*, 173, 190–95). See also Tadman, *Speculators and Slaves*, 192–94; "For Freight or Charter," New Orleans *Daily Crescent*, July 12, 1850; "Auction Sales Yesterday," *Charleston (S.C.) Mercury*, March 10, 1858; and Barelli v. Hagan, Supreme Court of Louisiana #3488 (May 1839) 13 La. 580.

14. Petitions, 1859 no. 90, State Library of South Carolina, Columbia; Charleston County Mortgage Book U-11, p. 149, Charleston County Registrar of Mesne and Conveyances; Bank of Charleston Records, SCHS.

15. Forret, "How Deeply They *Weed* into the Pockets."

16. An Act to Incorporate the Traders Bank of the City of Richmond (passed February 18, 1860); "Traders' Bank," *Richmond Daily Dispatch,* February 28, 1860. Hector Davis, for example, had previously been a director of the Bank of the Commonwealth, while Robert Lumpkin received substantial loans from the Farmers Bank of Virginia (Bank of the Commonwealth Records, Mss4B2257a1, Virginia Historical Society, Richmond [hereinafter cited as VHS]; Cashier's Checkbook, April 28, 1851, p. 74, Farmers Bank of Virginia Records, Mss3F2298a1, VHS).

17. Crouch v. Davis's Ex'or (1866), Richmond City Chancery Court, John Marshall Court House, Richmond, Virginia.

18. An Act to Incorporate the Traders Bank of the City of Richmond (passed February 18, 1860); "Trader's Bank," *Richmond Daily Dispatch,* February 28, 1860; Bodenhorn, *State Banking,* 12–13.

19. "Trader's Bank," *Richmond Daily Dispatch,* February 24, 1860; *The Bankers' Magazine and Statistical Register* 11, no. 1 (July 1861): 76; Hector Davis Account Book, Vol. II, Chicago History Museum Archives; *Richmond Daily Dispatch,* October 19, 1857. None of the bank books of the Traders' Bank of Richmond survive.

20. "Trader's Bank," *Richmond Daily Dispatch,* April 25, 1860.

21. *Bankers' Magazine and Statistical Register* 11, no. 1 (July 1861): 76; Eugene W. Ferslew, comp., *First Annual Directory for the City of Richmond, to Which Is Added a Business Directory for 1859* (Richmond: Geo. M. West, 1859).

22. Bodenhorn, *State Banking,* 30; Gibbon, *Banks of New York,* 26–27.

23. Gibbon, *Banks of New York,* 47–48; "Report of the President of the Bank," 1848, F. H. Elmore Papers #814, SHC.

24. Will of Hugh Hagan, Sumter District, South Carolina, dated June 25, 1839, and executed August 23, 1841.

25. Testimony of Alexander Hagan, Bank of Charleston v. John Hagan, Supreme Court of Louisiana; Southeast Coastwise Inward and Outward Slave Manifests, 1790–1860, Ports of Charleston, Savannah, and Augusta; New Orleans Slave Manifests 1807–1860.

26. Southeast Coastwise Inward and Outward Slave Manifests, 1790–1860, Ports of Charleston, Savannah, and Augusta; New Orleans Slave Manifests 1807–1860.

27. "$100 Reward," *The Southerner* (Tarboro, N.C.), January 26, 1856, 2; 1860 U.S. Census, Richmond, Virginia, "Hugh Hagan," Ancestry.com; "Democratic Nominations for the Legislature," *Richmond Daily Dispatch,* May 25, 1857, 2; "The Democratic Vigilance Committee," *Richmond Enquirer,* September 7, 1852, 2. After the Civil War, Solomon Davis relocated with his family to New York City, where he continued to work in the banking industry (1870 Census, City of New York, s.v. "Solomon Davis").

28. Succession of Lucy Ann Hagan, 21696 Civil District Court, Orleans Parish, Louisiana; Will of John Hagan, Orleans Parish Will #10362, vol. 10, filed June 9, 1856. For more on Lucy Ann

Cheatham and the sexual economy of the slave trade, see Alexandra Finley, "'Cash to Corinna': Domestic Labor and Sexual Economy in the 'Fancy Trade,'" *Journal of American History* 104 (September 2017): 410–30.

29. Testimony of A. Moise and Alexander Hagan, Bank of Charleston v. John Hagan, Supreme Court of Louisiana.

30. John Rist v. John Hagan, Supreme Court of Louisiana, Eastern District, Docket #4503, June 1844, 8 Rob. 106; The Bank of the State of South Carolina v. John Hagan, Fourth District Court Case #134, Orleans Parish, New Orleans Public Library.

31. Testimony of A. Moise, Bank of Charleston v. John Hagan, Supreme Court of Louisiana.

32. Bank of Charleston v. John Hagan, Supreme Court of Louisiana; *Report of the Special Committee on the Memorial of F. H. Elmore, President of Bank of State of S. Carolina* (1849), F. H. Elmore Papers #814, SHC.

33. Bank of Charleston v. John Hagan, Supreme Court of Louisiana; Bank of the State of South Carolina v. John Hagan, Fourth District Court, Orleans Parish.

34. Bank of Charleston v. John Hagan, Supreme Court of Louisiana; Clark, *History of the Banking Institutions*, 198.

35. Bank of Charleston v. John Hagan, Supreme Court of Louisiana; Bank of the State of South Carolina v. John Hagan, Fourth District Court, Orleans Parish.

36. In relative real wealth value, the $46,000 debt would be approximately $1,602,333.33 in 2020 (https://www.measuringworth.com/calculators/uscompare/).

37. Bank of the State of South Carolina v. John Hagan, Fourth District Court, Orleans Parish; "Ker Boyce," in *Biographical Directory of the South Carolina Senate, 1776–1985*, vol. 1, ed. N. Louise Bailey, Mary L. Morgan, and Carolyn R. Taylor (Columbia: University of South Carolina Press, 1986), 169–70.

38. Testimony of A. Moise and Thomas Ryan, Bank of Charleston v. John Hagan, Supreme Court of Louisiana; Bank of the State of South Carolina v. John Hagan, Fourth District Court, Orleans Parish.

39. *Report of the Special Committee*, 174; Lesesne, *The Bank of the State*, 71–88.

40. *Report of the Special Committee*, 176.

41. *Report of the Special Committee*, 176; Bank of Charleston v. John Hagan, Supreme Court of Louisiana; Bank of the State of South Carolina v. John Hagan, Fourth District Court, Orleans Parish.

42. *Report of the Special Committee*, 180.

43. Bank of Charleston v. John Hagan, Supreme Court of Louisiana; Bank of the State of South Carolina v. John Hagan, Fourth District Court, Orleans Parish.

44. Estate of John Hagan, Orleans Parish Will #10362, vol. 10, filed June 9, 1856. Hagan's estate has a 2020 relative real wealth value of $7,947,304 (https://www.measuringworth.com/calculators/uscompare/relativevalue.php).

45. Estate of John Hagan, Orleans Parish Will #10362.

46. Estate of John Hagan, Orleans Parish Will #10362.

47. 1870 U.S. Census; "Personals and Briefs," *Richmond Dispatch,* December 15, 1885, 1.

48. Colclough v. Colclough, Bill 347 (1849) and 1852, Bill 348 (1852), SCDAH; Green et al. v. McDonald et al., 1866 Bill 415, Sumter District Equity Court, SCDAH.

49. For the concept of slavery's capitalism, see Beckert and Rockman, eds., *Slavery's Capitalism.*

"How Deeply They *Weed* into the Pockets"

SLAVE TRADERS, BANK SPECULATORS, AND THE ANATOMY
OF A CHESAPEAKE WILDCAT, 1840–1843

JEFF FORRET

On October 12, 1840, the Commercial Bank of Millington, located on Maryland's Eastern Shore, closed its doors for the last time. Bigger-city papers condescendingly described Millington as "no great shakes of a place," a trifling, "obscure village . . . containing perhaps a store and blacksmith shop" and "about fifty houses." A stagecoach passed through three times per week, helping the town forge some commercial ties to Elkton, to the north, and Baltimore, across Chesapeake Bay. But despite Millington's generally sleepy countenance, it had nevertheless secured in 1836 a state charter for a bank, joining the proliferation of financial institutions that sprouted after President Andrew Jackson's attacks killed the centralized Second Bank of the United States. The Millington Bank did not become fully operational until 1838, when broker Moses Holmes "opened an account" on behalf of the Commercial Bank of Millington at the Chesapeake Bank of Baltimore, where its notes could be redeemed. That account closed later the same year, however, and the Millington Bank continued to languish, barely surviving the depression of 1839. Throughout this time, it eked out but "a nominal existence" with little influence outside the vicinity of Kent County. Its cashier presided over a "large ledger," according to one report, "but there were few or no entries made in it."[1]

The small, initially insignificant bank's fortunes rose fantastically and deteriorated just as dramatically after the arrival of the enigmatic "stranger" William Weed, his brother F. A. Weed, and a third investor, a man identified only as Sherwood from Buffalo, New York—probably the banker Merril B. Sherwood. Together they purchased the establishment's charter from Moses Holmes in November 1839 for $10,000. The partners then installed F. A. Weed as bank president, reopened the Millington account at the Chesapeake Bank, and adopted "the high pressure principle," embarking upon the reckless printing of banknotes with wanton disregard to the concern's specie reserves, an increasingly common practice absent the regulatory constraints of the Second Bank. The speculative bubble of the 1830s that had burst so spectacularly in 1837, ushering in widespread bank failures and the ignominious end of the "flush times," might have cautioned the Weeds against the irresponsible issuance of banknotes, but in a climate of national deregulation, in which bank oversight devolved entirely upon overwhelmed state governments, the prospect of realizing immense profits through overly generous lending policies proved too tantalizing. Issuing more paper than banks had specie in the vault backing it up had long been normative, but the practice was now carried to unprecedented extremes. As early as May 1840, the Millington Bank lacked the "funds or coin sufficient to redeem its circulation." By the time it finally exploded in October, joining the Patapsco Savings Fund and a slew of "other defunct shinplaster factories" and "swindling shops" of Baltimore, as much as a half million dollars in Millington money had been dumped into circulation across the United States. Yet when the hapless "people of the neighborhood took possession of the banking house" in Millington to seize "whatever valuable funds they could lay their hands on," they found but $565 lying in the vault. William and F. A. Weed fled Maryland to avoid the public's wrath.[2]

The Weed brothers' speculative ventures in the banking industry rendered them briefly notorious. Like so many others of their shady ilk, the Weeds functioned as agents of capitalist excess in the age of Jackson. In contrast to the elite bank directors described by Alexandra J. Finley in the previous essay in this volume, they "belong to the wild-cat species of financiers," condemned one newspaper in 1841. As historian Stephen Mihm has explained, the term "wildcat bank" originally referred only to "institutions founded by unscrupulous financiers in remote areas for the express purpose of making it difficult, if not impossible, for the notes to be exchanged for gold and silver." By 1840, the American public had generalized the phrase to apply to any banking concern whose paper issues vastly exceeded its specie in the vault and, hence, its ability to redeem its notes. By either definition, the Weeds' Millington enterprise qualified as one of the dozens of wildcat banks that sprouted between 1836 and the 1863 passage of the National Bank Act crafted to impose financial order on the reigning chaos. Only a blurry line separated legitimate from illegitimate financial institutions in the age of Jackson, however, so perhaps the Commercial Bank of Millington's progenitors had originally conceived it in good faith and with the best of intentions. At the same time, the uncertainties of the emerging nineteenth-century American capitalist system supplied ample opportunities for all manner of fraud. As one scholar has pointed out, "the darker forces of greed and deception . . . prosper in new frontiers of commerce." Cons and swindles thrive in such environments. Rather than dismiss the Millington as a rogue institution, then, we may use it to illustrate the innovative if ethically questionable ways in which antebellum-era wildcat banks sprang up, operated, and spread to new, unsuspecting communities.[3]

By employing the history of the Commercial Bank of Millington as a case study, this essay takes a microhistorical approach to the macroeconomic transformations afoot in the age of Jackson. Like many other banks that popped up in the 1830s and early 1840s, the Millington was located in a tiny, rural community filled with farmers and other working people. For the first time, common folk gained convenient access, right in their hometown, to the services of a financial institution emblematic of the evolving capitalist system. Most residents assumed that its presence would be beneficial to the area. As the Millington's wildcat status soon became evident, however, locals who lost their deposits quickly soured on the penetration of a capitalist banking institution into the Eastern Shore. The village of Millington, then, stood as a microcosm for the overwhelmingly pastoral America of the time, its citizens representative of the disillusioned masses often confounded by the mysteries of the emerging economy.

If the town's setting and residents were broadly typical of the country as a whole, the Millington debacle was uniquely devastating and widespread in its impact. The Commercial Bank of Millington served as an incubator for failure and scandal with nationwide implications. A mother wildcat, the Millington birthed at least two known cubs. Its notes underwrote the creation of a pair of other doomed institutions—the Farmers and Millers Bank of Hagerstown, Maryland, and, more infamously, the Gallipolis Bank of Ohio—and exerted disastrous ripple effects across the economies of several states. The sheer quantity of worthless paper the Millington Bank spewed forth set it apart. Its notes became the fodder for counterfeiting operations for the next two decades. Already in 1840, the *New York Times* dubbed the Millington fraud "the greatest shave extant," its spectacular demise thoroughly documented in newspapers and court cases. The scale of the Millington Bank's explosion and the scope of its consequences also prompted an investigation into its causes by the Maryland state legislature, the product of which was an exceptionally rich documentary record of the actions of a handful of greedy and opportunistic charlatans whose craftily engineered scams wreaked havoc on the American economy. Investigators extracted testimony that pries into the obscure, inner workings of the real but elusive scoundrels so influential in the evolution of American capitalism but oftentimes lost or overlooked in discussions of impersonal market forces and sweeping macroeconomic shifts.[4]

In churning out currency with reckless abandon, the Millington wildcat joined thousands of other, relatively more cautious and legitimate institutions in extending credit in the form of banknotes for the acquisition of land and slaves, the twin engines that drove the cotton economy and the development, as recent scholarship has shown, of American capitalism itself. Historians have demonstrated how antebellum banking institutions proved crucial cogs in the machinery of the domestic slave trade that redistributed surplus slaves from the Upper South southwestward to the advancing cotton frontier as well as to the cane fields of Louisiana. Banks fueled slave traders' entire operations by lending them the ready cash necessary to buy Chesapeake masters' excess slaves. As made clear by the peculiar history of the Commercial Bank of Millington, the relationship between banks and domestic slave traders could go deeper still.[5]

The propagation of all state-chartered banks in the 1830s demanded start-up capital. Stephen Mihm recently inquired, "Who provided the capital for banks to get off the ground?" The testimony gathered in the fallout of the Millington wildcat permits us to "follow the money" and offer one direct, albeit incomplete, answer to Mihm's query. Located in the southern, slaveholding state of Maryland, the Commercial Bank of Millington found one source of funds in slave traders themselves. Despite being denounced in public discourse as ruthless, loathsome, marginal figures, slave dealers were, on the whole, prominent, respectable individuals and at times among the wealthiest of all Americans. Calculating profit-seekers, they entertained a wide variety of

investment opportunities. With the monetary resources at their disposal, traders might underwrite the very banking ventures that later granted them credit
and kept them awash in paper money.[6]

Banking entrepreneurs understood their importance to slave traders' livelihood and sometimes appealed directly to the purveyors of human chattel to
capitalize their institutions. Unscrupulous bankers involved in risky wildcat
concerns probably would not have divulged fraudulent intentions when so-
liciting funds from prospective slave-trading financiers, for the slave dealers
would not have wished to alienate themselves with the local slave-selling public. At the same time, traders exhibited no qualms against profiting by economic endeavors other Americans condemned as morally objectionable and—
unflattering popular rhetoric about their profession notwithstanding—suffered
little by doing so. Wildcat bankers, in turn, appreciated traders' ability to circulate their dubious notes widely. Whether slave traders carried bank paper
dozens of miles away from the issuing institution to purchase bondpeople or
stuffed wads of bills in their pockets as they undertook slaving journeys across
the country to New Orleans, they delayed that paper's redemption for specie
by days, weeks, or even months. Relieved of the anxiety of their notes' prompt
return, wildcat banks such as the Millington could blissfully continue the irresponsible printing of paper money. At the Commercial Bank of Millington,
those who speculated in banks and those who speculated in enslaved black
bodies thus developed a close relationship, one at times symbiotic but at other
times riven by tension.[7]

Slave traders' occupation inherently demanded expertise in local money
markets. Their advertisements consistently promised "cash" for one hundred,
three hundred, four hundred or more "negroes," and they paid in banknotes
of various sorts, sometimes bowing to the preferences of the seller for paper
from a particular state or even a specific bank. Traders needed access to banks'
paper, along with an acute understanding of the relative values of the multifarious bills through which they might complete their transactions. These were
paramount to running a successful operation. Headquartered in Washington, D.C., slave dealers and occasional business associates William H. Williams
and Thomas N. Davis were as familiar with the currencies in circulation as anyone. When Williams first began advertising as an independent slave trader in

1835, he invited sellers to call at his residence or to visit him at Alexander Lee's Lottery and Exchange Office on the north side of Pennsylvania Avenue, where he was a partner.[8]

Although Williams eventually relocated to the Yellow House, his notorious slave pen within sight of the U.S. Capitol, it made ample sense for him to base his operations initially at a lottery and exchange office. One scholar suggested long ago that it was because frustrated lottery players could conveniently sell a slave to acquire the funds for more tickets, but this flippant remark overlooks the broader relationship between slave trading and finance in the Old South. Like slave traders, owners of lottery and exchange businesses understood money and grasped the emerging economic realities amid the dramatic transformations of the market revolution. Even as lotteries were growing more disreputable, proprietor Alexander Lee sold chances and drew "Lucky Numbers" at his establishment in the 1830s and 1840s. The geographic reach of his business was sprawling. Customers came from across the country as they visited the nation's capital, and Lee accepted orders by mail as well. His office thus attracted a wide assortment of banknotes. With such intimate acquaintance with the dizzying array of notes in circulation, Lee routinely exchanged currencies at his office, discounting more heavily those notes from suspect or faraway banks. The confused state of American currency permitted a lively business, and at some point before 1840 Lee had partnered with William H. Williams in the exchange office. Each man pursued the maxim "buy low, sell high" as they profited through speculation, whether by playing the money markets or by human trafficking.[9]

With a solid understanding of banknotes and the wider financial system in which they circulated, Williams and fellow Washington, D.C., slave trader Thomas N. Davis were both deeply involved in the Millington concern. Though more slave dealers than bankers per se, each had "exchanged with [William] Weed some thousands of dollars" in support of the Commercial Bank of Millington during its meteoric rise. They were invested in the institution, and the institution invested in them, channeling them the cash they needed. The system could theoretically function in ways mutually beneficial to bankers and slave traders alike, but the death of the Second Bank of the United States and the shockingly careless proliferation of little monitored state-chartered institutions permitted the formation of banking concerns erected on fragile foundations, their metaphorical edifices susceptible to even the slightest financial breeze.[10]

The founders of the Millington Bank sowed the seeds of the establishment's own destruction. Buffalo, New York, financier and founder of the Erie County Bank Merril B. Sherwood and two unnamed "others"—perhaps the Weed brothers?—launched the Gallipolis Bank in 1839 with $200,000 in capital, including $80,000 in Millington money "as a special deposit . . . not to be put in circulation" but "for the sole purpose of giving credit" to the institution so that it might commence operations. The Millington bills were supposed to sit in the vault and merely help accountants balance the Gallipolis Bank's books. The bank fraudulently put them into circulation, however, and in late August 1840 some $12,000 unexpectedly returned to the Millington Bank for redemption. The Millington paid on the notes, but at great cost. It "exhaust[ed]" its "coin & funds," sending the institution into the suicidal tailspin that ended in its October collapse. Steeped in fraud from its reinvention and in the throes of insolvency, the Millington Bank, in desperation, aggressively printed notes for traders such as Williams and Davis to "broadcast over the land," floating them "as far away from home as possible, so as to prolong the time before they would return for redemption." The longer the notes stayed out, the more paper the bank could print and thereby extend its life.[11]

Some contemporaries expressed serious reservations about the soundness of Millington notes well before the institution collapsed. Alexander Lee, William H. Williams's partner in the exchange office, observed that he knew "nothing of the character of the money except that it was bad." John Corse, who ran an exchange office in Alexandria, declared that "he would have nothing to do with Millington notes, and refused to Exchange" them. Washington, D.C., slave trader James H. Birch, infamous today for abducting the free black Solomon Northup, temporarily imprisoning him in Williams's slave pen, and selling him as a slave in Louisiana, insisted that he "did not consider the Millington money good & never did." Thanks to the institution's suspect reputation, "the only persons" Birch knew of who "circulat[ed] it in large amounts" were Williams and the "negro trader" Thomas N. Davis.[12]

The financial ties between the pair of slave dealers and the Commercial Bank of Millington compelled the traders, as investors, to try to prop up the dying institution once they realized it was in trouble. The best means of doing so was to get its notes into circulation, as far away as possible from sites of redemption in Millington or Baltimore. In late September and early October 1840, only weeks and days before the Millington Bank went under, William H. Williams and his two leading purchasing agents—his younger brother Thomas Williams and Ebenezer Rodbird, the jailer at his slave pen—conducted a brisk business, buying up slaves in northern Virginia and southern Maryland with Millington notes. After the Millington Bank's death, at least three sellers sued Williams, demanding recompense for the now-worthless money he or his agents had given them. Williams lost at least two, and probably all three, of these cases, the last in 1850, a full decade after the Millington failed.[13]

To rescue the institution, William H. Williams conspired with William Weed to hatch a concerted plot to disseminate notes from the Commercial Bank of Millington. At an unspecified date in the fall of 1840, prior to the Millington's failure, Williams rendezvoused with Thomas N. Davis at the railroad depot in Washington, D.C., and persuaded him to meet with "two gentlemen . . . who would propose a . . . scheme" through which Davis "might make a large sum of money." Intrigued, Davis consented to a meeting between the four. Williams and the mysterious "two gentlemen"—Millington Bank investor William Weed and co-conspirator Joseph T. Guthrie—pressed Davis to accept $100,000 in Millington notes so that he might dump them, at a discount, into circulation in Washington, D.C., in exchange for other, more valid funds. Even though the other bills would command a premium over Millington paper, Davis would be disposing of increasingly suspect Millington notes in favor of more sound currency that he could then forward to the Eastern Shore to keep the Millington afloat. Reports of this last-ditch effort to save the Millington confirmed that Williams most assuredly knew that the bills he and his agents Thomas Williams and Ebenezer Rodbird were using to purchase slaves in the fall of 1840 had been issued by a bank teetering on the brink.[14]

Ultimately, Davis "declined the . . . proposition" because his own suspicions of Millington paper made it too risky. Slave traders engaged in a sordid commerce, but they were also savvy, calculating businessmen. Although often portrayed as dealing in slaves only temporarily, until they could amass the wealth to purchase a plantation or invest in other ventures, professional slave traders bought and sold enslaved people as they engaged concurrently in a range of other economic pursuits. Some owned a stake in general stores or were merchants in various commercial enterprises. Throughout a good portion of his decades-long career as an active trader, William H. Williams partnered with George M. Grant to sell boots and shoes at 18 Camp Street in New Orleans. Slave dealers willingly backed any number of concerns, but it made sense for Williams and Davis to gravitate toward banking institutions that not only promised to generate revenue but also financed the slave trade itself. Nevertheless, traders' drive for profit and shrewd cost-benefit analyses superseded any loyalty to financiers whose schemes might jeopardize their bottom line. Davis's unwillingness to participate in the latest machinations of William Weed and Joseph T. Guthrie gave Williams pause as well. Suddenly anxious over the proposal, he lost his enthusiasm for the arrangement and likewise withdrew.[15]

Undeterred, William Weed and Joseph T. Guthrie forged ahead with their plan to salvage the Commercial Bank of Millington. Paradoxically, the plot they concocted hinged on launching a new bank, the Farmers and Millers Bank of Hagerstown, Maryland. Located about seventy-five miles northwest of Baltimore, Hagerstown in 1840 was a rural outpost of only a few thousand souls. Maryland's country folk had been clamoring for easier access to credit for years, so despite—and in fact, because of—Hagerstown's small size and relatively remote location, the Maryland legislature had incorporated the Farmers and Millers Bank in 1836 to appease lawmakers' rural constituents. The charter mandated the possession of $75,000 in specie, through any combination of gold and silver coin, before the bank could lawfully issue notes or commence operations. William Weed and Joseph T. Guthrie made it their mission to secure the necessary funds, for those monies were crucial to their plans. The pair calculated that they could raise sufficient resources to launch the Hagerstown bank and then, given Weed's connections to both institutions, divert a portion of the funds intended to capitalize the new institution for the purpose of propping up the struggling Commercial Bank of Millington.[16]

Slave traders William H. Williams and Thomas N. Davis had rebuffed Weed's and Guthrie's recent pleas to underwrite the Farmers and Millers Bank of Hagerstown and thereby indirectly funnel money into the Millington, but the determined entrepreneurs persevered. Both had a stake in the plan's success. Whereas Weed wanted the Millington Bank to survive, Guthrie was a significant shareholder in the Hagerstown concern. To fund the enterprise, Weed redirected funds that Williams and Davis had previously supplied the

Millington to the embryonic Hagerstown venture, without either slave deal-er's permission. But Weed's great coup came in securing for the Farmers and Millers Bank two specie certificates totaling $60,000, including one drawn on the Commercial Bank of Millington, to count toward the $75,000 specie requirement. "The Millington Bank at that time was in as good credit as any of the county banks in the State," boasted the *Baltimore Sun,* "their paper being at a discount of only ½ per cent in Philadelphia." In reality, as Weed surely knew, these were phantom funds. Specie certificates stated a bank's willingness to supply the quantity of gold or silver indicated on the paper; they did not guar-antee the bank was in actual possession of that specie. And the Millington was not. Nevertheless, banks routinely counted money that was only pledged on paper and not physically present in the vault. In August 1840, the treasurer of the Western Shore of Maryland dispatched a committee of three commission-ers to certify the Farmers and Millers Bank's specie reserves. After consulting the advice of legal counsel, the investigators, satisfied that the specie require-ment had been met, handed over the requisite certificate for the bank to go into operation. Counting monetary promises that existed only on paper, the Farmers and Millers Bank opened its doors on September 10, 1840. When the Millington failed a little more than a month later, its specie certificate had al-ready served its function, as qualified assets for the Hagerstown wildcat, and been cast, according to one chronicler, into the metaphorical waste basket. With the Millington's demise, William Weed promptly carried the institution's furniture, locks, and other portable assets to Hagerstown for use in the new fa-cility. Although the bank president in Hagerstown denied "any official connec-tion whatever" between the two establishments, truly the Farmers and Millers Bank was the specious "offspring" of the defunct Millington Bank.[17]

The Millington's spawn institution in Hagerstown fell into crisis soon af-ter its September opening. The Commercial Bank of Millington's failure the next month caused, as the *Baltimore Sun* reported, "wide spread ruin and dis-tress," and the Farmers and Millers Bank could not escape the deleterious ef-fects of its mother's death. Facing financial ruin, Hagerstown bank co-founder, stockholder, and cashier Joseph T. Guthrie consulted Thomas N. Davis. He informed the slave dealer in the spring of 1841 that the Farmers and Millers Bank had, in its first weeks of operation, been "doing well, but when the Mill-ington Bank . . . failed, the money came in on them very rapidly." It weathered the immediate storm, and by the time he spoke with Davis in 1841, Guthrie insisted that "the prospect was good." Nevertheless, the shifty Guthrie, now absent his absconded partner William Weed, devised a familiar strategy to relieve the Hagerstown bank from any similar fiscal misery in the future: He aimed to get another bank chartered and operational as quickly as possible. His particular focus was the salt manufacturing center of Kanawha, Virginia (now West Virginia). The "object" of establishing a bank there, Guthrie admitted, "was to keep the Farmers and Millers Bank good." He could certainly marshal funds from the Hagerstown bank to get the Kanawha venture "rightly under way," but he also required "some little specie" for launch. Guthrie confided to Davis that, behind the scenes, the proposed Kanawha concern "*could be broke*," but that was immaterial because "it was *away from home*," well more than two hundred miles from his base of operations in Hagerstown.[18]

Thomas N. Davis had made his customary fall slaving voyage to New Orleans, the South's foremost slave market, in late 1840, soon after the Millington Bank went under. While there, he not only occupied himself disposing of his enslaved cargo but also bumped into a pair of old acquaintances, the fugitives William and F. A. Weed, freshly absquatulated from Maryland. Though Davis discovered the Weeds in New Orleans, public conjecture held that the brothers were en route to Lafayette, Louisiana, to hole up, or perhaps to the Republic of Texas, a favorite destination in the late 1830s and early 1840s for those seeking to evade the reach of American law. Captain of the Watch H. S. Harper, keeper of New Orleans's Second Municipality prison on Baronne Street, and another officer took the brothers into custody on Monday night, November 30, or possibly December 1, at a Carrollton hotel. Prompting the arrest was an affidavit that Ambrose A. White, a Baltimore merchant, filed before Joshua Baldwin, recorder for the Second Municipality. White charged that F. A. Weed had "fraudulently obtained the presidency" of the Millington Bank and then "pass[ed] off and exchange[d], to a very large amount," its "worthless" paper "for the bills of other banks that were solvent." F. A.'s brother William, White added, had aided and abetted in the scheme.[19]

The Weed brothers' capture "created a great sensation" among the "'monied circles'" in New Orleans and across the country. Their pending trial before the recorder's court promised "to ascertain how deeply they *Weed* into the pockets" of the pair's unsuspecting victims, quipped one Natchez, Mississippi, newspaper. The Weeds made frequent appearances in court during December. On Wednesday, December 2, they pleaded not guilty in the recorder's court to the charge of fraud. Over the next several days, court testimony revealed that William Weed was involved with such "swindling" concerns as the Exchange Bank and Savings Institution of Philadelphia, an unnamed wildcat bank in Michigan, the Merchants' and Traders' Bank of Cincinnati, and one other Ohio bank not identified by name, but probably the Gallipolis. The most valuable testimony against the Weeds came from slave trader William H. Williams, then in New Orleans, having delivered his latest human cargo for auction. Of all the witnesses summoned, Williams marked the only one ever to receive Millington money directly from the defendants. The *Picayune* reported that "it was positively proven that William Weed had sold the notes of the Millington bank, in the capacity of its agent, and that he had uttered or expressed a wish that the notes of the bank might be circulated largely abroad and at a distance, so as to prevent their quick presentation at the bank for payment." One other purportedly incriminating piece of evidence also emerged in the press. When William Weed checked into the Verandah Hotel on Common Street, he signed the register as "Mr. Wood, of New York." His use of an alias struck the editors of the *Picayune* as "a circumstance calculated to excite suspicion," even though the difference between "Weed" and "Wood" may simply have been sloppy penmanship.[20]

The case against William and F. A. Weed concluded on Tuesday, December 8. Their counsel argued for their clients' release because prosecutors had failed to show how they had violated the laws of Maryland, the state where the alleged fraud had been committed. They maintained that the Weeds should not have been arrested unless or until the governor of Maryland had ordered it. Prosecuting attorney M. M. Cohen thought the testimony of William H. Williams sufficient to secure William Weed's conviction. He furthermore saw the wisdom in detaining the Weed brothers "for a reasonable time" until the court could determine the will of the Maryland governor, whom he believed legally entitled to have a say in the dispensation of the case. Joshua Baldwin agreed with the prosecution that the accumulated evidence was strong enough to merit the temporary detention of the Weeds until he could apprise the Maryland executive of their arrest. The recorder ordered the constable to take William and F. A. Weed into custody and deliver them to the Orleans Parish prison, where they would remain pending word from the Maryland governor.[21]

The Weeds dreaded further imprisonment in the calaboose and had no intention of remaining incarcerated a moment longer than absolutely necessary. Being jailed in an unfamiliar city and state, "in the midst of strangers," was bad enough, but with every passing day, the odds of Maryland's executive intervening in the Weeds' case increased, and the brothers surely understood the ill feeling their financiering had generated across the Chesapeake. Maryland, where hard economic times and the proximity of an adjacent free state combined to encourage masters to sell slaves to roving traders, bore the brunt of the Millington's failure. In Kent County, three Maryland small slaveholders initiated a suit against F. A. Weed's successor as bank president, J. C. H. Ellis, who inherited the Weeds' mess and then exacerbated it. His accusers alleged that Ellis had committed conspiracy and fraud by putting into circulation another $5,000 in Millington money almost a week after the bank had closed its doors. He was initially found guilty but secured a second trial and was acquitted in 1842. The seething anger of thousands of people in possession of worthless currency, but without the time, money, or inclination to pursue court action, went unsated.[22]

To avoid prolonged incarceration, William and F. A. Weed each petitioned Judge A. M. Buchanan of the First Judicial District Court on December 10, 1840, to obtain a writ of *habeas corpus* so that they might appear promptly before him to plead their case. Recorder Baldwin had "illegally & unjustly imprisoned" them, they explained. First, they pointed out that the State of Maryland had never prosecuted the Weed brothers, and the recorder lacked "authority to commit persons as fugitives from justice from other states, without proper evidence that the persons accused have been proceeded against criminally in the state from which they are alleged to have fled." Second, Baldwin had preemptively imprisoned the Weeds without instruction from Maryland's executive, but the recorder possessed "no authority to act in such cases except upon the requisition of the Governor of the state" in which the alleged crime was committed. Third, the Weeds' confinement was illegal because the offense for which they stood charged—an unspecified "felony"—was "unknown to the criminal laws" of Louisiana, and neither the rationale for it nor the term of imprisonment was clear. Nor were the brothers allowed to post bail. The Weeds asserted that the order for their incarceration had been "obtained by false pretences & by improper evidence," including "public reports or rumours, & hearsay testimony," motivated by the prosecution's desire to "detain [them] under colour of legal proceeding until civil suits can be instituted against [them]." The Weeds prayed that Buchanan issue them a writ of *habeas corpus* to discharge them from jail and get them an immediate hearing before the judge. Buchanan granted the writ the same day the brothers requested it and ordered Ursin Bouligny, sheriff of the criminal court and keeper of the Orleans Parish prison, to produce them in court.[23]

Handing down his decision, Judge Buchanan found most influential the Weeds' argument that they were being incarcerated on a charge of "felony." Louisiana law, Buchanan observed, did not recognize the generic term "felony" as a crime. He therefore ordered the Weeds' discharge because they stood accused of a crime that did not exist in his state. The dispensation of their case would not depend upon the Maryland governor's desired course of action after all. "Our executive," noted the *Baltimore Sun* wryly, "is therefore saved further trouble."[24]

The Weed brothers' confinement ended, but the litigation in New Orleans targeting them continued unabated. Starting in early December, immediately after the discovery and arrest of the Weeds, plaintiffs began filing civil suits in Louisiana's First Judicial District Court against the Commercial Bank of Millington. Baltimore merchant Ambrose A. White filed an affidavit on December 2 in which he claimed the institution was "justly & truly indebted" to him in the amount of $1,100 because he was "holder & owner of Sundry Bills" of the very institution driven to bankruptcy by the Weeds' mismanagement. White was not alone in seeking reimbursement from the brothers for the Millington's devalued paper. Peter John Cockburn, James McMaster, William Biggs, James Jameson, and the firm of Horace Bean & Co. all filed separate suits against the Commercial Bank of Millington in amounts ranging from $465 to more than $4,000.[25]

The plaintiffs all clamored for their share of the contents of two trunks confiscated from the Weed brothers at the time of their arrests. As Ambrose A. White explained, after the Millington collapse, the officers of the bank had "absconded with the greater portion of the assets" of the institution. Now, with the Weeds' apprehension, there were available "funds in Louisiana within the Jurisdiction" of the First Judicial District Court for use in compensating those taken in by the Millington fraud. Rumor held that the Weed brothers had "some twenty thousand dollars in current bank notes" in the chests they carried with them during their flight from Maryland. Recorder Baldwin confirmed that, at the time of the Weeds' arrests, the police seized two trunks and all of their contents. Although Baldwin had the trunks in his possession, he did not know if they were the Weeds' property or contained anything belonging to them, "they not having been opened." White implored the First Judicial District Court to cite Baldwin to open the trunks and "declare on oath what property rights[,] credits[,] moneys[,] and interests" of the Millington Bank were in his "custody or control."[26]

On February 11, 1841, William Weed strenuously protested the continued impoundment of his trunk, now withheld from him for more than two months, and demanded its return. The chest "contains . . . clothing[,] wearing apparel & other property" that was being "illegally withheld," he complained. "Baldwin has no right to the possession of said trunk, having taken it forcibly & illegally." The plaintiffs' claims upon the trunk and its contents were equally groundless, Weed continued. All belonged to him. Over Weed's objections, authorities opened his trunk on February 20 and inventoried its contents. Recorder Baldwin, attorneys from both sides, and Weed himself were present. Upon unlocking the trunk and raising the lid, inside they found, among other things, a number of bank books, memorandum books, receipts of various amounts (including a receipt of the Millington Bank), "three Gold Watches & chains," "thirty six drafts on Phoenix Bank" of New York, and "15 Bonds [of the] City of Vicksburg."[27]

In 1840, amid Mississippi's continued economic struggles in the wake of the painfully slow recovery from the depression, the city council of Vicksburg sought out investors in their town to finance such projects as the installation of a sewer system and the macadamization of the streets. It therefore dispatched the city financier to Baltimore for the purpose of selling city bonds—a first for Vicksburg—as a means of raising more immediate funds. Of all possible currencies he might have traded for, the city's agent returned from the Chesapeake bearing tens of thousands of dollars in Millington banknotes, mere weeks before the institution failed. Fifteen of the Vicksburg bonds, valued at $1,000 each, ended up in William Weed's trunk. Baldwin seized them and attached them to the civil suits pending against the Weeds, as assets for possible use in compensating the plaintiffs. He did not realize that the Mississippi river town, in an act of debt repudiation, had suspended payment on those very bonds two months earlier.[28]

The scramble for the funds the Weeds transported into Louisiana lasted into the late spring of 1841. In the suits initiated by White, McMaster, Cockburn, and Biggs, slave trader William H. Williams supplied the crucial testimony. As familiar as anyone with the Commercial Bank of Millington, he could verify the genuineness of both the Millington notes the plaintiffs produced in court and the signatures on them. He was also able to recount the bank's history to Judge Buchanan. That Williams had "no interest any way in any of these suits" lent his information weight and credibility. In June 1841, Buchanan ruled in favor of all the plaintiffs for whom the outcome of the civil suits is known, granting them the amounts they sued for, plus interest and court costs.[29]

One other holder of Millington notes approached William Weed in New Orleans to discuss the fallen bank: Thomas N. Davis. Either in late 1840 or early 1841, the slave trader encountered Weed and asked "how he came to act so badly." Weed "excused himself by saying he was deceived," although how or by whom he did not say. The trader next "asked him how I was to get my money back," referring to "the money which I had previously exchanged with him for the Millington concern." Had Davis pursued the matter smartly, he might have filed suit, as so many others had, against the Weeds to gain access to the "thousands in their trunks." But Davis had acquaintance with Weed and chose not to pursue the matter in court. Besides, Weed had a ready response to the trader's query. He replied that "he and Guthrie had the Farmers and Millers Bank at Hagerstown . . . we must look there for our money, as this was his only hope."[30]

And so, upon returning to Maryland in the spring of 1841, laden with the defunct Millington Bank notes still in his possession, Thomas N. Davis journeyed to visit Joseph T. Guthrie, seeking repayment. The Hagerstown cashier "appeared glad to see me," Davis recalled. The slave trader supposed it was "all owing to his fear of my exposing him" for his role in bringing the dubious Farmers and Millers Bank to fruition. To the contrary, Davis recollected, Guthrie was excited to divulge his latest scheme. The cashier warmly "solicited me to join *him*" in his proposed banking institution in Kanawha. Progress on the new venture was slow. In the summer of 1841, Guthrie invited Davis to Hagerstown so that they might more "fully understand ourselves as regards our future business." "I am determined to push the Virginia concern," declared the cashier, "and nothing, except the want of funds, shall hinder my putting her in operation. I can give you my views more fully after I see you." But the Kanawha project never met with success. "This all failed," Davis related, "as I supposed the means could not be raised."[31]

Guthrie rededicated his energies to making a go of the Hagerstown institution. He first resigned his public role as cashier in August 1841 to deflect any lingering concerns the community might have about his association with the controversial William Weed in getting the Farmers and Millers Bank under way. "My interest and influence will not by this act, be any the less," Guthrie boasted to Davis, for his relationship to the Hagerstown bank had not been severed entirely. Guthrie continued on behind the scenes as a member of the board of directors, to which he had been elected the previous May. The next step in reviving the Farmers and Millers Bank was to acquire an influx of capital that would enable it to print a substantial "new issue" of its currency, one that elicited greater public confidence than the old. By August 1841, Guthrie shared with Davis his growing desire "to make our money go current."[32]

Here was where slave trader Thomas N. Davis entered into the bank speculator's calculus. Guthrie's letters to Davis were filled with vague allusions to events and transactions only the two men would have fully understood, so his plan remains opaque at best. But its broad contours sound familiar, reminiscent of the Weed brothers' attempt to keep the Millington alive. Guthrie stated clearly that his scheme required Davis "merely to make exchanges," such that Farmers and Millers Bank notes should not be redeemed "at once or at least for a few days." Float "our notes in Philadelphia and Baltimore," he encouraged Davis. That would allow the Hagerstown institution "to raise our circulation and credit" because "all the [good] money we can raise together" would fund the "new issue." Davis would take the good notes he received and give them to Guthrie, who, in turn, would use them as collateral to get bank loans to underwrite the Hagerstown enterprise. In short, Guthrie's plan was to run a bank with borrowed money. To start this process, he gave Davis $1,000 in Farmers and Millers Bank notes to place in circulation.[33]

Guthrie had grand visions, but all of his plans required capital. His correspondence thus repeatedly impressed upon Davis the urgency of raising the operational funds for the Farmers and Millers Bank. "If you ever raised a dollar in your life," Guthrie wrote, "do it now." He was relentless, and with the passage of time grew only more desperate for the slave trader's cooperation, promising that "it will lead to a good business for you and I both." Struggling to maintain good credit with the banks that financed his own, Guthrie implored Davis, "if you cant bring $1000 bring $500, and if you cannot do that, bring less to exchange; this will keep the good feeling. . . . I will work with you in good faith." But whatever you do, he reiterated, "*act promptly,*" and remember that "we . . . are doing nothing we are ashamed of."[34]

But Davis's patience with the speculator was running thin. The slave trader had gotten sued upon a draft that Guthrie had instructed him not to pay because the Farmers and Millers Bank lacked the means. As a consequence, their relationship had grown testy. Davis, increasingly disgusted, claimed to have had enough of Guthrie's entreaties. "I found from his letters that my money was all his aim," Davis declared in October 1841, "and of course he got no more out of me." On October 22, the same date as Guthrie's latest plea for funds, Davis departed with a cargo of bondpeople for New Orleans. He and Guthrie did not communicate at all for several months.[35]

Yet when Davis returned in the spring of 1842, his resentment had abated. Guthrie again pleaded for money, asking, as Davis recounted, "if I would give them some Virginia and other funds" in exchange for Farmers and Millers Bank notes. Probably feeling flush after his recent slaving voyage, Davis relented and channeled some of his profits back into the Hagerstown concern: "I gave them some thousand or eleven hundred dollars, part in Virginia [paper] and part in gold." He also accepted Guthrie's invitation to invest $1,000 in a flour store in Georgetown, the anticipated profits of which were to be funneled to the Hagerstown bank. Guthrie's fiscal mismanagement doomed the Georgetown enterprise before it began.[36]

Throughout 1842, the Farmers and Millers Bank struggled on, chronically undercapitalized. In July, Guthrie groused about the "heavy demand" upon the bank for specie from notes coming "home rapidly." It "keeps us poor," he grumbled. The "brisk" "redemption of our own paper" during the November term of court, when Washington County's citizens descended upon Hagerstown en masse, exacerbated the drain on the institution's resources. Seeking relief, Guthrie turned, once again, to traders, consulting William H. Williams's slave-dealing younger brother Thomas Williams in his Washington, D.C., office. Thomas, surely cognizant of Guthrie's increasingly toxic reputation, refused to cash a $500 bank draft Guthrie presented him. Guthrie next consulted his old accomplice Thomas N. Davis, complaining that he was "strapped hard" and "wanted money." "I would of [sic] exchanged some more" for him, Davis insisted, but the timing did not work out. "I had no money," he recalled. Guthrie then convinced Davis to take the $500 bank draft he had been unable to cash and present it on his behalf at Thomas Williams's office, presumably thinking that Williams would accept it if it came from Davis rather than himself. Having already visited Williams but not admitting that to Davis, Guthrie asked him to "take it and see." Alone, Davis ventured over to meet his fellow trader, but Williams was no fool. As Davis recounted, Williams "looked at [the draft] and read it, and handed it back to me." When Davis returned to Guthrie bearing only the draft, the bank speculator "was quite out of temper, because he could not get the money."[37]

Convinced that Guthrie could not "raise five hundred dollars at that time," Davis predicted a dim future for the Farmers and Millers Bank of Hagerstown, and he resolved to extract himself fully from the concern: "I . . . really abandoned it as all lost," he stated. "I wrote to Guthrie to make arrangements to pay the acceptance I was sued on, and pay me my expenses, and I wanted nothing more to do with them." Guthrie arranged with a different gentleman "to take the notes of the Farmers and Millers Bank west to circulate" and to secure $5,000 in specie to have on hand while filing the bank's annual statement for the Maryland legislature. The collapse of that plan prompted one last-ditch appeal to Davis, sometime between Christmas Day 1842 and January 1, 1843, to "procure . . . any amount of specie, say from one to five thousand dollars." Even if Davis had access to that quantity of gold or silver, by then he had determined to divorce himself from the Hagerstown wildcat.[38]

In addition to a shortage of hard currency, another major liability that the Farmers and Millers Bank never overcame was the public's nagging association between it and the corrupted Commercial Bank of Millington. The *Baltimore Sun*, long a booster of both institutions even as they struggled to remain solvent, denied any such connection. In December 1842, the newspaper printed a public letter signed by the Hagerstown bank's president, cashier, and board of directors stating that the rumored ties were "without even the shadow of foundation." They acknowledged that some of the original stockholders of the Farmers and Millers Bank, such as William Weed, "were known to be deeply implicated in the Millington fraud, but they have long ceased to have any connexion with this Bank." Although technically that was true, the Hagerstown bank, conceived in deception, could not shake public skepticism about the institution's integrity, and without public confidence, banks' notes amounted to nothing. In December 1842, eighteen citizens of Washington County, Maryland, and its environs petitioned the state legislature to investigate suspected fraud at the institution. The *Baltimore Sun* staunchly defended the Hagerstown bank from the aspersions cast upon it, primarily by smearing its accusers. The *Sun* denied that any of the petitioners hailed from "within twenty-five miles of Hagerstown." Almost all of them, the newspaper charged, did not even reside in Maryland; a number lived in Harpers Ferry, Virginia (now West Virginia). Some of these men were purportedly disgruntled simply because the Farmers and Millers Bank had repeatedly refused them loans. Unable to borrow money, out of "a spirit of cruel and gratuitous vengeance" and "vindictive malice," they purportedly mailed anonymous letters to Hagerstown threatening to publicly impugn the institution's character. Their petition to the legislature marked the fulfillment of that threat, intended "perhaps to depreciate the value of the notes, and enable speculators to profit by the panic." The *Sun* unilaterally dismissed the letter writers' accusations of a link between the Farmers and Millers Bank and the disgraced institution in Millington. "We believe the banking laws of this State are sufficiently rigid to protect the community," the paper declared, and should the legislature initiate an investigation, "this institution is prepared."[39]

The *Sun's* confidence in the Farmers and Millers Bank could not have been more poorly placed. On January 13, 1843, the Maryland House of Delegates appointed a five-man select committee to investigate the institution's affairs. The Washington County, Maryland, sheriff arrested Thomas N. Davis on a writ sought by Joseph T. Guthrie, to compel the slave trader to appear as a witness before the committee. Davis gave his testimony on January 20 and 21 and entered his extensive correspondence with Guthrie into evidence. Once Davis concluded his testimony, the committee chairman secured his discharge. Guthrie denied many of Davis's sworn statements and attempted to discredit the slave trader by arguing that he occasionally sent "letters containing threats that unless the Farmers and Millers Bank did loan him as much money as he wanted, he would blow her up" by divulging what he knew about the institution. "I have been told" secondhand, Guthrie added, "that Davis has stated that if I would give him a thousand dollars he would go away."[40]

Based on the whole of the assembled evidence, including incriminating statements from the institution's employees, the select committee reported that the Farmers and Millers Bank of Hagerstown originated in "the most base and fraudulent pretences," "that it was the purpose and design of the principal agents of the bank to perpetrate a most stupendous fraud upon all who should be credulous enough to trust them," and that it was nothing but "a fraudulent device to plunder the unwary and confiding portion of the community." Little more than a crooked "offshoot of the exploded Millington Bank, . . . it never had any legal existence" because it had failed to attract the obligatory $75,000 in legitimate specie required by charter to open. "The Bank," reported the committee, "was frequently sustained by borrowed money." While filing yearly reports, bank officials borrowed specie, counted it toward the bank's annual statements, and removed it the same day. At its nadir, the concern housed "only four dollars [in] bankable funds . . . and no specie excepting some boxes of cents." The select committee, by a margin of three to two, elected to "introduce resolutions directing the Attorney General to issue an injunction suspending the operations of the Bank until it shall be determined if the charter has been forfeited." When news of the institution's troubles reached the public, a run on the bank ensued, driving it under.[41]

With the 1843 collapse of the Farmers and Millers Bank of Hagerstown, the elaborate con game that began three years earlier in the unassuming village of Millington reached its conclusion. The Millington Bank fiasco and its aftermath chronicle the type of sketchy, corrupt business practices enabled by the frenzied economic climate of the time. The Millington and Hagerstown wildcats illustrate, in particular, how such economically irresponsible banks, formed first and foremost to enrich their initial investors, could function in the context of southern, slaveholding states. In the wake of the flush times of the 1830s, the Chesapeake played host to a mesmerizing kaleidoscope of unscrupulous shysters—in the Millington's case, confidence men who masqueraded professionally as respectable bankers and slave traders. Peddling currencies and enslaved bodies, respectively, those occupational categories graced opposite sides of the same slug in the Millington drama, bound as tightly as the wads of banknotes that filled their pocketbooks. The collaboration between professional slave traders such as William H. Williams and Thomas N. Davis and bank speculators such as the Weed brothers and Joseph T. Guthrie contained the potential for them to realize astounding profits through their participation in a financially sophisticated shell game in which the traders, needing ready money, conveyed bankers' notes as far away as possible from sites of redemption. Trafficking in commodified black bodies proved so lucrative for the slave dealers that they then turned around to finance new banking ventures that might rescue old ones and perpetuate the mutually beneficial cycle. But as the Millington and Hagerstown concerns also demonstrated, traders and bankers played a dangerous game. Banks' overly aggressive issuance of paper in an economy unregulated at the national level magnified the risks for those involved. Slave traders jeopardized their professional standing and faced legal action when they passed bad notes, and erstwhile banking entrepreneurs could be vilified by the press and transformed overnight into scam artists out to dupe the public. With such high economic stakes hanging in the balance, tensions between slave-trading and banking allies and co-conspirators occasionally bubbled over, but because they were equally ensnared in the pervasive "spirit of speculation" of the time, their fortunes rose and fell in tandem.[42]

Notes

1. *New Orleans Times-Picayune,* December 5, 1840 (first, third, fifth through seventh quotations); *Vicksburg (Miss.) Tri-Weekly Sentinel,* September 30, 1840 (second quotation); Edward E. Baptist, *The Half Has Never Been Told: Slavery and the Making of American Capitalism* (New York: Basic, 2014), 254; Cassedy v. Williams (1843), Records of the U.S. District Court for the District of Columbia, Case Papers, 1802–1863, Civil Trial #98, Box 663, National Archives, Washington, D.C. (fourth quotation).

2. Cassedy v. Williams (first quotation); *Times-Picayune,* December 5, 1840 (second quotation); Joshua D. Rothman, *Flush Times and Fever Dreams: A Story of Capitalism and Slavery in the Age of Jackson* (Athens: University of Georgia Press, 2012) (third quotation); Stephen Mihm, *A Nation of Counterfeiters: Capitalists, Con Men, and the Making of the United States* (Cambridge, Mass.: Harvard University Press, 2007), 9; Baptist, *The Half Has Never Been Told,* 230; Jessica M. Lepler, *The Many Panics of 1837: People, Politics, and the Creation of a Transatlantic Financial Crisis* (New York: Cambridge University Press, 2013), 15–23; Wilkinson v. Williams (1850), Records of the U.S. District Court for the District of Columbia, Case Papers, 1802–1863, Civil Trial #15, Box 739, Folder 15, National Archives, Washington, D.C. (fourth quotation); *Boston Post,* October 20, 1840 (fifth quotation); *Vicksburg Tri-Weekly Sentinel,* September 30, 1840 (sixth quotation);

Times-Picayune, December 3, 1840 (seventh and eighth quotations). For a history of banking in Maryland, see Howard Bodenhorn, *State Banking in Early America: A New Economic History* (New York: Oxford University Press, 2003), 123–24, 135, 137–40.

Joshua R. Greenberg defines shinplasters as unregulated, legally questionable paper notes that functioned as money. Real rather than counterfeit, they were used in local or regional money markets. In the late 1830s and early 1840s, the meaning of "shinplaster" evolved to include any note, legal or not, in which the public placed no confidence (Greenberg, "The Era of Shinplasters: Making Sense of Unregulated Paper Money," in *Capitalism by Gaslight: Illuminating the Economy of Nineteenth-Century America,* ed. Brian P. Luskey and Wendy A. Woloson [Philadelphia: University of Pennsylvania Press, 2015], 55–56, 73).

3. *Philadelphia Public Ledger,* March 30, 1841 (first quotation); Mihm, *Nation of Counterfeiters,* 8 (second and third quotations), 186, 239; William H. Dillistin, *Bank Note Reporters and Counterfeit Detectors, 1826–1866* (New York: American Numismatic Society, 1949), 59; Ian Klaus, *Forging Capitalism: Rogues, Swindlers, Frauds, and the Rise of Modern Finance* (New Haven, Conn.: Yale University Press, 2014), 3 (fourth quotation), 5. On the contested etymology of the term "wildcat," see Dillistin, *Bank Note Reporters,* 59–66.

4. Mihm, *Nation of Counterfeiters,* 185; Wilkinson v. Williams; *New York Times* quoted in *Louisiana Courier* (New Orleans), November 12, 1840. On hidden, obscure, and/or shady historical economic actors, see the essays in *Capitalism by Gaslight,* ed. Luskey and Woloson. Lepler, *The Many Panics of 1837,* also does a particularly admirable job of keeping human beings at the heart of her story of economic change.

5. Calvin Schermerhorn, "Slave Trading in a Republic of Credit: Financial Architecture of the US Slave Market, 1815–1840," *Slavery & Abolition* 36, no. 4 (2015): 586; Steven Deyle, "Rethinking the Slave Trade. Slave Traders and the Market Revolution in the South," in *The Old South's Modern Worlds: Slavery, Region, and Nation in the Age of Progress,* ed. L. Diane Barnes, Brian Schoen, and Frank Towers (New York: Oxford University Press, 2011), 111.

Recent works on the relationship between slavery and capitalism include Walter Johnson, *River of Dark Dreams: Slavery and Empire in the Cotton Kingdom* (Cambridge, Mass.: Belknap Press of Harvard University Press, 2013); Baptist, *The Half Has Never Been Told;* Sven Beckert, *Empire of Cotton: A Global History* (New York: Vintage, 2015); and Calvin Schermerhorn, *The Business of Slavery and the Rise of American Capitalism, 1815–1860* (New Haven, Conn.: Yale University Press, 2015).

6. Stephen Mihm, "Follow the Money: The Return of Finance in the Early Republic," *Journal of the Early Republic* 36 (Winter 2016): 795 (first quotation); 783 (second quotation); Michael Tadman, *Speculators and Slaves: Masters, Traders, and Slaves in the Old South* (Madison: University of Wisconsin Press, 1989, 1996), chap. 7.

7. Deyle, "Rethinking the Slave Trade," 106, makes passing reference to traders' involvement with antebellum banks, but the work presented here offers a more detailed case study.

8. Deyle, "Rethinking the Slave Trade," 112–13; *Daily National Intelligencer* (Washington, D.C.), April 5, 1836; E. A. Cohen & Co., *For 1834. A Full Directory, for Washington City, Georgetown, and Alexandria* (Washington City: Wm. Greer, 1834), 58, 33, unpaginated advertisement for A. Lee's Lottery and Exchange Office.

9. Frederic Bancroft, *Slave Trading in the Old South,* introd. Michael Tadman (1931; Columbia: University of South Carolina Press, 1996); Cohen, *Full Directory, for Washington City,* n.p. (quotation); Mihm, *Nation of Counterfeiters,* 236; Cassedy v. Williams.

10. *Report of the Select Committee Appointed to Investigate the Affairs of the Farmers and Millers Bank of Hagerstown* (Annapolis, Md.: Geo. & Wm. Johnston, 1843), 19.

11. *Nashville (Tenn.) Union,* August 30, 1841; John Jay Knox, *A History of Banking in the United States* (New York: Bradford Rhodes, 1903), 678 (first quotation); Wilkinson v. Williams (second through fifth quotations); Thomas J. C. Williams, *A History of Washington County, Maryland, from the Earliest Settlements to the Present Time,* vol. 1 (Hagerstown, Md., 1906; repr., Salem, Mass.: Higginson Book Company, 1990), 239 (sixth and seventh quotations).

12. Cassedy v. Williams.

13. Matthias Snyder, Jr. v. William H. Williams (1842), Alexandria County Circuit Court, in *Baltimore Sun,* October 11, 1842; Cassedy v. Williams; Wilkinson v. Williams.

14. Wilkinson v. Williams (all quotations); *Report of the Select Committee,* 19. Although it cannot be absolutely certain, these two disparate sources appear to discuss the exact same meeting.

15. Wilkinson v. Williams (quotation); Steven Deyle, *Carry Me Back: The Domestic Slave Trade in American Life* (New York: Oxford University Press, 2005), 120–23; Tadman, *Speculators and Slaves,* 47; Michael Tadman, "The Reputation of the Slave Trader in Southern History and the Social Memory of the South," *American Nineteenth Century History* 8 (September 2007): 260, 262; Deyle, "Rethinking the Slave Trade," 105; *Gibson's Guide and Directory of the State of Louisiana, and the Cities of New Orleans & Lafayette* (New Orleans: John Gibson, 1838), 214; *New-Orleans Directory for 1842* (New-Orleans: Pitts & Clarke, 1842), 422; *Times-Picayune,* November 9, 1842; *New-Orleans Annual and Commercial Directory, for 1843* (New Orleans: Justin L. Sollée, 1842), 341–42; Carlile Pollock, vol. 66, act no. 222, November 28, 1843, New Orleans Notarial Archives; *Times-Picayune,* August 28, 1845.

16. Bodenhorn, *State Banking in Early America,* 139–40; Williams, *History of Washington County,* 239; "Report of the Select Committee Appointed to Investigate the Affairs of the Farmers and Millers Bank of Hagerstown," *Baltimore Sun,* February 6, 1843; *Report of the Select Committee,* 19.

17. *Baltimore Sun,* February 11, 1843 (first and second quotations); *Report of the Select Committee,* 14 (third quotation), 19, 31, 49, 56; Williams, *History of Washington County,* 239; Joshua D. Rothman, "The Contours of Cotton Capitalism: Speculation, Slavery, and Economic Panic in Mississippi, 1832–1841," in *Slavery's Capitalism,* ed. Sven Beckert and Seth Rockman (Philadelphia: University of Pennsylvania Press, 2016), 128–29; "Report of the Select Committee," *Baltimore Sun,* February 6, 1843 (fourth quotation).

18. "Report of the Select Committee," *Baltimore Sun,* February 6, 1843, italics in original.

19. Walter Johnson, *Soul by Soul: Life Inside the Antebellum Slave Market* (Cambridge, Mass.: Harvard University Press, 1999); *Report of the Select Committee,* 19; *Times-Picayune,* December 6, 1840; *Public Ledger,* December 14, 1840; *Times-Picayune,* January 7, 1841; *Times-Picayune,* December 3, 1840 (all quotations).

20. *Times-Picayune,* December 3, 1840 (first, second, and fourth quotations); *Mississippi Free Trader* (Natchez), December 8, 1840 (third quotation); *Times-Picayune,* December 5, 1840; *Times-*

Picayune, December 9, 1840; *Times-Picayune*, December 8, 1840 (all remaining quotations); *Times-Picayune*, April 28, 1840.

21. *Daily Picayune*, December 9, 1840 (quotation); First Judicial District Court, Habeas Corpus Records #50–51, New Orleans Public Library (hereinafter cited as NOPL).

22. *Daily Picayune*, December 9, 1840 (quotation); Max Grivno, *Gleanings of Freedom: Free and Slave Labor along the Mason-Dixon Line, 1790–1860* (Urbana: University of Illinois Press, 2011); grand jury inquest, September 17, 1841, Kent County Circuit Court, Kent County Courthouse, Chestertown, Maryland; *Easton (Md.) Gazette*, April 9, 1842. To pay off its depositors and other creditors, the Commercial Bank of Millington meanwhile filed several lawsuits to recoup the money it was owed, including a successful suit in 1844 against the Phoenix Bank of New York, for the unimpressive sum of $77 (see *New York Tribune*, November 2, 1844).

23. First Judicial District Court, Habeas Corpus Records, #50–51 (quotations). The wording is identical in the respective petitions of William and F. A. Weed.

24. *Times-Picayune*, December 12, 1840; *Times-Picayune*, December 13, 1840; *Mississippi Free Trader*, December 15, 1840; *Baltimore Sun*, December 24, 1840 (quotations).

25. Ambrose A. White v. Commercial Bank of Millington, Case #19741, First Judicial District Court, NOPL; Peter John Cockburn v. Commercial Bank of Millington, Case #19750, First Judicial District Court, NOPL; James McMaster v. Commercial Bank of Millington, Case #19744, First Judicial District Court, NOPL; William Biggs v. Commercial Bank of Millington, Case #19768, First Judicial District Court, NOPL; Horace Bean & Co. v. Commercial Bank of Millington, Case #19756, First Judicial District Court, NOPL; *Times-Picayune*, December 3, 1840.

26. Ambrose A. White v. Commercial Bank of Millington (first, second, and fourth through sixth quotations); *Times-Picayune*, December 3, 1840 (third quotation).

27. Peter John Cockburn v. Commercial Bank of Millington (first through third quotations); Ambrose A. White v. Commercial Bank of Millington; Horace Bean & Co. v. Commercial Bank of Millington (fourth through sixth quotations).

28. *Vicksburg Tri-Weekly Sentinel*, September 28, 1840; *Vicksburg Tri-Weekly Sentinel*, October 2, 1840; *Vicksburg Tri-Weekly Sentinel*, November 4, 1840; *Vicksburg (Miss.) Daily Whig*, December 23, 1840.

29. Ambrose A. White v. Commercial Bank of Millington; James McMaster v. Commercial Bank of Millington; Peter John Cockburn v. Commercial Bank of Millington (quotation); Horace Bean & Co. v. Commercial Bank of Millington; William Biggs v. Commercial Bank of Millington.

30. *Report of the Select Committee*, 19 (first through fourth and sixth quotations); *Times-Picayune*, December 5, 1840 (fifth quotation).

31. *Report of the Select Committee*, 19 (first through third quotations), 63 (fourth through sixth quotations), 20 (seventh and eighth quotations).

32. *Report of the Select Committee*, 65 (first and second quotations), 63 (third quotation), 64, 20, 47.

33. *Report of the Select Committee*, 64 (first, second, and fourth quotations), 65 (third, fifth, and sixth quotations), 12, 20.

34. *Report of the Select Committee*, 65 (first and second quotations), 66 (third and fifth quotations), 67 (fourth quotation), 68 (fifth quotation).

35. *Report of the Select Committee,* 20 (first and second quotations), 66.

36. *Report of the Select Committee,* 20 (first and second quotations), 21, 61.

37. *Report of the Select Committee,* 61 (first quotation), 62 (second and third quotations), 68 (fourth and fifth quotations), 21 (sixth through twelfth quotations).

38. *Report of the Select Committee,* 21 (first through third quotations), 22 (fourth and fifth quotations).

39. *Baltimore Sun,* December 29, 1842 (quotations); Williams, *History of Washington County,* 239. On the importance of public confidence, see Lepler, *The Many Panics of 1837,* 9, 15, 28, 30.

40. *Report of the Select Committee,* 34.

41. *Report of the Select Committee,* 59, 44, 33; "Report of the Select Committee," *Baltimore Sun,* February 6, 1843 (first and second quotations); *New-York Tribune,* February 9, 1843 (third through eighth quotations); Williams, *History of Washington County,* 239.

42. Edwin Adams Davis, ed., *Plantation Life in the Florida Parishes of Louisiana, 1836–1846: As Reflected in the Diary of Bennet H. Barrow* (New York: Columbia University Press, 1943), 170.

Bernard Kendig

ORCHESTRATING FRAUD IN THE MARKET
AND THE COURTROOM

MARIA R. MONTALVO

ernard Kendig was a New Orleans slave trader. Because he left behind
no personal papers, what we can learn about his life comes from the
surviving records of his violent business. Several of the acts of sale he
signed tell us that he had a wife named Jane Miller, and court records indicate
that he was buying and selling enslaved people in the Crescent City as early as
1839, if not sooner.[1] Contracts and court records provide only a limited glimpse
of Kendig himself. What they do tell us, however, is that Bernard Kendig was in
the business of buying and selling human beings, and sometimes he lied about
the people he sold. Between 1840 and 1860, Kendig's customers sued him at
least nine different times, alleging that he had used Louisiana's redhibitory
warranties to misrepresent the enslaved people he had sold them. In this essay,
I rely on court records from these slave-centered warranty disputes to examine
the world in which Bernard Kendig lived and worked; the legal, rhetorical, and
archival strategies that enslavers employed in their attempts to make money
and defraud their customers in the market; and the means that slave dealers
used to protect themselves from liability for their deception in the antebellum
courtroom.[2]

On February 4, 1858, in New Orleans, Thomas Gatlin, a resident of Sem-
inary, Arkansas, purchased Jim Gale and an enslaved child named John from
Bernard Kendig for $2,200. When Kendig sold enslaved people in New Or-
leans, he did so under the shadow of Louisiana's Civil Code, which included
specific laws regarding the obligations of buyers and sellers, the exchange of
information during a slave sale, and requirements about how parties were to
document and register these acts of sale if they wanted to be able to enforce the

terms of their agreements in the future. If the enslavers who bought and sold enslaved people in Louisiana wanted to be able to rely on Louisiana's courts to enforce their contracts, they had to record the terms of their sales in writing and register them with the state. Louisiana's Civil Code set the rules that governed North America's largest slave market, but the ways in which enslavers and traders such as Bernard Kendig used these regulations were of their own design.[3]

When Bernard Kendig sold Jim Gale and John to Thomas Gatlin, both he and Gatlin relied on Louisiana's redhibition laws to negotiate the terms of the sale. Redhibition, according to Louisiana's Civil Code, was "the avoidance of a sale on account of some vice or defect in the thing sold, which renders it either absolutely useless, or its use so inconvenient and imperfect, that it must be supposed that the buyer would not have purchased it, had he known the vice."[4] Anyone who purchased an enslaved person in Louisiana, documented the purchase in an act of sale, and later discovered that the individual in question suffered from some "hidden" or "redhibitory" vice could sue the seller to secure a refund. In addition to any "hidden" defects—those that would not be visible by "simple inspection" at the time of a sale—Louisiana's Civil Code listed six redhibitory vices that were unique to enslaved people.[5] Those who sold enslaved people in the state and wanted to avoid being held liable for the person in the future would need to modify the state's implied warranty by informing a buyer if the person in question was addicted to theft, had previously committed a capital crime, was in the habit of running away, or suffered from leprosy, madness, or epilepsy.[6] Louisiana did not prohibit enslavers from selling people with hidden ailments or redhibitory defects; it simply made sellers liable if they signed an act of sale and knowingly withheld specific information about an enslaved person.[7]

Those who bought and sold enslaved people in New Orleans relied on Louisiana's peculiar market regulations when negotiating the terms of a sale, when seeking out information about an enslaved person, and when deciding what information about an enslaved person to disclose and preserve in a contract. Enslavers constructed warranties rooted in Louisiana's redhibition laws that could but did not always alter the state's implied warranty. By including a full or mitigated guarantee—for example, a warranty where a seller guaranteed an enslaved person against the vice of running away but not epilepsy—in an act of sale, a seller not only influenced the terms of a sale and shaped their future liability for the person sold; they also shaped what information about an enslaved individual was conveyed to the buyer and was both preserved and readily available in the future. For instance, when Bernard Kendig sold Jim Gale and John to Thomas Gatlin, he sold them with a full guarantee "against the prohibitory vices and maladies prescribed by law."[8] Kendig's guarantee essentially restated Louisiana's implied warranty, promising that, to his knowledge, Jim Gale and John did not possess any hidden or redhibitory vices or defects and emphasizing that he could be held liable for their value and utility for the upcoming year.

When slave sellers and traders such as Bernard Kendig offered to include a redhibitory guarantee in an act of sale, they presumably offered buyers specific information about the person in question as well as provided them with the opportunity to return an enslaved person in the event that they displayed some vice or defect. Prominent New Orleans auctioneer Joseph A. Beard, while testifying in a civil suit tried in the Fifth District Court of New Orleans in May 1849, described the circumstances wherein a slave seller might be asked to offer a redhibitory guarantee. "It frequently happens," Beard observed, "with other traders, that purchasers require a city guarantee, and it is sometimes done as a matter at business and at others as a matter of courtesy." "It daily happens," he continued, "when the vendor is not known that the purchasers require [a] city guarantee and particularly when the slaves come from common law states."[9] Louisiana's redhibition laws guaranteed buyers protections unavailable in common law states, where a dissatisfied buyer could typically sue for a refund only if they had obtained an express warranty or if the seller had knowingly deceived them during a sale.[10] With a written bill of sale and Louisiana's implied warranty, buyers could look to the courts in the event that they discovered their newly purchased enslaved property possessed some hidden vice or defect before the sale took place.

The mere existence of redhibition laws did not determine how enslaved people were bought and sold, however. Slave buyers, sellers, and traders transformed these regulations into tools of the trade that they used to depict enslaved people as products worth buying. There were benefits to purchasing an enslaved person in Louisiana—even without an express redhibitory guarantee—in that every buyer enjoyed the protections of the state's implied warranties. Buying an enslaved person without a documented redhibitory warranty in Louisiana did not automatically mean that a seller was freed from the possibility of a redhibition lawsuit. If a buyer discovered and could prove that a seller had misrepresented a slave on paper, regardless of whether or not they had purchased the person in question with an express redhibitory guarantee, they could then sue the seller for redhibition, asking a court for a full refund as well as damages. Louisiana's implied warranty meant that if a seller knew that an enslaved person was ill or had a history of running away and wanted to avoid being held liable for that person in the future, they needed to disclose that specific information at the time of the sale. There could always be legal and financial penalties if they neglected to do so. A buyer who discovered and could prove that a seller had withheld information about an enslaved person's hidden defects or redhibitory vices could sue a seller for redhibition at any time within one year of discovering the vice in question.[11]

When enslavers bought and sold enslaved people in New Orleans, they did so with Louisiana's redhibition laws and its courtrooms in mind. Indeed, the state's courts were where enslavers encountered the risks, possibilities, and consequences of their actions in the market. When Thomas Gatlin asked Bernard Kendig to sign a bill of sale on February 4, 1858, and to sell Jim Gale and John with a full redhibitory guarantee, Kendig initially refused, as he thought the act of sale "too binding."[12] Whereas Gatlin was working to protect his investment in Jim Gale and John, Kendig was attempting to avoid being held liable for their quality and utility after the sale. Thomas Gatlin would have known that it was in Bernard Kendig's interest to portray his enslaved property as both sound slaves and sound investments. He also knew enough about Louisiana's laws to ask for a written act of sale that stated the terms of Louisiana's redhibitory guarantee, not because it told him everything he wanted to know or could want to know about Jim Gale and John but because it created a written record of Kendig's representations in the market and likely made his investment in enslaved property seem safer. While Kendig eventually relented, signed his name to an act of sale, and sold Jim Gale for $1,200, his liability for Gale was not automatic. Selling an enslaved person with a redhibitory guarantee did not mean that if Gatlin asked to return Jim Gale or John, Kendig had to oblige. Kendig could refuse, and Gatlin could then file a redhibition suit, relying on the act of sale that contained the terms of their agreement as evidence.

Enslavers relied on Louisiana's redhibition laws to manage the risks involved in a sale, especially when it came to deciding what information about an enslaved individual to disclose, withhold, document, and archive. While the state's redhibition laws were important tools that enslavers relied on to negotiate the terms of a sale, the real battle centered on whether to construct an act of sale and what information to include and omit from its pages. Sellers crafted limited and incomplete portraits of their enslaved property because it was in their immediate and long-term economic interests to define what others could learn about a particular enslaved person before, during, and after a sale. When dissatisfied buyers did pursue redhibition suits, they encountered the archival limits that previous buyers and sellers had created in the interest of defining enslaved people as valuable commodities while still protecting themselves from being held liable for the people they sold.

On May 2, 1858, less than three months after returning to Arkansas, the recently purchased Jim Gale absconded. Despite making what he would later describe as "all efforts to apprehend the slave," Gatlin was unable to locate Gale for some time, and he eventually traveled to New Orleans to ask Kendig for a refund. When Kendig refused to reimburse Gatlin or to provide him with any information about Gale's past, Gatlin sought counsel from two attorneys and partners in a New Orleans law firm, Lewis E. Simonds and Charles E. Fenner. Simonds and Fenner informed their client that in order to successfully sue Kendig for redhibition, he would need to "prove the existence of the vice of running away, previous to the sale." As he had no such evidence in his possession, Gatlin returned to Arkansas without a refund and without filing a lawsuit against Kendig.[13]

Simonds and Fenner were quite right to inform Gatlin that if he could not prove that Jim Gale was in the habit of running away before the sale, then he did not have a case against Kendig. To establish cause for redhibition, Gatlin would not only have to present the act of sale that Kendig had signed as evidence but would also have to build a history of Jim Gale, the habitual runaway. The burden of proof in these disputes rested squarely on a buyer's shoulders, as Louisiana's Civil Code held that the "buyer who institutes the redhibitory action must prove that the vice existed before the sale was made to him."[14] To demonstrate that an enslaved person had a history of running away, a buyer had to show that he or she had "absented himself from his master's house twice for several days, or once for more than a month."[15] While these regulations had certain exceptions, plaintiffs were usually in a position where they needed to demonstrate that a vice existed before a sale, a task that often proved difficult. During redhibition suits, buyers and their attorneys became historians of slaves, seeking out previous acts of sale, notarial contracts, and mortgages, interrogating enslaved people as well as subjecting them to invasive physical examinations, working to locate and subpoena witnesses, and attempting to convince sellers to disclose information regarding an enslaved person's past. Plaintiffs worked to construct a believable, well-evidenced history of an unsound slave, whereas defendants simultaneously worked not only to deny their knowledge of an enslaved person's past but also to obscure it from view. Court records from these disputes thus contain competing historical accounts of the lives of enslaved people that begin with a single transaction and move forward and backward in time.

Like Bernard Kendig, other slave sellers in Louisiana often decided to sell an enslaved person with an unmodified redhibitory guarantee despite knowing that the individual in question had a history of running away or was suffering from a specific illness, in order to convince buyers to pay higher prices. When Kendig sold Jim Gale to Thomas Gatlin, he knew that Gale had run away at least three times in the previous year. Unbeknownst to Gatlin when he made his purchase, Kendig had sold Gale to John F. Williams—an attorney, judge, and resident of Marshall, Texas, located in Harrison County—for $1,300 or $1,400 in either February or March 1857. Three months after the sale, Gale ran away. In July or August of that same year, Gale was captured and imprisoned as a runaway in the Rusk County jail, in Henderson, Texas, just southwest of Harrison County. John Williams was able to reclaim Jim Gale from confinement and transport him back to Marshall. Just one week later, Gale absconded again and remained missing until November or December 1857, when he was captured and imprisoned as a runaway in Fredericksburg, Texas, located farther east, in Gillespie County. After reclaiming him from yet another Texas county jail, Williams transported Jim Gale to New Orleans, where he informed Bernard Kendig that he "regarded the boy Jim as a notorious runaway, and was determined not to keep him." Kendig "readily consented to take him back," and Williams exchanged Gale with Kendig for another enslaved man, whom Williams and Kendig agreed was of similar value, on January 31 or February 1, 1858.[16] Soon after John F. Williams returned Jim Gale to Bernard Kendig, a man by the name of Mr. Foster, whom Williams recognized as Kendig's agent, informed Williams that Gale had run away from Kendig the first night after he was returned. Williams later testified in *Gatlin v. Kendig* (1860) that "he was not informed of anything of the history of the boy 'Jim' by the Defendant [Bernard Kendig]" before his purchase. Thomas Gatlin was similarly ignorant of Jim Gale's pattern of behavior when he agreed to purchase him, as neither Kendig nor Gale had informed him about Gale's history of running away.[17]

Bernard Kendig intentionally withheld information about Jim Gale's past in order to sell him with a full guarantee and to convince Thomas Gatlin to pay $1,200. Gatlin, however, was eventually able to locate Gale as well as to secure the evidence necessary to pursue a redhibition suit.[18] With a history of buying and selling enslaved people since at least 1839, Kendig was no stranger to the business of slavery in New Orleans, and he was well aware that his actions in the city's slave pens could lead him to its courtrooms.[19] Richard Tansey's extensive analysis of notarial records reveals that between 1852 and 1860, Kendig sold at least 758 people in New Orleans using notarial contracts.[20] But as we do not have access to Kendig's personal records, we have no way of knowing the number of verbal transactions he participated in or how many of his sales may have gone unregistered with the City of New Orleans.[21] Indeed, Kendig likely bought, sold, and exchanged more enslaved people than we will ever know. Imprecisions aside, we do know that Gale was one of hundreds of enslaved people Kendig sold over the course of at least two decades. We also know that Jim Gale was one of at least ten enslaved people whom Bernard Kendig sold who eventually found themselves at the center of a redhibitory lawsuit.

Between 1840 and 1860, Kendig was involved in at least ten slave-centered redhibition suits. Kendig was accused of misrepresenting the enslaved people he sold using redhibitory guarantees in nine of these disputes. The defects at the center of these lawsuits included habitual running away, epilepsy, disease, and drunkenness.[22] Richard Tansey sampled 158 notarial contracts, filed between 1852 and 1860, that included the terms of slave sales involving Bernard Kendig and discovered that Kendig purchased "thirty-one physically and morally defective slaves and then sold these slaves under full warranties. Twenty-five of the thirty-one defective slaves were sold to Kendig as known runaways."[23] Tansey's findings as well as the redhibitory lawsuits involving Bernard Kendig suggest that Kendig, in all likelihood, regularly purchased enslaved people from sellers who expressly disclaimed Louisiana's implied warranty—by disclosing specific information about an enslaved person's value, utility, and past—and subsequently relied on redhibitory guarantees to portray them as both sound slaves and secure investments to mark up their prices and sell them at a profit. Court records from redhibitory lawsuits in which Kendig was involved further illuminate the extended consequences of his guarantees.

When Bernard Kendig sold Jim Gale to Thomas Gatlin in 1858, James B. Milner, a farmer, resident of Arkansas, and Gatlin's friend and neighbor, was also present. Milner later testified in *Gatlin v. Kendig* (1860) that, initially, "Mr. Kendig refused" to sign an act of sale, "as it was too binding." Eventually, however, Kendig provided his signature. For Kendig, the bill of sale was evidence not only that the transaction had taken place but also that he had sold Jim Gale with a full redhibitory guarantee. In truth, Kendig had exchanged Gale with John F. Williams only days earlier because the bondman had proven "a notorious runaway." Nevertheless, the slave dealer still made the decision to sell him with a redhibitory guarantee.[24]

Bernard Kendig's initial reluctance to sign any act of sale at all is understandable when we consider that he was, at that moment, embroiled in a different redhibitory lawsuit wherein the courts would remind Kendig of the "binding" nature of written guarantees. Oliver Palms, a resident of New Orleans, sued Bernard Kendig for redhibition in the Fourth District Court of New Orleans on December 11, 1857. In his petition, Palms explained that he had purchased an enslaved woman named Clara, who was then twenty-five years of age, from Rufus R. Rhodes for $1,300 on April 20, 1857. Rhodes and Palms had signed a notarial contract before New Orleans notary James H. Graham. According to the agreement, Rhodes "fully guaranteed" Clara "against the vices and maladies rendered redhibitory by the laws of this state." He had purchased her only four months earlier "from Bernard Kendig of this city . . . on the 23 day of December 1856."[25]

Rufus R. Rhodes's decision to include information about Bernard Kendig in the notarial contract was no mere formality. Rhodes did so because he was selling Clara with a redhibitory guarantee less than a year after he had purchased her from Kendig with a redhibitory guarantee. Should Oliver Palms then discover that Clara suffered from some redhibitory vice or defect before December 23, 1857, and file a lawsuit against Rhodes, Rhodes could then call in Bernard Kendig to defend himself because Kendig's guarantee would still be in effect. Rhodes had included Kendig's name and warranty in the act of sale as a means of minimizing the risk of offering a warranty himself, indicating that there were instances in which information about not only enslaved people but also previous buyers and sellers could prove valuable during and after a sale. In this case, shortly after his purchase, Palms noticed that Clara had a "varicose ulcer on her right leg, and a bad varicose state of the veins," which he maintained "existed before the said sale to petitioner from said Rhodes, and before the sale to said Rhodes from said Bernard Kendig." As a result of her condition, Clara was "of no use or benefit" to Palms and had become "a source of great trouble and expense." He therefore asked the court to order Bernard Kendig to pay him the $1,300 he had paid to purchase Clara as well as $200 in damages.[26]

By using New Orleans's notarial records, Oliver Palms was able to determine that Bernard Kendig purchased Clara without a warranty and subsequently sold her with a full guarantee, not once, but twice. On August 8, 1856, before the same New Orleans notary James Graham, Kendig purchased Clara from Julia Ann Palmer, a white woman and resident of New Orleans, for $800. According to the notarial contract, Palmer guaranteed Clara "as to title only, and not against the vices and maladies prescribed by the laws of this state, of which said purchaser hereby takes cognizance and renounces all recourse for said vices and maladies." Palmer, who testified on behalf of Oliver Palms, later clarified that she did not sell Clara with a full guarantee "on account of that sore leg," which she "informed Kendig of." On August 15, 1856, seven days after purchasing Clara, Bernard Kendig once again appeared before James Graham and sold the enslaved woman to New Orleans resident Charles C. Brier, with a full redhibitory guarantee, for $1,050. The notarial contract indicates that Kendig informed Brier that he had purchased Clara from Julia Ann Palmer but not that he had done so without a full guarantee. After calling a physician to examine Clara within days of his purchase, Brier discovered that she was suffering from "varicose veins and ulcers" in her right leg and promptly "sent her back to Kendig." Kendig accepted Clara on return, only to reappear before James Graham four months later and sell her to Rufus R. Rhodes for $1,150, again with a full guarantee "against the vices and maladies rendered redhibitory by the laws of this state." He included no mention of Julia Ann Palmer or Charles C. Brier in this contract.[27]

When Kendig sold Clara and Jim Gale with full guarantees, he did so with the knowledge that he was risking a redhibition suit. He had purchased Clara for $800 without a warranty, and by offering Rufus R. Rhodes a full guarantee, he was eventually able to sell her for $1,150, an increase in price of almost 44 percent. Technically, by including a redhibitory guarantee in an act of sale, a seller was simply restating Louisiana's implied warranty. But putting the guarantee in writing had power, as sellers could use it to portray enslaved people as useful, valuable, and secure investments. Buyers, in turn, were willing to pay handsomely for enslaved individuals covered by a warranty. By including redhibitory guarantees in acts of sale, enslavers shaped how enslaved people were bought and sold as well as what information about them was preserved and available in the future. Kendig relied on warranties to buy low and sell high, and in the process, he effectively shaped what information about an enslaved person was recorded in an act of sale, known to a buyer, and, as Thomas Gatlin would discover, readily available during a lawsuit.[28]

As a buyer, it was in Gatlin's interest to know as much about Jim Gale as he could, not only because he would have wanted to be sure that he was making a wise investment but also because he would have wanted to make sure that he was buying an enslaved person who could and would work on his farm. Bernard Kendig's willingness to sell Jim Gale with a redhibitory guarantee and to sign an act of sale, at Gatlin's request, may have convinced Gatlin that he knew who he was buying. At the very least, the terms of the sale, Kendig's reassurances, and Gale's willingness to remain silent regarding his past likely led Gatlin to the conclusion that even if Gale proved unsatisfactory, he could rely on Louisiana's redhibition laws to recoup his investment.[29]

Thomas Gatlin would not begin building his case against Bernard Kendig until October or November 1859, when he received word that Jim Gale was imprisoned as a runaway in the Rusk County jail in Henderson, Texas. Gale had been incarcerated there for some time. On May 11, 1859, a year after the bondman had fled Gatlin's farm in Ouachita County, Arkansas, A. P. Kirksy and Constable James H. Nelms arrested Gale and placed him in confinement. At the time of his imprisonment, Gale was suffering from what Thomas Gatlin would later describe as a "severe gunshot wound" in his thigh, an injury that resulted in "heavy charges for medical attendance and jail fees." Witnesses in *Gatlin v. Kendig* (1860) refrained from discussing the circumstances surrounding Gale's injury, but it is possible that Kirksy or Nelms shot Gale while attempting to capture him. Gale spent the next six months in the Rusk County jail, where he was likely interrogated by Sheriff John D. Hamilton. At some point, probably in May 1859, Gale informed Hamilton that he was indeed a runaway and "belonged to Tom. Gatlin of Arkansas," information that Hamilton used in his efforts to locate Gale's owner. On June 4, 1859, Sheriff Hamilton published a notice in the Austin (Tex.) *State Gazette* that included a physical description of Jim Gale and a request for Thomas Gatlin to "come forward, prove property, pay charges and take said negro away or he will be dealt with as the law requires."[30]

As Sheriff Hamilton's notices regarding Gale's capture bore Gatlin's name, it seems plausible that either Gatlin saw the notice or someone with whom he was acquainted brought it to his attention. In any case, soon after discovering where Gale was, Thomas Gatlin and James B. Milner set out for the Rusk County jail, where they found Gale, still ailing from his gunshot wound. While in Henderson, Gatlin met with James H. Nelms, the forty-year-old Rusk County constable and one of the two men who had arrested Gale on May 11. Nelms told Gatlin that this was not the first time that he had encountered Jim Gale. The very same enslaved man had been arrested and imprisoned in the Rusk County jail as a runaway two years earlier, in 1857. At the time, Nelms informed Gatlin, Gale was "proved out by a man named Williams of Harrison County, Texas"—his previous owner, Marshall attorney and judge John F. Williams.[31]

Thomas Gatlin was not the only enslaver who arrived at the Rusk County jail in November 1859 to reclaim Jim Gale. R. H. Graham, a physician and resident of Henderson, Texas, maintained that Gale was his property and had run away from him several years earlier. If Gatlin attempted to contest Graham's claim, he did not do so for long. After signing an affidavit and paying approximately $188 in jail and medical fees, Graham removed Jim Gale from the Rusk County jail on November 22. Although Thomas Gatlin was no longer Gale's owner, at least according to the State of Texas, he by no means ceased working to gather enough information about Gale's past to file a redhibition suit against Bernard Kendig. Before attempting to locate John F. Williams or filing a lawsuit, however, Gatlin once again attempted to convince Bernard Kendig to cancel the sale and save himself the trouble of a lawsuit.[32]

On December 21, 1859, Thomas Henderson, one of Gatlin's agents in New Orleans and a member of the firm of Henderson, Terry, and Company, personally delivered a letter to Bernard Kendig. In the letter, Gatlin's representatives explained that Jim Gale had been apprehended in Rusk County, Texas, and was then suffering from a gunshot wound, which had resulted in "heavy charges for jail fees and medical attendance." He was furthermore claimed under a "prior title" by R. H. Graham. The letter also accused Kendig of knowingly withholding information from Gatlin regarding Gale's history of running away and demanded that he cancel the sale immediately. Kendig refused to reimburse Gatlin and denied having prior knowledge of Gale's history. He also declined to disclose any information regarding the previous instances in which he had purchased and sold Gale, explaining, "he had so many 'Jims' in his house, he could not tell from where he had got the boy, and to whom he had sold him."[33]

Finally, on March 24, 1860, Thomas Gatlin filed a lawsuit against Bernard Kendig in the Fourth District Court of New Orleans. Gatlin accused Kendig of misrepresenting Gale, who, clearly not "free from all redhibitory vices of body and character," was in the habit of running away. Between December 1859 and March 1860, Thomas Gatlin and his attorneys, Lewis E. Simonds and Charles E. Fenner, used information that they obtained from James H. Nelms, and possibly Jim Gale himself, to reach out to Gale's former owner, John F. Williams, as well as six other witnesses from Louisiana, Texas, and Arkansas. In his petition, Gatlin explained that it was Bernard Kendig who had sold Jim Gale to Williams. After Gale ran away from Williams's home in Marshall, Texas, Williams apprehended Gale and returned him to Bernard Kendig a few days before Gatlin made his purchase. Gatlin's attorneys thus asked that the Fourth District Court of New Orleans order Bernard Kendig to pay Thomas Gatlin $1,200 (Jim Gale's sale price), plus $500 in damages.[34]

To build his case against Bernard Kendig, Gatlin relied not only on seven witnesses, all white men, but also on Jim Gale. On May 11, 1860, a day before John F. Williams was deposed in *Gatlin v. Kendig* (1860), Gatlin, James B. Milner, and Jim Gale met Williams in Marshall. According to Milner, who would testify on Gatlin's behalf, he and Gatlin "accompanied said boy Jim to the City of Marshall, Harrison County, Texas, for Judge Williams to identify." Williams corroborated Milner's statement, confirming that Gatlin had indeed arrived with "a negro boy by the name of 'Jim,' which said boy I purchased of the Defendant in the City of New Orleans, some time about the last days of January or the first day of February A.D. 1858."[35]

Exactly how and why Jim Gale fell into Thomas Gatlin's possession in May 1860 remains unclear. Sheriff John D. Hamilton of Rusk County, Constable James H. Nelms, and James B. Milner each stated that Dr. R. H. Graham had claimed Jim Gale as his enslaved property in November 1859. Yet on May 14, 1860, in testimony before a justice of the peace in Rusk County, Graham denied knowing Jim Gale, remarking, "No. I know of no such boy." While Hamilton testified that Graham signed an affidavit, produced a title, and presented a witness who was able to corroborate his claim, any documents reflecting his efforts were not included in court records from *Gatlin v. Kendig* (1860). Such omissions, while frustrating, are hardly surprising since Graham's claim was not pertinent to the matter at hand: whether Bernard Kendig had knowingly sold Thomas Gatlin an enslaved man who was in the habit of running away.[36]

To establish that Jim Gale was in the habit of running away and that Bernard Kendig was well aware of his history, Thomas Gatlin relied on witnesses to recognize Gale and to disclose specific information about his past. Because Gatlin was able to locate Gale and to gather information from officials at the Rusk County jail, he was able to demonstrate successfully that Jim Gale was in the habit of running away and that Kendig had misrepresented Gale when he sold him with a full redhibitory guarantee. For other disgruntled buyers who did not have access to the enslaved person at the center of a redhibition suit—for example, in instances wherein an enslaved person had run away and could not be located or had fallen ill and passed away—constructing a history of a slave who was unsound before a sale was still of the utmost importance.

When Thomas Gatlin filed his redhibition suit against Bernard Kendig, he claimed that he was not in possession of Jim Gale. Gale's absence, however, did not prevent Gatlin and his attorneys from convincing the Fourth District Court of New Orleans that Gale was a habitual runaway prior to his purchase and that Kendig had misrepresented Gale using a full redhibitory guarantee. According to Louisiana's Civil Code, "The redhibitory action may be commenced after the loss of the object sold, if that loss was not occasioned by the fault of the purchaser."[37] Gatlin's was a redhibitory lawsuit, and he was not attempting to maintain possession of Gale. Indeed, he was working to rid himself of the troublesome human property without losing his investment in someone he deemed useless. Because Thomas Gatlin did not need to be in possession of Jim Gale to secure a refund and because of contradictory testimony regarding precisely who maintained possession of Gale, our history of Jim Gale ends on May 11, 1860, in Marshall, Texas.[38]

Between 1840 and 1860, Bernard Kendig was involved in no fewer than ten redhibitory lawsuits. While he lost the majority of these legal battles, his willingness to sell enslaved people with redhibitory guarantees does not seem to have dissipated with each subsequent lawsuit. What motivation was there to change his methods? It was profitable to portray an enslaved person as a product free from the redhibitory vices and maladies prescribed by law, it was profitable to buy an enslaved person without a warranty at a low price and to sell them with a full guarantee, it was profitable to obscure the details of an enslaved person's history within an act of sale and during the course of a redhibitory lawsuit, and it was profitable for Bernard Kendig to take on the risk of a redhibitory lawsuit. After all, as Richard Tansey demonstrated, between 1852 and 1860, Kendig sold at least 758 people in New Orleans via notarial contracts. Although probably not each and every civil suit wherein Bernard Kendig was a plaintiff or defendant has been located, it is extremely unlikely that a majority or even one-tenth of his sales resulted in a civil suit. Probably no more than 1 or 2 percent of all of Kendig's slave sales resulted in redhibitory actions against him. The cost of reimbursing a plaintiff and paying court costs, attorney's fees, and damages in a paltry number of redhibitory lawsuits must have paled in comparison to the profits Bernard Kendig made while relying on the Louisiana guarantee to shrewdly navigate the spaces of the market and the courtroom.[39]

Notes

1. Bernard Kendig's wife, Jane Miller, is referenced in *Riggin v. Kendig* (August 1855), Case #9118, Fourth District Court of New Orleans, and several other cases. The redhibitory lawsuit of *Voorhees v. Dubois and Kendig* (July 1840), Case #13130, Orleans Parish Court, New Orleans, contains a notarial contract that documented the sale by Bernard Kendig and his partner Oliver Dubois of an enslaved woman named Susan to Marcus T. Voorhees on August 16, 1839.

2. I have located ten redhibitory lawsuits in which Bernard Kendig was involved between 1840 and 1860; however, it is possible that there are more such disputes that I have yet to discover. Kendig's disgruntled customers accused him of defrauding them in nine out of the ten disputes. Those cases and, in some instances, their corresponding civil suits appealed to the Louisiana Supreme Court, are the following. Verdicts, if known, are given in brackets: Voorhees v. Du-

bois and Kendig (July 1840), Case #13130, Orleans Parish Court, New Orleans [verdict unknown]; Gay v. Kendig (June 1841), Case #8939, City Court of New Orleans [verdict in favor of the plaintiff Gay]; Gay v. Kendig (June 1842), Case #4804, Louisiana Supreme Court [verdict affirmed]; Riggin v. Kendig (August 1855), Case #9118, Fourth District Court of New Orleans [verdict in favor of the defendant Kendig]; Riggin v. Kendig (June 1857), Case #4718, Louisiana Supreme Court [verdict reversed]; Buie v. Kendig (August 1857), Case #5483, Sixth District Court of New Orleans [verdict in favor of the plaintiff Buie]; Buie v. Kendig (June 1860), Case #6356, Louisiana Supreme Court [verdict affirmed]; Singleton v. Kendig (October 1857), Case #11920, Fifth District Court of New Orleans [verdict in favor of the plaintiff Singleton]; Palms v. Kendig (December 1857), Case #11899, Fourth District Court of New Orleans [verdict in favor of the plaintiff Palms]; Palms v. Kendig (April 1859), Case #6279, Louisiana Supreme Court [verdict affirmed]; Belknap v. Kendig (November 1858), Case #14786, Second District Court of New Orleans [verdict in favor of the defendant Kendig]; Belknap v. Kendig (April 1860), Case #6199, Louisiana Supreme Court [verdict affirmed]; Morris v. Kendig (January 1859), Case #12949, Fifth District Court of New Orleans [verdict in favor of the plaintiff Morris]; Morris v. Kendig (June 1860), Case #6385, Louisiana Supreme Court [verdict affirmed]; Cochrane v. Kendig (January 1860), Case #13377, Fifth District Court of New Orleans [verdict in favor of the defendant Kendig]; Gatlin v. Kendig (March 1860), Case #13731, Fourth District Court of New Orleans [verdict in favor of the plaintiff Gatlin]; Gatlin v. Kendig (November 1860), Case #6894, Louisiana Supreme Court [verdict affirmed].

3. Those who bought and sold enslaved people in Louisiana were required to record their agreements in writing, either in authentic acts or in acts made under private signature (see *A Digest of the Civil Laws Now in Force in the Territory of New Orleans, with Alterations and Amendments Adapted to Its Present System of Government* [New Orleans: Bradford and Anderson, 1808], Book III, Title VI, Chapter I, Article 2 [hereinafter cited as the Louisiana Civil Code of 1808]; and Thomas Gibbes Morgan, *Civil Code of the State of Louisiana: With the Statutory Amendments, from 1825 to 1853, Inclusive; and References to the Decisions of the Supreme Court of Louisiana to the Sixth Volume of Annual Reports* [New Orleans: Bloomfield and Steel, 1854], Book III, Title VII, Chapter I, Article 2415, p. 325 [hereinafter cited as the Louisiana Civil Code of 1825]).

4. Louisiana's Civil Code was a site of contention between the state's judiciary and legislature throughout the nineteenth century; however, during the antebellum period, the state's definition of redhibition remained much the same. The 1808 Civil Code, which remained in effect between 1808 and 1825, when it was replaced with the state's 1825 Civil Code, defined redhibition as "the cancelling of the sale on account of some defect in the thing sold, such as may be sufficient to oblige the seller to take it back again and have the sale annulled." The definition in Louisiana's 1825 Civil Code changed somewhat but maintained the same sentiment and is quoted word for word in the text. The Louisiana Civil Code's definition of redhibition did not change after 1825 (see Louisiana Civil Code of 1808, Book III, Title VI, Chapter III, Section III, Article 65; Louisiana Civil Code of 1825, Book III, Title VII, Chapter I, Section III, Article 2496, p. 334; and Thomas J. Semmes, "History of the Laws of Louisiana and of the Civil Law," *Journal of Civil Law Studies* 5 [2012]: 313–44).

5. Louisiana Civil Code of 1825, Book III, Title VII, Chapter I, Section III, Article 2497, p. 334.

6. Louisiana Civil Code of 1808, Book III, Title VI, Chapter III, Section III, Articles 79–80 *https://digestof1808.law.lsu.edu/index.php*; Louisiana Civil Code of 1825, Book III, Title VII, Chapter I, Section III, Articles 2502 and 2505, p. 335.

7. For more on redhibition laws in Louisiana, see Judith K. Schafer, "'Guaranteed against the Vices and Maladies Prescribed by Law': Consumer Protection, the Law of Slave Sales, and the Supreme Court in Antebellum Louisiana," *American Journal of Legal History* 31, no. 4 (October 1, 1987): 306–21; Judith Kelleher Schafer, *Slavery, the Civil Law, and the Supreme Court of Louisiana* (Baton Rouge: Louisiana State University Press, 1994), 127–48; Thomas D. Morris, *Southern Slavery and the Law, 1619–1860* (Chapel Hill: University of North Carolina Press, 1996), 112–13; Walter Johnson, *Soul by Soul: Life inside the Antebellum Slave Market* (Cambridge, Mass.: Harvard University Press, 1999), 4, 12–13, 53; Ariela J. Gross, *Double Character: Slavery and Mastery in the Antebellum Southern Courtroom* (Athens: University of Georgia Press, 2006), 73, 92–93; and Maria R. Montalvo, "The Slavers' Archive: Enslaved People, Power, and the Production of the Past in the Antebellum Courtroom" (Ph.D. diss., Rice University, 2017).

8. A copy of the act of sale that contained Bernard Kendig's warranty was used as evidence and included in court records from *Gatlin v. Kendig*, Case #13731.

9. Joseph A. Beard was a witness in the civil suit, *Dunbar v. Connor* (May 1849), Case #2496, Fifth District Court of New Orleans.

10. For more on slave warranties and legal protections in common law states, see Andrew Fede, "Legal Protections for Slave Buyers in the U.S. South: A Caveat Concerning *Caveat Emptor,*" *American Journal of Legal History* 31, no. 4 (October 1987): 322–58; Jenny Bourne Wahl, *The Bondsman's Burden: An Economic Analysis of the Common Law of Southern Slavery* (Cambridge: Cambridge University Press, 1998), 27–48; and Thomas D. Morris, *Southern Slavery and the Law, 1619–1860* (Chapel Hill: University of North Carolina Press, 1996), 104–12.

11. Louisiana Civil Code of 1825, Book III, Title VII, Chapter I, Section III, Articles 2523 and 2524, p. 337. Article 2523 reads as follows: "The seller who knows the vice of the thing he sells, and omits to declare it, besides the restitution of the price and repayment of the expenses, is answerable to the buyer in damages." Article 2524 states: "In this case, the action for redhibition may be commenced at any time, provided a year has not elapsed since the discovery of the vice. This discovery is not to be presumed; it must be proved by the seller."

12. Quoted testimony from James B. Milner in Gatlin v. Kendig, Case #13731.

13. Gatlin v. Kendig, Case #13731. Lewis E. Simonds and Charles E. Fenner were attorneys and partners who maintained a law office at 9 Commercial Street in New Orleans, Louisiana (see W. H. Rainey, ed., *Business Directory with a Map, Compiled and Arranged by W. H. Rainey, to be Published Annually, Containing the Name and Address of Every Business or Professional Man in the City, Classified According to Their Respective Avocations. Also, a Business Directory of Algiers, Baton Rouge, Natchez, Vicksburg, Bayou Sara, Clinton, and Port Hudson. 1858* [New Orleans: A. Mygatt & Co., 1858], 14).

14. Louisiana's Civil Code imposed certain temporal constraints on redhibition suits. According to the Louisiana Civil Code of 1825, Book III, Title VII, Chapter I, Section I, Article 2508, p. 335: "The buyer who institutes the redhibitory action must prove that the vice existed before

the sale was made to him. If the vice has made its appearance within three days immediately following the sale, it is presumed to have existed before the sale." This article was amended in 1834 to state that buyers who filed redhibition suits on the grounds that an enslaved person was a habitual runaway or a thief were not "bound to prove that such vice existed before the date of the sale, whenever said vice shall have been discovered within two months after the sale." Those who discovered "any redhibitory, bodily or mental maladies" were given the same leeway if they discovered these vices within fifteen days of the sale.

15. Louisiana Civil Code of 1825, Book III, Title VII, Chapter I, Section III, Article 2505, p. 335.

16. Census records indicate that John F. Williams was approximately fifty-five years of age when he purchased Jim Gale and was living with his wife and children in Marshall, Texas. Williams would eventually testify on Thomas Gatlin's behalf in *Gatlin v. Kendig*, but he did not disclose the exact date when he purchased Jim Gale. He did, however, provide more specific information regarding the weeks and months when Gale ran away and was captured. By relying on the information that Williams did provide, I have determined that Williams likely purchased Jim Gale from Bernard Kendig in New Orleans in February or March 1857 (Gatlin v. Kendig, Case #13731).

17. John F. Williams's quote was taken from his testimony in *Gatlin v. Kendig*.

18. Testimony in *Gatlin v. Kendig* reveals that Bernard Kendig intentionally withheld information regarding Jim Gale's past from Thomas Gatlin during the course of the sale and during the subsequent lawsuit (Gatlin v. Kendig, Case #13731).

19. Voorhees v. Dubois and Kendig.

20. Richard Tansey, "Bernard Kendig and the New Orleans Slave Trade," *Louisiana History* 23, no. 2 (Spring 1982): 162. Tansey states that "there is no evidence that he sold slaves outside of New Orleans." Petitions filed in states such as Alabama and Tennessee suggest, however, that Kendig's business may have been more expansive than previously acknowledged.

21. Tansey, "Bernard Kendig," 162. Tansey acknowledges that "the absence of Bernard Kendig's ledger books prevents any definitive account of his slave trading business."

22. See note 2.

23. Tansey, "Bernard Kendig," 170.

24. Quoted testimony from James B. Milner and John F. Williams in Gatlin v. Kendig, Case #13731.

25. Palms v. Kendig, Case #11899.

26. Quoted text from Oliver Palms's petition to the Fourth District Court of New Orleans in Palms v. Kendig, Case #11899.

27. Quoted text from Julia Ann Palmer's testimony and the notarial contract that reflected the terms of Bernard Kendig's and Rufus R. Rhodes's agreement (see Palms v. Kendig, Case #11899).

28. Palms v. Kendig, Case #11899; Palms v. Kendig, Case #6279; Gatlin v. Kendig, Case #13731; Gatlin v. Kendig, Case #6894.

29. Gatlin v. Kendig, Case #13731.

30. Gatlin v. Kendig, Case #13731; "Notice," *Austin (Tex.) State Gazette*, June 4, 1859, 3.

31. Quoted text from James H. Nelms's testimony in Gatlin v. Kendig, Case #13731.

32. Gatlin v. Kendig, Case #13731.

33. Quoted text from Thomas Henderson's testimony in Gatlin v. Kendig, Case #13731.

34. Above information from Thomas Gatlin's petition to the Fourth District Court of New Orleans in Gatlin v. Kendig, Case #13731.

35. Quoted text from John F. Williams's and James B. Milner's testimony in Gatlin v. Kendig, Case #13731.

36. Quoted text from R. H. Graham's deposition in Gatlin v. Kendig, Case #13731.

37. Louisiana Civil Code of 1825, Book III, Title VII, Chapter I, Section I, Article 2514, 336.

38. Gatlin v. Kendig, Case #13731; Gatlin v. Kendig, Case #6894.

39. Tansey, "Bernard Kendig," 162.

William A. Britton v. Benjamin F. Butler

OCCUPIED NEW ORLEANS, CONFISCATION, AND THE DISRUPTION
OF THE COTTON TRADE IN WARTIME NATCHEZ

JEFF STRICKLAND

On August 1, 1862, Confederate troops attacked Union pickets five miles above Carrollton, Louisiana, a town not far upriver from New Orleans, but were repelled. Early the next morning, the outer line of pickets captured an unnamed white southerner, presumably a Confederate spy, attempting to enter New Orleans under cover of darkness with three bank drafts worth $7,500, drawn on the accounts of William A. Britton & Co. of Natchez, Mississippi, which the mystery agent planned to cash at a Crescent City bank. This variety of anticipated financial transaction would have required authorization from the occupying forces, and the man had not obtained clearance to conduct it. The Union soldiers seized the southerner, confiscated his bank drafts, and turned man and money over to their commanding officer, who carried them to Major General Benjamin F. Butler's headquarters in New Orleans. Although his troops had thwarted the planned cashing of bank drafts this time, Butler feared someone would eventually withdraw money from New Orleans financial institutions and use it to provide material support to the Confederate army. Butler therefore cashed the bank drafts himself and deposited the money into the War Treasury.[1]

Secession and Civil War severely disrupted the southern cotton economy. Prior to the war, slaves planted and harvested nearly all of the cotton grown in the South, making the United States the largest cotton producer in the world by far. New Orleans thrived as a seaboard commercial center based on the cotton economy. From 1860 to 1861, the port of New Orleans exported 1,849,212 bales of cotton, but with the onset of the war, the total number of cotton bales exported from New Orleans fell to 38,880 from 1861 to 1862. That figure would not improve until the 1864–65 season.[2] By the end of the Civil War, the global cotton economy had changed considerably. In the wake of emancipation, sharecroppers, tenant farmers, and peasants grew ever-greater quantities of cotton, and a significant portion of cotton production moved to India, Egypt, West Africa, and Brazil. This led to a global empire of cotton that stimulated the growth of capitalism worldwide. While the Lower Mississippi River delta continued to grow the best-quality cotton in the world, Mississippi took nearly thirty-five years to recover its prewar position.[3]

Natchez was the commercial and manufacturing center of Mississippi. In 1860, slaves toiling on Natchez, Mississippi, plantations produced 400,000 bales of cotton, 10 percent of the southern total.[4] Natchez cotton brokers sent their cotton downriver to New Orleans. Prior to the Panic of 1837, agency houses in New Orleans, backed by seven English banking houses, issued sixty- or ninety-day bills of exchange payable when the cotton reached England. At the same time, the Second Bank of the United States issued "bank drafts" to agency houses that functioned much like the bills of exchange. In practice, the Second Bank of the United States and the seven houses borrowed their money from the same English country banks. Land speculation schemes led English banks, including the Bank of England, to contract the flow of credit. The majority of the seven houses failed, as did many agency houses in the United States. The prices of cotton and slaves nosedived. Planters relied heavily on the credit system, purchasing slaves on credit. In the wake of the Panic of 1837, banking houses took possession of those slaves whom the planters could no longer afford. The cotton economy and associated credit system rebounded slowly, with the price of cotton and slaves not rising considerably until the second half of the 1840s.[5]

In the 1840s, planters relied on short-term bills of exchange to finance the fall harvest, particularly the transportation of cotton to market. Banks in New Orleans issued bills of exchange for promissory notes, which served as currency throughout the Lower Mississippi Valley, including Natchez. William A. Britton & Co., a lottery and exchange brokerage, functioned as Natchez's chief financial institution in the 1840s and 1850s.[6] Britton & Co. did not call itself a bank, although it definitely acted like one. The brokerage maintained popularity among Natchez planters who were highly suspicious of banks. Certainly, the brokerage helped found a uniquely southern brand of capitalism. The firm bankrolled the slave economy of Natchez for two decades, supplying credit to cotton planters and manufacturing interests in Natchez. No better evidence of the Civil War's disruption of the cotton economy in Natchez exists than the fact that William A. Britton & Co. disbanded as the war commenced.

Although William Britton made his living as a broker in the South, he was a citizen of New York State. Shortly after the conclusion of the Civil War, he filed an officer suit against General Benjamin F. Butler in New York City court to re- cover the $7,500 in bank drafts seized from him during the Union's occupation of New Orleans. As he did so, William attempted to portray himself as a loyal northerner, even though his strongest ties remained to his brother, Audley C. Britton, and other cotton planters in Natchez, Mississippi. A planter and large slave owner in his own right, Audley Britton's depravity far exceeded William's. His greatest misdeed entailed the attempt to violate the Non-Intercourse Act of July 1861, which declared that "all goods, and chattels, wares, and merchan- dise" coming from a state in rebellion to other parts of the United States should be forfeited. General Butler strictly enforced this law during the occupation of New Orleans and withdrew all of William A. Britton & Co.'s funds on deposit in New Orleans. More than twenty-five years later, Audley Britton deliberately misled Congress in a failed attempt to recover the confiscated money.[7]

Civil War Disruption

In a conservative move to stabilize their economic position, New Orleans banks issued fewer notes and bills of exchange beginning in the fall of 1860 as the national election approached, and by December, they ceased issuing new loans completely. Cotton factors could not obtain the short-term bills of exchange that they used to move the fall cotton harvest, which led some firms to suspend operations. The banks' outstanding short-term paper, most of which consisted of the ninety-day loans on which the export trade relied, fell signifi- cantly between November 1860 and April 1861, from $24.4 million to $14.1 million. An economic slowdown became evident in early 1861 due in part to the lack of currency. Fewer commodities in circulation meant less money in circulation. At the same time, the Confederacy relied on available currency to finance wartime production. As the war began, the $13.6 million in specie on reserve in New Orleans banks ranked second only to the value amassed in New

York City.[8] In May 1861, the U.S. naval blockade of the Port of New Orleans restricted the number of ships arriving at the port and disrupted Mississippi River traffic generally.

Many white northerners in the antebellum decades had relocated to New Orleans and its hinterlands to participate in its burgeoning slave economy. William A. Britton moved to Natchez hoping to capitalize on the region's growth in the early 1830s, and his brother Audley joined him several years later. With sectional tensions boiling over, southern whites committed to secession questioned the loyalties of Yankees in their midst. The overwhelming majority of Louisiana merchant capitalists supported the Confederacy. When the war began, William Britton went home to New York City and, from there, managed his banking transactions and business connections in Natchez and New Orleans. Audley, meanwhile, operated his Eutaw Plantation in Natchez from his residence in the Crescent City. The Britton brothers refrained from discussing their loyalties in their personal correspondence, but both men had become wealthy in Natchez's slave economy. Following the election of President Abraham Lincoln in November 1860, the threat and eventual outbreak of Civil War disrupted the customary routines of slavery and capitalism in the Lower Mississippi River Valley. In Natchez, cotton planters continued to maintain tight control over their slaves, but they found it difficult to obtain credit.[9]

The Union military invasion and occupation of New Orleans and its surrounding area in May 1862 presented a more serious interruption. New Orleans was an economic ghost town when General Benjamin F. Butler and the infantry arrived on May 1. President Lincoln had instructed Butler to obtain cotton by any means necessary for fear that the northern economy would suffer from a shortage of the crop. Confederate troops had burned cotton bales stockpiled on the city's wharves as federal forces approached the city. Butler quickly imposed martial law over New Orleans, confiscating Confederate property and imposing strict limits on banking and business activity.[10] As Butler seized money from Confederate sympathizers, the federal government approved the general's punitive approach. Historians have tended to question Butler's integrity, but he appears to have targeted for confiscation disloyal southerners as well as northerners loyal to the Confederacy, all of whom deserved what they got.[11]

Proponents of confiscation hoped to punish Confederates, emancipate enslaved men and women, and begin the process of Reconstruction even as the war was still being fought. Whereas opponents of confiscation considered the measures extreme and unconstitutional, most supporters viewed it primarily as a military expedient. Some regarded it as an appropriate means to punish the South. It made sense to take southern property, including slaves, but even many advocates for confiscation had little interest in reforming southern society or assisting freedpeople. During the war, President Lincoln supported confiscation for military reasons.[12]

Confiscation

Congress passed the First Confiscation Act without much debate on August 6, 1861, authorizing the federal government to confiscate "property devoted to hostile use." Therefore, it targeted the property of those participating directly in the rebellion.[13] Less than a year later, on July 17, 1862, Congress approved the Second Confiscation Act, implementing a court system for the confiscation of Confederate property and authorizing the military to assist in confiscation proceedings in areas where the courts had ceased to function.[14] The law empowered the federal government to seize the property of anyone who supported the Confederacy.[15] Five days later, on July 22, Lincoln issued an executive order to military commanders authorizing the seizure and use of rebel property for military purposes and the employment of freedmen as wage laborers.[16]

The passage of the Second Confiscation Act was the product of numerous proposals, six months of debate, and the deliberations of two Judiciary Committees, two Select Committees, and a Committee of Conference between the two houses of Congress. It narrowly escaped Lincoln's veto. Much of the debate revolved around the proposed role of the federal courts.[17] In most cases, no federal courts existed to process the confiscation of property, especially cotton, as the Union army occupied southern territory.[18] The Second Confiscation Act did not grant the federal government permanent title to the confiscated property, and the government could only hold confiscated property during the individual Confederate propertyholder's lifetime.[19]

During his occupation of New Orleans, General Butler intended to penalize Confederates and Confederate sympathizers, and he confiscated more property than did any other Union commander anywhere in Confederate territory.[20] In September 1861, the banks in New Orleans suspended specie payments and began issuing Confederate notes. They sent the specie away, hiding it outside of the city. Of the $9 million on deposit in New Orleans banks when the war began, collectively only a half million dollars remained in town when Butler arrived in May 1862. As of June 30, however, just two months into the occupation, Butler had seized $262,534, including $215,820.89 from the Citizens' Bank, $24,076.11 from the Louisiana State Bank, $16,773.90 from the Bank of Louisiana, $2,850 from the Bank of America, $2,500 from the New Orleans Canal and Banking Company, and $513.10 from the Southern Bank. On occasion, black New Orleanians informed Butler of hidden money, which he also then confiscated.[21]

Union occupation of the city meant the rapid depreciation of Confederate notes, but the banks continued to pay them out while refusing to accept them on deposit. In General Order Number 30, issued May 16, 1862, Butler moved to bring back the bank bills and abolish Confederate currency. He made three important demands of the banks. First, the incorporated banks must cease issuing Confederate notes to depositors and creditors and pay all deposits in the bills of the bank, United States Treasury notes, gold, or silver. Second, all private bankers must pay all deposits in current bills of city banks, United States Treasury notes, gold, or silver. Third, the savings banks must pay depositors or creditors in their own bills, current bills of city banks, United States Treasury notes, gold, or silver, to an amount not exceeding one-third of their deposits.[22]

Bankers hid half of the money until Butler managed to convince them to return it. New Orleans bankers requested assurances that the restored funds would remain in the bank vaults upon their return. Butler agreed, and gradually, $4 million in specie filtered back into New Orleans bank vaults by the time Butler departed the city in December 1862. The cashier of the Bank of America journeyed up the Red River to retrieve $650,000 in specie belonging to that institution.[23]

Several historians have written important studies about Civil War property confiscation and the rapid return of property to ex-Confederates in the name of reconciliation. Some of the most notable studies have focused on Union efforts to obtain cotton.[24] As reported officially in May 1868, the gross proceeds from the sale of cotton from February 1862 to October 1866 were $29,518,041, while gross proceeds from miscellaneous property totaled $1,309,650. The net total derived from captured and abandoned property was $25,257,931.[25] On September 24, 1862, sixty days after the Second Confiscation Act became law, Butler ordered Confederate sympathizers to take an oath of allegiance on or before October 1 as well as submit a list of their property. Four thousand Confederates refused to take the oath, registered as enemies, and left the city with little property.[26]

Butler also confiscated millions of dollars in gold and silver from foreign consuls on deposit in New Orleans banks, sparking international outrage. Although the consuls seemed sympathetic to the Confederate cause, they remained officially neutral. Secretary of State William H. Seward sent Reverdy Johnson, a former U.S. attorney general and Maryland senator, to investigate the situation.[27] Military officials had apparently auctioned off real estate and personal effects, with proceeds amounting to $1 million.[28] Butler's aggressive confiscation policies against the consuls, bankers, and merchants led President Abraham Lincoln to recall him on December 16, 1862.[29]

The Britton Brothers

Many northerners residing in the South during the Civil War took advantage of their Union citizenship. Although like the foreign consuls in New Orleans neutral in their outward appearance, politically they sympathized with the Confederacy. At times, they provided material support for the Confederacy and then later claimed Union loyalties.[30] The Britton brothers in Natchez, Mississippi, did exactly that.

The burgeoning cotton economy of the Lower Mississippi Valley proved highly attractive to young white men on the make. William A. Britton, a native of Rhode Island and part-time resident of both New York City and Kent, Connecticut, maintained strong ties to New York City. He began operating his lottery and exchange business in Natchez, Mississippi, in 1834, at about the age of twenty-three. William likely received financial support from his father to set up operations. His business connections in New York City presented him with the opportunity to sell life insurance for the Nautilus Insurance Company and probably other companies as well. It is difficult to ascertain how much money his ventures made him.[31]

The federal and Mississippi manuscript censuses reveal William Britton's migratory life. In 1850, the federal census enumerator encountered William, by then thirty-nine years old and married to Mary Ann, age thirty-eight, living in Kent, Connecticut. The couple had three children, ages nine, five, and nine months. Three Irish women lived in the household, probably as domestic servants. William did not own any property, according to the enumerator.[32] The 1853 Mississippi census captured William living alone in Natchez.[33] In 1860, William had a household appear in both the Kent and New York City censuses. In Kent, the enumerator indicated real estate holdings of $10,000 and a personal estate worth $100,000. Two Irish domestic servants and an Irish coachman lived in the same household. In New York City's Twenty-First Ward, the enumerator listed William as a banker by occupation, who owned $60,000 in real estate and personal estate valued at $5,000. It does not appear he owned any enslaved people in 1850 or 1860, but he did profit from the institution of slavery.[34]

William Britton sold life insurance policies for the Nautilus Insurance Company, the precursor to the New York Life Insurance Company. He mainly sold policies on slaves, although he did sell some life insurance to white planters and merchants as well, earning a 10 percent commission on each life insurance policy premium. His total commission from slave life insurance policies was less than $50 per year, but his willingness to sell such policies implied support for the slave system he would increasingly bankroll. It also helped establish relationships with planters who would later conduct business with his brokerage house. One customer joined his firm. On May 10, 1847, William sold policies to a white man named George W. Koontz on domestic servants Burrell and Elizabeth, age twenty-five and twenty, respectively, each valued at $500. The premiums cost $8.75 apiece for the year. The following year, pressure from New York abolitionists compelled Nautilus to cease selling life insurance policies on the enslaved.[35]

Although Audley C. Britton arrived in Natchez in the 1840s, several years after his brother, he remained there permanently. Born in New York City in 1821, he did not maintain connections to the city as his brother did. In 1850, Audley lived in a house by himself and listed his occupation as broker. He did not yet own any real estate. By 1853, Audley had married, and the couple had one child.[36] By 1860, Audley had amassed $135,000 in real estate and $15,000 in personal property. He and his wife, Eliza McCrery, the daughter of a Mississippi planter, had three children. Audley's sister Ruth rounded out the household. The manuscript slave census for the same year indicates that Britton owned thirty-seven slaves, including seven males and five females sixteen and older. He was the largest slave owner in Natchez. The most arresting aspect of his enslaved labor force was its youth: twenty-five were children, including seventeen who were six years old or younger. The oldest was eleven. Only four of Britton's female slaves were old enough to reproduce, and that included a forty-five-year-old and a seventeen-year-old. Britton must have acquired some of the children through purchase and mortgage defaults.[37] Like his brother, Audley made his fortune on the backs of slaves.

George W. Koontz, a banker from Pennsylvania, joined the Britton brothers' firm in the 1850s. Koontz had arrived in Natchez a short time before 1845. He married Mary Beltzhoover, also from Pennsylvania, in October 1845, and she bore seven children. In 1850, Koontz claimed $8,500 in real estate and owned six slaves. By 1860, he possessed $95,000 in real estate and $70,000 in personal property. He had increased his holdings in enslaved people to thirty-three. Audley Britton lived in his household.[38]

Officially, William A. Britton & Co. ceased operations when the war commenced, and William returned to New York City. Although William had become wealthy in the plantation economy of the Lower Mississippi Valley, he did not own slaves and spent several months each year in the Northeast, never adopting the South as his true home. Audley, on the other hand, remained in Mississippi year-round and embraced his identity as a white southerner and slave owner. Like other planters and bankers who maintained ties with their northern counterparts throughout the war, Audley continued to conduct what amounted to fraudulent business through his brother in New York City.[39]

The Enslaved at Eutaw Plantation

During the war, Audley moved to New Orleans to look after his investments while his overseer, James W. Melvin, operated Eutaw Plantation and continued to plant cotton throughout the war. Although Natchez planters did not cease cotton production during the Civil War, minimal cotton trading occurred through 1863. Business improved somewhat when the federal government appointed treasury agents to purchase cotton within Union lines on July 2, 1864.[40] Importantly, Natchez planters maintained considerable control over their slaves, and they were able to harvest the crop and take it to market. Cotton speculators traded goods and supplies with planters and/or the Confederate government in exchange for cotton. Doing so entailed the dangerous practice of bringing ships and supplies into Confederacy. Federal law required the speculators to acquire the cotton first before taking the items to the Confederates. The Confederate government required the opposite. That meant that cotton speculators often circumvented federal regulations because they stood to make tremendous profits. It was difficult to obtain a permit to trade, which often depended upon personal connections to officials in Washington, including President Lincoln himself, so permit holders lacking friends in the federal government often resorted to bribery.[41] Meanwhile, planters forced their enslaved work forces to plant and harvest cotton.

The treatment of the slaves on Audley's Eutaw Plantation serves as evidence of his villainy. It is difficult to imagine the degree of suffering that the bondpeople on Eutaw Plantation endured. Audley's overseer James W. Melvin continued to plant cotton while adding edible crops of corn, pumpkins, and peas. Occasionally, he slaughtered livestock to feed his family. The blockade of New Orleans and the Civil War generally decreased the availability of dry goods and medicine. Slaves and livestock on Eutaw Plantation faced persistent sickness throughout the war.[42] Melvin, his wife, and daughter appear to have fared much better than the slaves, an indication that he reserved the best-quality foods for his family. On September 29, 1862, Melvin wrote Audley Britton, "There has been [a] great deal [of] sickness on [the] plantation, but at this time all are on the mend." Melvin added, "Matilda, John's wife, was taken about five weeks ago with swelling of the face, which I took to be a rising. I applied a poultice, when lo! There droped [sic] out of her nose three of the largest maggets [sic] I ever saw in my life. I had made Elder tea, and injected up the nose, when there came out about fifty from first to last more than a double hand full." The doctor could not diagnose the condition because it did not appear in his medical manuals but predicted that she would die in three or four days. Meanwhile, Matilda could feel "the motion of worms" behind her ear, a condition that lasted for several weeks.[43] In late October, Melvin reported, "not an ox, mule, horse, cow, calf, or hog that receives a scratch, but gets immediately full of maggots or small worms." Worms had also infected a slave named Old Bill, and Melvin feared he would die. But Melvin wrote a few days later that

Bill was "on the mend," although worms continued to "come out from time to time."[44]

Worms presented just one of many physical challenges to Audley Britton's enslaved workers. The bondwoman Delphy suffered from tuberculosis.[45] The enslaved Black Bill survived a dangerous bout with pneumonia. To make matters worse, Melvin sent slaves to work on Confederate fortifications when called upon, as planters were required to send one slave for every five. Confederate officers required those slaves to work from sunup until sundown.[46] On January 1, 1863, the day President Lincoln's Emancipation Proclamation went into effect, the enslaved woman Rosetta bore a child into unhealthy and inhumane conditions on Eutaw Plantation. The slaves patched their tattered clothing together and made moccasins out of rawhide because they lacked shoes. Disease continued to ravage the farm. Black Bill died of typhoid fever on January 31. Although Melvin wrote that the slaves were "in tolerable good health," he proceeded to document more illnesses.[47] In the summer of 1863, Melvin observed "10 hands and 5 children sick with chills and fever" on June 29, and on July 7, "8 hands [were] sick, and Rose badly sick with chills—myself not very well."[48]

The Eutaw slaves also coped with the forced separation of loved ones as Audley Britton took several bondpeople to New Orleans. Melvin wrote, "I am glad to hear Cely is doing so well. Tell her [illegible] hopes she will be a good girl. Her mother is pretty well. Willis sends his love to his son wants him not to leave where he is, that he may some time chance to see him again. All are pretty well, some few have colds."[49] Of course, slaves had always suffered from forced separation, and Audley, as a slave owner, and both of the Britton brothers, as brokers and bankers, had long sanctioned these transactions.

William and Audley rarely discussed slaves in their correspondence, and William appeared only vaguely interested in their well-being. In late December 1863, he wrote his brother: "What do you have from your plantation? Has any of your people left you? I hope not, but fear some have."[50] Melvin did not mention any runaways in his correspondence with Audley. In August 1864, William again wrote Audley: "I am sorry to hear that you report some sickness in Natchez. I hope you will not face an epidemic."[51] The enslaved population of Eutaw Plantation had been suffering from epidemic disease since the war began.

The captives at Eutaw Plantation had endured the brutality of slavery at the hands of Audley Britton and James Melvin long enough. When the war ended in April 1865, they looked forward to freedom. Melvin reported to his employer that all of Britton's slaves had fled the plantation, using a flatboat to transport themselves. Tragically, however, in late April or early May, the flatboat capsized at Daniel's Ferry, and many of those freshly liberated from bondage drowned. Only sixteen survived.[52] This traumatic experience of watching family members die at the very moment of freedom remained on their minds for the rest of their lives.

Officer Suits

When the war ended, Audley Britton still owned land and an unknown amount of money. Enough of his wealth survived the war to enable him to reestablish his banking business in 1866. William, however, remained in New York. He was already attempting to recoup money confiscated during the Union occupation of New Orleans and portions of Louisiana.

The confiscation of property in Confederate territory presented a variety of legal problems for the federal government. Section 7 of the Habeas Corpus Suspension Act of 1863, amended in 1866, officially titled "An Act relating to Habeas Corpus, and regulating Judicial Proceedings in Certain Cases," required plaintiffs to file officer suits within two years of an alleged incident. Federal judges dismissed several officer suits against Major General Benjamin F. Butler because the plaintiffs initiated their complaints after the two-year window had closed. As the war progressed, increasing numbers of Republicans believed that the confiscation of rebel property was a legitimate wartime measure.[53]

The law could be invoked not only by southerners but also by northerners living or with property interests in Confederate territory. They, too, filed civil lawsuits for monetary damages against Union officers. Several cases against General Butler originated in the New York City Court of Common Pleas. All but one of these lawsuits ended up in the United States Circuit Court in the Southern District of New York. The officer suits provide insight into the behavior of northerners in the Confederacy. Historians have largely neglected these lawsuits, some of which Butler discussed in his memoirs.[54]

On June 16, 1865, attorneys for the firm Vose & McDaniel of New York filed a civil suit against Butler on behalf of plaintiff William A. Britton in the New York City Court of Common Pleas to reclaim the $7,500 that had been confiscated from him in New Orleans. It had been nearly three years since the confiscation and well beyond the two-year statute of limitation.[55] The case ended up in the U.S. Circuit Court in the Southern District of New York. It's worth noting that the plaintiff's allegiance to the United States never became an issue during these proceedings. In fact, not a single document reveals the nature of William A. Britton & Co.'s business dealings in Natchez and New Orleans, nor the extent of Audley C. Britton's slaveholding.

Plaintiffs could sue government officers not only for the value of the confiscated property but also for damages. Congress investigated thousands of requests for bills to reimburse claims for property seized during the war. Eventually, Congress created the Court of Claims to handle the overwhelming number of requests, and it limited the claimants to property damages.[56] If an officer had acted reasonably, the federal government protected him, including by paying the attorney's fees. In cases where the officer exceeded his authority, the federal government refused such protection.[57]

William Britton's attorneys argued that intercourse between Natchez and New Orleans was illegal during the Civil War, and therefore no person should have been able to cash the checks, including Butler himself. The money had legally remained in New Orleans. In addition, the lawyers pointed out that their client was a loyal citizen, and the First Confiscation Act did not authorize the seizure of the bank bills from loyal men. Britton's counsel further contended that Butler was liable for damages and not protected by the fact that he was an officer in the army of the United States.[58]

John Hackett, Butler's attorney, responded to the complaint. He did not dispute the fact that Butler had confiscated $7,500 from William A. Britton & Co. and never returned it. Instead, he argued that Butler confiscated the money legally. Hackett observed that, acting under the order and direction of the president and commander in chief of the United States, Abraham Lincoln, Butler had served as major general in command of the Department of the Gulf in Louisiana from February 24, 1862, until December 16 of the same year. Actions Butler took during that time therefore enjoyed the sanction of the highest authority. Hackett also laid out a timeline showing that the statute of limitations concerning suits for indemnification had already expired.[59]

In early 1867, the New York City law firm of Develin, Miller, & Trull, representing Butler, petitioned the Supreme Court of New York to move the case to the U.S. Circuit Court. Their memorial stated that federal army pickets stationed on the outer lines of New Orleans captured a spy attempting to sneak into the city from Natchez, in Confederate territory. The spy acted "in the interest of the enemy," concealing $7,500 in bank drafts or bills of exchange from banks in New Orleans "to the credit of such enemies of the United States who had drawn said drafts of bills for the same." The pickets arrested the spy and brought him before Butler, who believed the $7,500 would end up aiding the Confederacy, in violation of Congress's Non-Intercourse Acts. As commanding general acting under the authority of the president, Butler signed the drafts and had them cashed in the currency and bills of the banks of the state of Louisiana at a large discount. Butler then had the money converted into U.S. currency and, after paying expenses and commissions, had the money "accounted for and credited in his accounts with the United States." Hackett concluded that the money was "duly passed upon, audited, and credited to him by the order of the President of the United States in settlement of his said accounts." William Britton therefore held no valid claim. On May 30, the New York Supreme Court held a hearing regarding Butler's petition. Vose & McDaniel continued to represent Britton. Judge J. C. Smith, Jr., presided over the hearing at City Hall. Judge Smith approved the petition and ordered the case moved to the U.S. Circuit Court for the Southern District of New York.[60]

The case made its way onto the docket at the U.S. Circuit Court on October 31, 1867. Two and one-half months later, on January 15, 1868, William A. Britton raised the amount of the lawsuit to $15,000 in a complaint filed with the clerk of the Circuit Court. But it would take another five years before a judge would rule on the case. On January 29, 1872, Britton's attorneys claimed that Butler never deposited the money in the War Treasury, as the general claimed. No entry existed in the Treasury records for the confiscated bank drafts.[61]

District Judge Samuel Blatchford presided over a hearing on February 24, 1872. Develin, Miller, & Trull appeared for Butler, and Vose & McDaniel for Britton. John E. Develin, Butler's attorney, made two special pleas. First, he noted that Butler acted under orders of the president of the United States in confiscating the bills of exchange "drawn by a rebel banker in Natchez." Second, the statute of limitations had expired on March 3, 1865. District Judge Samuel Blatchford, a Republican who would eventually serve on the U.S. Supreme Court, ruled in favor of Britton, finding that Butler had seized the money illegally. By Blatchford's reckoning, the money had been confiscated in loyal territory—New Orleans—and Britton was not an "enemy" or "insurgent." The judge's interpretation of the First and Second Confiscation Acts revealed their weaknesses. As Blatchford opined, "The mere declaration of war does not confiscate enemy property, or debts due to an enemy, nor does it so vest the property or the debts in the government, as to support judicial proceedings for the confiscation of the property or debts, without the expression of the will of government, through its proper department, to that effect." Blatchford ruled that the statute of limitations did not apply in the case because he considered the suit "an action of *assumpsit*, and . . . not a suit for an arrest or imprisonment made, or a trespass or a wrong done or committed, or an act omitted to be done, during the rebellion." He further added that the bill of exchange should have been void because commerce between the Union and Confederacy had been deemed illegal. Finally, the capture of the bill of exchange did not authorize Butler "to collect and confiscate the money." Blatchford did not decide whether Butler should repay the money or not.[62]

More than a year later, U.S. Circuit Court Judge Lewis Woodruff of the Second Judicial Court heard the case on October 30, 1873. William A. Britton had waived his right to a jury trial, leaving it to the judge to decide the outcome of the case. Now sixty-one years old and retired in Kent, Connecticut, Britton did not personally appear in court, but his attorney Everett P. Wheeler made use of a deposition that Britton had given on October 25, 1872, to portray him as a loyal northern man caught up in secession and Civil War. Britton stated that he had left Natchez on April 10 or 11, 1861, just a day or two prior to the Confederate attack on Fort Sumter, and arrived in New York late that same month. Britton had left money on deposit with the Citizens' Bank of Louisiana, indicative of his intention to return. But Britton did not return to Natchez until after the war ended. Upon cross-examination, he recalled that he moved to Natchez in 1834 and had always wintered there. He spent summers in New York City, where his immediate family lived, and sometimes visited Kent. Britton typically spent the summer and fall in the North and returned to Natchez in November, December, or January. Each year, then, he spent six to eight months in the South. His wife and children remained in the North, although occasionally his wife visited him in Natchez for a few months.[63]

Next, Britton's counsel portrayed him as a successful entrepreneur. Britton had formed William A. Britton & Co. as an exchange business, but the firm later expanded into banking, conducting extensive business with the Citizens' Bank and the Canal Bank in New Orleans. As Britton explained his business, "Our remittances consisted of planters' notes, drafts, and merchants' bills of exchange which we bought, and then we sent them down there to be collected, and the Citizens' Bank placed them to our credit when paid."[64]

Butler's lawyers, U.S. District Attorneys George Bliss and John E. Develin, portrayed William as a white southerner—including in his politics—who had intentionally violated federal law. They pressed him on his voting record. Britton claimed merely to have voted for town and city officers in Natchez, having abstained from the national elections of 1856 and 1860. In fact, he stated that the only time he had voted for president "was for Henry Clay in 1844." Though possible, it seems highly unlikely that Britton stayed home given the antebellum period's record of high voter turnout for presidential elections.[65] Britton indicated he had not done any business in the South since April 1861. Prior to the war, William A. Britton & Co. were "doing a very large business" and each partner had a one-third interest in the firm. Britton kept meticulous records of his operations, yet when Butler's attorneys pressed him to answer how much money he had on deposit in the Citizens' Bank of New Orleans, he repeatedly stated that he did not know. Interestingly, the planters' directory listed an entry for William but not Audley.[66] Butler recollected that he had asked the man why he had "three drafts in different rights, different interests and different dates in payment of a single debt," and why he tried to sneak past the pickets if it were an honest transaction. The general demanded the man tell him the truth because "he had not time to spend on prevarications." The man volunteered that he had met with bankers at Natchez, and they told him if he could get their money out of the Citizens' Bank in New Orleans, they would give him a 20 percent commission. He accepted the terms and carried drafts payable to those bankers.[67]

Butler had feared the spy would find a way to withdraw the money, and the Confederacy would end up benefiting from the funds. Therefore, Butler sent for a bank representative from Judson & Co., the firm listed on the drafts. The banker believed the drafts covered all of the money William A. Britton & Co. had on deposit in New Orleans. Butler explained to him, "I must have possession of the money because, although I have caught this man I may not catch the next one if I leave it where it is." The banker responded, "But General, what justification shall I have for paying it?" Butler replied: "We will make no secret of this sir. You endorse the draft to me, and I will put my name to it so that I may always be responsible to whomsoever it may concern for having received this money." "You make that as a military order?" the banker asked. "I do sir," Butler answered. The general indicated that he received payment of the bank drafts in bank bills and passed them to a financial agent of the War Department, who used a broker to exchange them into U.S. currency. The War Department had "duly accounted" for the money upon the settling of his affairs, and Butler kept detailed records of his transactions. As the August 2, 1862, entry in Butler's account book stated, "Check drawn by a secessionist in Natchez on a house in New Orleans, who were not then loyal, and which was being smuggled through the lines in the pocket of a spy, $5,000, which is this transaction." The financial agent charged $1,600 for the $5,000 draft. During the war, discounts ranged from as low as 17 percent to as high as 25 percent. The notes on the different banks of Louisiana were at different rates of discount. Some were worth a mere half of their face value.[68]

Attorney John E. Develin focused on the statute of limitations, arguing that William Britton had failed to sue Butler within the two-year window mandated in the legislation.[69] While Butler commanded forces in Virginia and North Carolina, the Norfolk courts were open, and Britton could have served him there. Butler acknowledged the United States courts in New Orleans were closed while he commanded the occupation of the city. He added, however, that it would have been easy for Britton to sue him in Massachusetts court: "During all that time I had real and personal property in the State of Massachusetts to a much larger amount than the amount claimed in this suit, open to attachment, and by the laws of Massachusetts I could have been served there with legal process by publishing a notice." Butler ended his testimony by answering a question about whether he had expended the money for public purposes, replying that he had only spent money on purposes approved by the government.[70]

In October 1873, Judge Woodruff ruled that the firm of William A. Britton & Co. had dissolved in April 1861. When William Britton left Natchez, only his former partners remained, and the money that Butler confiscated was not necessarily Britton's. Furthermore, Section 7 of the 1863 Habeas Corpus Suspension Act required plaintiffs to file officer suits within two years. Therefore, the statute of limitations had passed. Butler won the case, and the confiscated money remained in Butler's possession.[71] Britton remained free to turn the case into a bill of exceptions, but he died soon after.[72] In the *Confiscation Cases* decided earlier that same month, the U.S. Supreme Court had affirmed the legality of the confiscation of property in New Orleans. The decision offered strong support for the goals of confiscation as long as basic common law guarantees prevailed. The court also sympathized with the officers authorized to administer confiscation.[73] Judge Woodruff's ruling thus aligned with the Supreme Court's.[74]

New Evidence

At some point in the early 1880s, and for reasons unknown, Audley C. Britton hired a lawyer to investigate General Butler's confiscation of the bank drafts nearly thirty years earlier. The attorney misidentified the object of the suit as a confiscation that had occurred just two weeks earlier. Then, years later, in 1891, Britton filed a claim with Congress for $19,436.81, or more than $511,000 in 2020.[75] Most likely, the former slave owner knew the facts surrounding the original case, but he allowed his attorneys to pursue the claim based upon false evidence, in what amounted to an attempt to defraud the federal government.

In 1855, Alexander C. Ferguson had been appointed receiver in a federal court case, and he held $19,436.81 on deposit with William A. Britton & Co. When the Civil War commenced, Confederate Judge Alexander M. Clayton ordered Ferguson to transfer the funds to the Confederate Treasury. Ferguson obtained two bank drafts from Britton & Co., dated November 22, 1861—one for $10,000, drawn on the Canal and Banking Company of New Orleans, the other for $9,436.81, drawn on the Citizens' Bank of Louisiana, also of New Orleans. Both were payable to the order of Judge Ferguson. The money remained in the Bank of Louisiana when General Butler occupied New Orleans, until he confiscated it on July 19, 1862.[76]

The U.S. Circuit Court for the Southern District of Mississippi appointed Audley Britton receiver in the case, probably in 1885. In February of that year, Britton filed a petition with the court requesting permission to present his claim to Congress. On February 9, the Circuit Court approved his request. A member of the Committee on Claims wrote: "It may be presumed . . . that his appointment as receiver was for the purpose of setting on foot the application which has since been made to Congress for the moneys. It is in his capacity as receiver alone that the claim is presented by him." Britton's attorneys claimed that Butler had failed to deposit those funds into the Treasury because they could not locate them in House Executive Document 101, which detailed Butler's confiscations in New Orleans.[77]

The Committee on Claims did not recommend paying the claim because the claimant lacked evidence and it fell well outside the statute of limitations. In addition, Audley Britton did not provide any reason for failing to file the case in the U.S. Circuit Court for the Southern District of Mississippi. The long delay in filing the claim made it difficult for the government to ascertain the facts in the case. O. L. Spaulding, acting secretary of the treasury, wrote the Committee on Claims that George Law of New York had already filed a successful claim to recover the money that Ferguson had held on receivership and that Butler had confiscated. On April 24, 1880, Congress had ordered a payment of $15,861.50 to Law. Examining the facts available to him, Spaulding concluded, "It is not perceived this matter has any connection with the claim of Mr. Britton." Senator William F. Vilas, a Democrat from Wisconsin and chair of the committee, wrote Butler to ask for clarification about the confiscation and lack of an entry in the treasury records or in House Executive Document 101.[78]

On April 5, 1892, Butler wrote Vilas from Lowell, Massachusetts, informing the senator that the various federal government departments had filed the records away, but he recalled that the Britton confiscation took place in July 1862. "I think [Britton] is wholly mistaken," Butler wrote. "The transaction had nothing to do whatever with the cash accounts reported to be settled in the letter of the Treasury in the House document which you sent me." Butler had only been responsible for a report dated June 1862, while General Nathaniel P. Banks filed a report the following year. Butler added that he had deposited $15,000 in the Treasury of the United States, and George Law later claimed the money.[79]

Butler shed light on the events surrounding the confiscation of the Britton & Co. bank drafts. Many citizens of the Confederacy had considerable sums of money to their credit in the banks of New Orleans, and the Non-Intercourse Act prevented them from withdrawing those funds. "Of course all sorts of devices were entered into to surreptitiously get them out," Butler confided. He recalled that his pickets captured two men who claimed to be New Yorkers and agents for a New York firm collecting debts at Natchez. The drafts represented their payments. Butler cross-examined them, and they confessed that they were trying to get the money, which belonged to the Confederate states, out of New Orleans. Butler confiscated the drafts and ordered them paid and credited to Butler's civil fund, "which contained many thousand dollars . . . used in the service of the United States." Butler added that William Britton had already sued him unsuccessfully. The general concluded, "I do not obtrude any advice to you as to the validity of this claim, but I will say it has not been fairly and truthfully presented."[80]

The Senate referred Bill 1893 to the Committee on Claims on January 21, 1892. On May 11, the committee reported adversely on it and postponed it indefinitely.[81] On January 11 of the following year, Benjamin F. Butler died at age seventy-four, one day after arguing a different case before the Supreme Court in Washington, D.C. He left an estate worth $7 million, or more than $206 million today. Audley C. Britton died fifteen months later, on April 18, 1894. One Vicksburg, Mississippi, newspaper lamented the loss of a notable banker well known and universally esteemed across the state. Although "a native of New York," he "had resided in Natchez for half a century."[82]

Conclusion

The Britton brothers moved from New York City to Natchez, Mississippi, in search of economic opportunity, and both men realized tremendous wealth in the slave economy of the Lower Mississippi Valley. William A. Britton began selling slave insurance policies and brokering cotton. He fled Mississippi when the Civil War commenced, but he continued to conduct business with his brother from afar, technically a violation of federal law. Benjamin F. Butler confiscated what may have been William's last remaining cash on deposit in New Orleans. As Britton labored for the return of his riches, he attempted to portray himself as a loyal Union man, but his efforts failed to sway a U.S. Circuit Court judge, who simply used the statute of limitations to rule against him. Upon William's death on March 19, 1874, he left real estate and personal property worth more than $100,000 (in excess of $2.3 million in 2020 dollars) to his two surviving sons, plus $3,500 to an aunt and three cousins.[83]

Audley C. Britton operated the most important bank in Natchez and became the largest slave owner in the city. He returned to the banking business as soon as the war ended, forming Britton & Koontz Bank with antebellum-era partner George W. Koontz. Although Mississippi did not surpass prewar levels of cotton production until 1894, Britton thrived. He used the wealth he had amassed through the forced labor of slaves, including his own, to diversify his portfolio in the postwar period, investing in such enterprises as the Natchez Cotton Mills in 1877.[84] Audley Britton died a millionaire.[85] In his obituary, one Natchez newspaper considered him "a shrewd businessman . . . for many years, one of the wealthiest men of this section . . . [and] one of our largest real estate owners." He "owned stock in many of our largest business enterprises of Natchez." The city lamented the loss of Audley Britton, to whom it owed much of its prosperity and development.[86]

Yet Audley Britton was also an attempted swindler who schemed to defraud the federal government. During the Civil War, nearly eighteen months after his brother returned to New York City, he tried to withdraw William A. Britton & Co.'s money from a bank in occupied New Orleans in violation of the Non-Intercourse Act of 1861. General Benjamin F. Butler confiscated the money and successfully rebuffed William Britton's suit to recover it. Audley Britton knew the entire case history yet filed a claim with Congress, submitting false evidence. In short, he endeavored to cheat the federal government out of more than a half million dollars, when adjusted for inflation. More than a century later, in November 2013, Home Bancorp, a billion-dollar holding company for Home Bank of Lafayette, Louisiana, acquired B&K Capital Corp., the holding company for Britton & Koontz Bank, for $34.5 million.[87] Not surprisingly, the press release failed to mention the Britton brothers' mendacity.

Notes

1. William A. Britton v. Benjamin F. Butler (1867–1873), Law Case File 3-101, United States Circuit Court, Southern District of New York, National Archives, New York Branch (hereinafter cited as William A. Britton v. Benjamin F. Butler).

2. *Debow's Review*, ser. 2, 1 (January 1866): 49.

3. Sven Beckert, "Emancipation and Empire: Reconstructing the Worldwide Web of Cotton Production in the Age of the American Civil War," *American Historical Review* 109, no. 5 (December 2004): 1405; Sven Beckert, *Empire of Cotton: A Global History* (New York: Knopf, 2014), esp.

chap. 10, "Global Reconstruction"; Department of Commerce and Labor, Bureau of the Census, Bulletin 100, Cotton Production 1908 (Washington, D.C.: Government Printing Office, 1909), 20.

4. Michael Wayne, *The Reshaping of Plantation Society: The Natchez District, 1860–1880* (Urbana: University of Illinois Press, 1990), 7.

5. Scott Reynolds Nelson, *A Nation of Deadbeats: An Uncommon History of America's Financial Disasters* (New York: Knopf, 2012), 102–19; Jessica M. Lepler, *The Many Panics of 1837: People, Politics, and the Creation of a Transatlantic Financial Crisis* (New York: Cambridge University Press, 2013).

6. William A. Britton was no known relation to Abe Britton, president of the New Orleans Cotton Exchange in the early 1900s and member of the prominent Jewish mercantile family of that name in the Lower Mississippi Valley.

7. Stephen C. Neff, *Justice in Blue and Gray: A Legal History of the Civil War* (Cambridge, Mass.: Harvard University Press, 2010), 34, 116–18, 125; *Gay's Gold*, 80 U.S. 358 (1871) (quotation).

8. Scott P. Marler, "'An Abiding Faith in Cotton': The Merchant Capitalist Community of New Orleans, 1860–1862," *Civil War History* 54, no. 3 (September 2008): 253–54, 256–57; Scott P. Marler, *The Merchants' Capital: New Orleans and the Political Economy of the Nineteenth-Century South* (New York: Cambridge University Press. 2015), 128–30.

9. Marler, "An Abiding Faith in Cotton," 256–60; William Ashley Vaughan, "Natchez during the Civil War" (Ph.D. diss., University of Southern Mississippi, 2001), 73–74, 77, 81.

10. Butler was one of the most recognizable figures of the second half of the nineteenth century. He began his career as a Democrat, became a Lincoln Republican during the Civil War, and served in Congress as a Radical Republican from 1866 to 1875. Early in his congressional tenure, he helped lead the effort to impeach Andrew Johnson. In 1878, voters elected Butler to Congress on the Greenback ticket. He rejoined the Democratic Party in 1880, and two years later, Massachusetts voters elected Butler governor. The Greenback Party nominated Butler for president in 1884. He died in 1893 with an estate worth $7 million, or about $200 million in 2019 dollars, when adjusted for inflation.

11. Glenn David Brashear, *The Peninsula Campaign and the Necessity of Emancipation: African Americans and the Fight for Freedom* (Chapel Hill: University of North Carolina Press, 2012), 164–67.

12. John Syrett, *The Civil War Confiscation Acts: Failing to Reconstruct the South* (New York: Fordham University Press, 2011), 1, 43–44, 54.

13. Daniel W. Hamilton, *The Limits of Sovereignty: Property Confiscation in the Union and the Confederacy during the Civil War* (Chicago: University of Chicago Press, 2007), 1.

14. Syrett, *Civil War Confiscation Acts*, 22.

15. Hamilton, *Limits of Sovereignty*, 1.

16. Presidential Proclamation 93, also known as the Preliminary Emancipation Proclamation, in *The Collected Works of Abraham Lincoln*, ed. Roy P. Basler, vol. 5 (New Brunswick, N.J.: Rutgers University Press, 1953), 337–38.

17. Patricia M. L. Lucie, "Confiscation: Constitutional Crossroads," *Civil War History* 23, no. 4 (December 1977): 307–8.

18. James G. Randall, "Captured and Abandoned Property during the Civil War," *American Historical Review* 19, no. 1 (1913): 65–66; Report, Secretary McCulloch, November 8, 1866, House Ex. Doc. No. 97, 39th Cong., 2d sess., 2–3.

19. Anthony J. Gaughan, *The Last Battle of the Civil War: United States Versus Lee, 1861–1883* (Baton Rouge: Louisiana State University Press, 2011), 25.

20. Hamilton, *Limits of Sovereignty*, 146.

21. Funds Seized at New Orleans, House Ex. Doc. No. 101, 49th Cong., 1st sess., 9.

22. Benjamin F. Butler, *Private and Official Correspondence of Gen. Benjamin F Butler during the Period of the Civil War in Five Volumes*, vol. 1: *April 1860–June 1862* (Norwood, Mass.: Plimpton, 1917), 505.

23. B. F. Wade and Daniel W. Gooch, *Report of the Joint Committee on the Conduct of the War at the Second Session, Thirty-Eighth Congress*, vol. 3 (Washington, D.C.: U.S. Government Printing Office, 1865), 359–60.

24. Marler, *Merchants' Capital*; Chester G. Hearn, *When the Devil Came Down to Dixie: Ben Butler in New Orleans* (Baton Rouge: Louisiana State University Press, 2000); Benjamin F. Butler, *Butler's Book: Autobiography and Personal Reminiscences of Major-General Benj. F. Butler: A Review of His Legal, Political, and Military Career* (Boston: A. M. Thayer & Co., 1892); Ludwell H. Johnson, *Red River Campaign: Politics and Cotton in the Civil War* (Baltimore: Johns Hopkins University Press, 1958); D. Clayton James, *Antebellum Natchez* (Baton Rouge: Louisiana State University Press, 1968); William Blair, "Friend or Foe: Treason and the Second Confiscation Act," in *Wars within a War: Controversy and Conflict over the American Civil War*, ed. Joan Waugh and Gary W. Gallagher (Chapel Hill: University of North Carolina Press, 2009).

25. Randall, "Captured and Abandoned Property," 69; Hugh McCulloch, Sales of Captured and Abandoned Cotton, S. Ex. Doc. No. 56, 40th Cong., 2d sess., 2–13, 52.

26. Syrett, *Civil War Confiscation*, 81.

27. Hearn, *When the Devil Came Down to Dixie*, chaps. 8, 10. Voters elected Johnson, a Maryland Democrat, to the U.S. Senate, and he served from March 4, 1863, until he resigned in July 1868.

28. Gerald M. Capers, *Occupied City: New Orleans under the Federals: 1862–1865* (Louisville: University Press of Kentucky, 1965), 86–87, 93, 95.

29. Marler, *Merchants' Capital*, 162–63. Historians, including his numerous biographers, have long debated whether General Butler was a corrupt villain who had enriched himself during his military occupations in Virginia/North Carolina and Louisiana. Some of his contemporaries called him "Spoons" Butler, alleging he had confiscated silver spoons from a Confederate woman's house for his own use. That myth was debunked a century ago in William Dana Orcutt, "Ben Butler and the 'Stolen Spoons': The Documents in the Case, from His Unpublished 'Private and Official Correspondence,'" *North American Review* 207, no. 746 (1918): 66–80.

30. Several northerners living in the South filed officer suits against Butler, claiming Butler had failed to recognize their Union citizenship and loyalties.

31. D. Clayton James, *Antebellum Natchez* (Baton Rouge: Louisiana State University Press, 1968), 203.

32. Manuscript Census Returns, Seventh Census of the United States, 1850, City of Kent, Litchfield County, Connecticut, Schedule 1, Free Population, NAMS M-432, reel 43, p. 58B.

33. Mississippi State Census, 1853, Natchez, Adams County.

34. Manuscript Census Returns, Eighth Census of the United States, 1860, City of Kent, Litchfield County, Connecticut, Schedule 1, Free Population, NAMS M-653, reel 81, p. 301; Manuscript Census Returns, Eighth Census of the United States, 1860, 2nd District, 21st Ward, New York, New York, Schedule 1, Free Population, NAMS M-653, reel 819, p. 5.

35. Nautilus Life Insurance Company, Slavery Era Ledgers, Schomburg Center for Research in Black Culture, New York Public Library; W. A. Britton Account Book, Mss. 923, Audley Clark Britton and Family Papers, Louisiana and Lower Mississippi Valley Collections, Special Collections, Hill Memorial Library, Louisiana State University, Baton Rouge. The policies that appear in the Nautilus ledgers match the personal account book that William kept. There was a one-dollar fee to write each policy. On the topic of slave life insurance, see Sharon Ann Murphy, "Securing Human Property: Slavery, Life Insurance, and Industrialization in the Upper South," *Journal of the Early Republic* 25 (Winter 2005): 615–52; and Todd L. Savitt, "Slave Life Insurance in Virginia and North Carolina," *Journal of Southern History* 43 (November 1977): 583–600.

36. Manuscript Census Returns, Seventh Census of the United States, 1850, City of Natchez, South, Adams County, Mississippi, Schedule 1, Free Population, NAMS M-432, reel 368, p. 4A; Mississippi State Census, 1853, Natchez, Adams County.

37. Manuscript Census Returns, Eighth Census of the United States, 1860, City of Natchez, Adams County, Mississippi, Schedule 1, Free Population, NAMS M-653, reel 577, p. 46; Manuscript Census Returns, Eighth Census of the United States, 1860, City of Natchez, Adams County, Mississippi, Schedule 2, Slave Population, NAMS M-653, reel 595, p. 27; Edward E. Baptist, *The Half Has Never Been Told: Slavery and the Making of American Capitalism* (New York: Basic, 2014).

38. James, *Antebellum Natchez,* 203.

39. Wayne, *Reshaping of Plantation Society,* 38. The Britton Brothers corresponded throughout the war.

40. Elisabeth Joan Doyle, "Greenbacks, Car Tickets, and the Pot of Gold: The Effects of Wartime Occupation on the Business Life of New Orleans, 1861–1865," *Civil War History* 5 (December 1959), 348, 352–53; *Debow's Review,* ser. 2, 1 (January 1866): 48–50.

41. Ludwell H. Johnson, "Northern Profit and Profiteers: The Cotton Rings of 1864–1865," *Civil War History* 12, no. 2 (June 1966): 101–2; and David G. Surdam, "Traders or Traitors: Northern Cotton Trading during the Civil War," *Business and Economic History* 28, no. 2 (Winter 1999): 301–4.

42. On enslaved people's health during wartime, see Jim Downs, *Sick from Freedom: African-American Illness and Suffering during the Civil War and Reconstruction* (New York: Oxford University Press, 2012).

43. John Melvin to A. C. Britton, September 29, 1862, 28774b, Mss. 1403, Audley Clark Britton and Family Papers.

44. John W. Melvin to A. C. Britton, October 1862, 28774b, Britton Papers.

45. John W. Melvin to A. C. Britton, October 1862, 28774b, Britton Papers.

46. John W. Melvin to A. C. Britton, November 20, 1862, 28774b, Britton Papers.

47. John Melvin to A. C. Britton, April 16, 1863, 28774d, Britton Papers.

48. John Melvin to A. C. Britton, July 5, 1863, 28774d, Britton Papers.

49. John Melvin to A. C. Britton, December 20, 1863, 28774d, Britton Papers.

50. William A. Britton to A. C. Britton, December 22, 1863, 28774d, Britton Papers.

51. William A. Britton to A. C. Britton, August 12, 1864, 28774d/e, Britton Papers.

52. John W. Melvin to A. C. Britton, May 10, 1865, 28774e, Britton Papers.

53. Eric Foner, "Thaddeus Stevens, Confiscation, and Reconstruction," in *The Hofstadter Aegis: A Memorial*, ed. Stanley M. Elkins and Eric L. McKitrick (New York: Knopf, 1974), 158–59.

54. Hearn, *When the Devil Came Down to Dixie*, 162–63.

55. William A. Britton v. Benjamin F. Butler.

56. Vicki C. Jackson, "Suing the Federal Government: Sovereignty, Immunity, and Judicial Independence," *George Washington International Law Review* 35, no. 3 (August 2003): 555–56.

57. Louis L. Jaffe, "Suits against Governments and Officers: Damage Actions," *Harvard Law Review* 77, no. 2 (1963): 213–18.

58. William A. Britton v. Benjamin F. Butler.

59. William A. Britton v. Benjamin F. Butler.

60. William A. Britton v. Benjamin F. Butler; *New York Times*, July 1, 1867.

61. William A. Britton v. Benjamin F. Butler.

62. "United States Circuit Court, Southern District of New York, William A. Britton v. Benjamin F. Butler," *American Law Register (1852–1891)* 20, no. 5 (May 1872): 293–301; "U.S. Circuit Court, S.D. of New York," *Chicago Legal News* 4, no. 23 (March 16, 1872).

63. Britton v. Butler (1872), Case #1903, West Law 4 Fed. Cas., 177; *Britton v. Butler* (1873), Case #1904, West Law 4 Fed. Cas., 182; *The Internal Revenue Record and Customs Journal* 18, no. 20 (November 15, 1873): 157; *New York Herald*, November 7, 1873; *New York Evening Post*, November 7, 1873. Britton was deposed at 23 Madison Avenue in New York City, in the presence of attorneys representing both men, and of notary public Michael Phillips.

64. William A. Britton Deposition, October 25, 1872, Audley Britton Case File, Papers Supporting Specific Bills and Resolutions, Sen 52A-E1, Box 6, Record Group 46: Records of the U.S. Senate, 52nd Congress, National Archives, Washington, D.C.

65. Glenn C. Altschuler and Stuart M. Blumin, "Limits of Political Engagement in Antebellum America: A New Look at the Golden Age of Participatory Democracy," *Journal of American History* 84, no. 3 (1997): 875–85.

66. Charles Gardner, *Gardner's New Orleans Directory, for 1861: Including Jefferson City, Gretna, Carrollton, Algiers, and McDonogh, with a New Map of the City, a Street and Levee Guide, Business Directory, an Appendix of Much Useful Information, and a Planters Directory Containing the Names of the Cotton and Sugar Planters of Louisiana, Mississippi, Arkansas and Texas* (New Orleans: Charles Gardner, 1861), 525.

67. Benjamin F. Butler Testimony, U.S. Circuit Court Trial, October 3, 1873, Audley Britton Case File, Papers Supporting Specific Bills and Resolutions, Sen 52A-E1, Box 6, Record Group 46: Records of the U.S. Senate, 52nd Congress, National Archives, Washington, D.C.

68. Benjamin F. Butler Testimony.

69. Butler had been a resident of Massachusetts since 1828. He had landed in New Orleans on May 1, 1862, and remained there until December 16 of the same year. After that, he went to Washington, D.C., and met with federal officials before his arrival in New York on January 1, 1863. Then he went home to Lowell, Massachusetts, in May 1863. On November 10, he assumed command of the Department of Virginia and North Carolina. In April 1864, General Ulysses S. Grant placed Butler in command of the Army of the James. In November, authorities in Washington sent Butler to New York City to quell a Confederate plot to burn New York City and protect it from any violence that might erupt on Election Day. On November 15, Butler returned to his command in Virginia. Following the defeat at the Battle of Fort Fisher, General Grant removed him from command, on January 8, 1865, with President Abraham Lincoln's approval. Butler then returned to Lowell.

70. Benjamin F. Butler Testimony.

71. William A. Britton v. Benjamin F. Butler (1867–1873), Law Docket, vol. 3, 1866–1873, U.S. Circuit Court, Southern District of New York, National Archives, New York Branch.

72. The case was dismissed without prejudice on May 4, 1918.

73. Syrett, *Civil War Confiscation,* 167.

74. Supreme Court of the United States, "The Confiscation Cases," *U.S. Reports,* 87 U.S. (20 Wall.) 92 (1874).

75. Robert C. Sahr, *Inflation Conversion Factors for Years 1774 to Estimated 2028* (2016), https://liberalarts.oregonstate.edu/spp/polisci/research/inflation-conversion-factors (accessed January 26, 2020).

76. Manuscript Senate Bill 1893, 52nd Cong. 1st sess., Audley Britton Case File, RG 46, Records of the U.S. Senate, 52nd Cong. 1st sess., Papers Supporting Specific Bills & Resolutions, SEN52A-E1, Box 6, National Archives, Washington, D.C.

77. Manuscript Senate Bill 1893.

78. Manuscript Senate Bill 1893.

79. Manuscript Senate Bill 1893.

80. William Freeman Vilas, Senate Report No. 643, May 11, 1892, 52nd Cong. 1st sess., 5–6.

81. Manuscript Senate Bill 1893.

82. *Vicksburg (Miss.) Daily Commercial Herald,* April 20, 1894.

83. Probate filed September 27, 1878.

84. Wayne, *Reshaping of Plantation Society,* 106.

85. One person in the *Daily Commercial Herald,* April 19, 1894, estimated his net worth at $1 million.

86. *Saturday Evening Banner* (Natchez, Miss.), April 18, 1894.

87. *Natchez (Miss.) Democrat,* November 6, 2013.

Devils at the Doorstep

CONFEDERATE JUDGES, MASTERS OF SEQUESTRATION

RODNEY J. STEWARD

D uring the Civil War, shysters and con men abounded on the southern home front. Arguably the greatest concentration of villainous characters was found within the halls of Confederate justice. District court judges, receivers, and grand juries armed with the Confederate Act of Sequestration presided over a campaign of confiscation and intimidation to enforce loyalty to the South and to squelch dissent. By April 1865, millions of dollars of debts owed to northern creditors, along with hundreds of thousands of pieces of real estate and personal property, were seized and sold at auction. Untold numbers of common people were stripped of their property, fined, or threatened. Some were imprisoned, or worse. The financial devastation resulting from the sequestration of property and the collection of debts seized from so-called alien enemies of the Confederacy would last for generations. Crippling debt-peonage and crushing poverty stretching well into the next century became the legacy of property seizure on the Confederate home front.

Officers of the Confederate district courts were the authors of financial ruination for many ordinary southern folk. The 1861 Act of Sequestration empowered southern district court judges, receivers, and grand juries to engage in acts of legal turpitude perpetrated against their fellow southerners. Tyranny, greed, and corruption abounded as court officials often enriched themselves with property confiscated from those accused, sometimes falsely, of disloyalty to the Confederate cause. Acting with impunity, district court officials menaced the home front, seizing and selling property at will. The Act of Sequestration and its lasting impact on the Confederate home front is one of only a handful of Civil War topics that remains understudied, yet a close examination of the day-to-day application of this law reveals that it was designed to control and intimidate ordinary folk, its nefariousness hidden behind a veil of judicial secrecy and unseen by the public eye. It was characterized by a widespread disregard for civil liberties, personal property rights, and a vicious *Realpolitik* overlooked by historians of the Civil War. Perhaps most significantly, the Act of Sequestration pulls the curtain back on the depth and strength of home front loyalty, revealing a rapacious court bureaucracy and a Confederate government deeply suspicious of its own people.

Official government confiscation of private property during the Civil War began on August 6, 1861, when the United States Congress approved the First Confiscation Act, which laid the legal groundwork for federal forces to confiscate southerners' private property being used to aid the rebellion. Although not directly mentioned in the act itself, it was understood, and later confirmed by executive order, that "property" included slaves, or "contraband," as they would become known.[1]

With slaves now under direct threat by federal confiscation, the Confederate government in Richmond was compelled to act. A resolution introduced by Louisiana congressman Duncan F. Kenner urged the Confederate Congress to consider "the expediency of reporting a general confiscation bill." With that, drafting a reciprocal policy of confiscation became the Confederate government's top priority.[2] On August 30, 1861, Confederate lawmakers passed the Act of Sequestration in direct response to federal confiscation policy. Its preamble charged that "the government and people of the United States have departed from the usages of civilized warfare in confiscating and destroying the property of the Confederate States of all kinds, whether used for military purposes or not." As a result, "our only protection against such wrongs is to be found in such measures of retaliation as will ultimately indemnify our own citizens for their losses, and restrain the wanton excesses of our enemies." Such provocative language is noticeably absent from the northern confiscation law, suggesting the value that Confederates attached to private property, especially slave property, and their disdain for northern attempts to violate its sanctity.[3]

Ostensibly, the Confederate Congress intended sequestration to strike a blow at northern financial interests within the Confederacy. It called for duly appointed Confederate officers to locate "all and every lands, tenements, hereditaments, goods and chattels, rights and credits within these Confederate States and every right and interest therein held, owned, possessed or enjoyed by or for any alien enemy." Such property would be "sequestered by the Confederate States of America" and, in turn, sold, with the proceeds paid into a fund administered by the Confederate Treasury Department. A board of three sequestration officials would hear indemnity claims made by "loyal Confederates" whose personal property had fallen prey to confiscation by the Union. The board would then pass on its recommendation to the Confederate Congress, and after a special hearing, Congress would approve or reject the claims. Those claims approved by the Confederate Congress would then be sent back to the Treasury to issue an indemnity to the claimant. The circuitous route established for indemnity claims ultimately gave Congress the final word on compensation.[4]

The wording of the indemnity clause, however, was problematic, for it stated that personal property confiscated by the U.S. government was eligible to be "held for full indemnity of any true and loyal citizen or resident of these Confederate States or other person aiding said Confederate States in the prosecution of the present war with the United States." Nowhere did the act define or offer any criteria for identifying "true and loyal citizens." The ambiguity established by the Confederate Congress in defining loyal citizens eligible for indemnity created a veil of secrecy behind which the disbursement of compensation would operate. It also signaled that the southern Congress, wary of the depth and strength of home front loyalty, was reluctant to offer a definition specifically identifying "loyal Confederates." Perhaps Confederate officials wanted to ensure that planters whose slave property was being confiscated by federal armies were the only sort of "loyal Confederates" who could expect to be compensated for their losses.[5]

Southerners bore the brunt of property confiscation during the Civil War. Like federal confiscation, which was enforced primarily by military officers as Union armies advanced into Confederate territory, sequestration would also be enforced on the Confederate home front. The difficulty with enforcing the law lay in locating alien-owned debts and property. As a matter of practicality, Confederate legislators dismissed concerns about privacy and the sanctity of attorney-client privilege and chose to target business, tax, and legal records as useful tools for shedding light on the whereabouts of some of it. The bulk of information regarding the location of liable property and debts, however, came from ordinary citizens. The authors of the Sequestration Act intended to squeeze the home front for information. As historian Brian Dirck has noted, "The Sequestration Act required every Southerner to turn informant for the government." The act specifically stated, "It is, and shall be, the duty of each and every citizen of these Confederate States speedily to give information to the officers charged with execution of this law." Indeed, should anyone prove reluctant to provide the government the information it sought, sequestration officials were granted extraordinary punitive powers to search out and seize all suspect real estate, property, and debts.[6]

Enforcement of the law fell to two arms of the Confederate district courts repurposed specifically to help administer sequestration: receivers and federal grand juries. Receivers were lawyers appointed by district court judges and tasked with overseeing legal procedure, taking custody of sequestered debts and property, and arranging the public sale of sequestered goods. Federal grand juries, consisting of as many as twenty-three men, were impaneled in every receiver district. They aided receivers by hearing testimony and interrogating those suspected of knowing the whereabouts of liable property as well as those people whose loyalty to the Confederate cause was questionable.[7]

Operating like a secret police force, both receivers and grand jurymen randomly interrogated individuals and diligently kept a probing, suspicious eye on citizens in their districts. Attorneys, agents, and former business partners were of keen interest to the courts. The authors of the sequestration law made it clear that those who in the past represented the interests of one now accused of being an alien enemy were, by default, guilty by association: "It shall be the duty of every attorney, agent, [or] former partner . . . holding or controlling such . . . goods or credits . . . for any such alien enemy, speedily to inform the Receiver . . . and to render an account thereof . . . and to place the same in the hands of such Receiver; whereupon such person shall be fully acquitted of all responsibility of all property reported and turned in." To drive the point home the authors of sequestration warned that "any such person willfully failing to give such information . . . shall be guilty of a high misdemeanor." Armed with these extraordinary powers, receivers and grand juries were a threatening presence on the home front. "Are you not agent for a man named Alexander an alien enemy who has interests in lands known as the Campbell Survey[?]" wrote receiver Archimedes Davis to William Nash of Abingdon, Virginia. "Tell all you know in regard to that or any other lands owned by alien enemies."[8]

To ensure success at locating alien assets, the Sequestration Act required—and the district courts demanded—that all residents be immediately forthcoming in reporting all alien assets in their possession and inform the government of any such assets possessed by a neighbor. For some, the opportunity to exact revenge on a rival or the prospect of personal gain was a luring temptation to provide receivers and grand juries false information about a neighbor's property. In December 1861, Virginia receiver Archimedes Davis took delivery of a letter from Lipscomb Pomeroy informing him that, in 1859, Pomeroy had sent "a certain small horse belonging to Alexander E. Adams," from Letcher County, Kentucky, to Washington County, in southwestern Virginia, some fifty or sixty miles away. Pomeroy alleged that Adams, formerly of Washington County but a resident of Kentucky since 1859, was disloyal and had joined the Union army. He further stated that the horse in question had since been given to Adams's father, William, and that he reckoned its value at $150. Pomeroy later falsely informed Davis that Alexander Adams also owned the house in which his father, William, was living. To be sure, Adams was, indeed, serving in the Union army, but the horse in question belonged to his father, who had since sold it for $175. Unfortunately for William Adams, the court took action against him, seizing the value of the horse and sequestering his house.[9]

Failure to comply with the district court was dangerous. The act empowered officials to fine and jail individuals refusing to answer questions regarding the whereabouts of alien assets. Violation of the law was a high misdemeanor, and those caught concealing liable property or debts faced a fine double the value of the hidden property as well as the regular fine and imprisonment for as long as five years. Furthermore, sequestration proceedings, for property and real estate particularly, fell into the category of an *in rem* action to determine title to property. Defendants named in such a proceeding were not required to be present for sequestration to go forward. Most significantly, those to whom interrogatories were sent and the hundreds of thousands against whom garnishment proceedings were initiated were considered disloyal by Confederate officials, and they became vulnerable to abuse at the hands of unscrupulous district court officials. For example, in October 1862, Virginia receiver Francis L. Smith petitioned Judge James D. Halyburton of the District Court for the Eastern District of Virginia for a writ to sequester "[a] large amount of real and personal property an exact description of which is to your petitioner unknown." Smith claimed that the undescribed property belonged to alien enemies "whose names and domiciles are unknown to your petitioner." Nevertheless, Smith was certain that the undescribed property belonging to unknown alien enemies was "in the possession of William Tarenner of Loudoun County." In still another case highlighting the courts' abuse of power, in October 1862, Virginia receiver Thomas N. Campbell accused J. T. Young of Petersburg of being indebted to unknown alien enemies. Although Campbell did not know the names of the people Young allegedly owed, he was certain that they lived in "New York, Pennsylvania, Mass[achusetts]. And other states of the United States." Furthermore, Campbell charged in his petition that "J. T. Young . . . may have paid over some of said debts since the 22nd of May 1861," which was in effect an accusation of treason, which, upon conviction, carried the death penalty.[10]

The Sequestration Act charged the Confederate attorney general with putting the law into effect. It set no parameters or limitations on the power of receivers and grand juries to acquire information and to seize property and debts. Furthermore, the act was silent on nearly all interpretive matters, thus placing the awesome responsibility of defining the terms "loyal Confederate" and "alien enemy" entirely in the hands of local sequestration officials. Moreover, unlike other federal laws passed by the Confederate Congress, including conscription, impressment, and tax-in-kind, which were administered by state officials, sequestration proceedings were the exclusive jurisdiction of the Confederate district courts. Judges thus wielded unprecedented and concentrated authority.[11]

For district court judges with jurisdictions immediately along the Atlantic and Gulf coasts, the first order of business was clearing the admiralty and prize dockets. Once that business was settled, judges then turned their full attention to ordering their courts and implementing the sequestration law. Acquiring the right cadre of court officers was paramount, and judges carefully selected men known for their devotion to the Confederate cause. Receivers and clerks of court were the top priority, followed by marshals and bailiffs. In most states, receivers were responsible for selecting men to serve on the grand jury, and, perhaps not surprisingly, the men they chose were loyal to them. Across the Confederacy, stay laws drastically reduced the number of criminal and civil cases allowed to be brought before the district courts, leaving sequestration proceedings and cases involving treason as their sole business. As soon as the courts were set in order, sequestration proceedings could begin.

Thomas Bragg, the first attorney general of the Confederacy, established procedures for the courts by issuing a series of standard legal forms used mainly by receivers and clerks of court to facilitate sequestration proceedings. The first form was known as a garnishment, which summoned an individual or agent of an alien enemy to appear before the bench to give answer as to the whereabouts of liable materials in their possession. An individual received a garnishment based on information obtained by members of the grand jury through interrogations. The recipient of a garnishment was automatically suspected of Unionist sympathies by virtue of the fact that he had not been forthcoming with information about the confiscable property in his possession. He was also liable to pay a fine or suffer imprisonment as per the stipulations of the sequestration law. Along with the garnishment was sent a bill of interrogatories containing five very specific and probing questions defendants were required to answer in writing. Most people receiving the bill of interrogatories found it necessary to hire an attorney to help draft their written response to the court. Such was the case for Mary Barnhardt and Adeline White, both of Cabarrus County, North Carolina. Both women were illiterate, elderly, and living alone on land left to them by deceased husbands. They both had sons set to inherit land, but each was said to be living in California. Without bothering to confirm the whereabouts of the two men, Asa Biggs, the judge for North Carolina, declared the sons alien enemies and ordered their respective lands sequestered and sold. Both Mary and Adeline were left destitute and dependent upon the goodwill of neighbors and friends for their maintenance.[12]

Women alone on the home front were easy targets for some court officials, and judges applied the sequestration law with cold indifference to circumstance. Those with no political connections or legal recourse were at the greatest risk of losing property, whether they were associated with alien enemies or not. The case of Catherine Young of Abingdon, Virginia, is a prime example of the risks to which women on the home front were exposed as a result of the Confederate government's policy of sequestration. Young was the youngest of three children. Her father seems to have died when Catherine was just a small girl, so she grew up in the care of her mother, Mary. In an affidavit to Confederate judge John Brockenbrough of the Western District of Virginia, Catherine's uncle Jacob Lynch described her as "being of weak and imbecile mind." Catherine's mother died in 1857, but upon her deathbed requested that her daughter be encouraged to move to Iowa to live with her older sister Eliza Ann and her husband. In his affidavit, Jacob Lynch explained that "Catherine was induced by her friends to dispose of some property, which she had acquired from her brother Joseph E. Young (deceased)." A neighbor, William M. Grim, purchased the property, which "was all she [Catherine] owned or possessed," in 1859 for $1,400. According to Lynch, the terms of the sale required Grim to pay half the price up front, with the balance due in December 1861. The proceeds of the sale were intended for Catherine's future maintenance, but receiver Archimedes Davis seized upon the debt Grim owed Catherine, and Judge Brockenbrough, in spite of the unusual circumstances of the case, ordered it sequestered and paid into the sequestration fund. Catherine was left with nothing. Her fate remains unknown.[13]

The cases of Mary Barnhardt, Adeline White, and Catherine Young demonstrate the Confederate court's willingness to exploit the vulnerable. In each case, the courts were technically conforming to the letter of the law, but they were also sending a clear and threatening message to others on the home front—that real power was in the hands of the judicial bureaucracy.

The Confederate district courts were single-minded in their quest to deprive anyone of all they possessed, especially if their circumstances appeared questionable or out of the ordinary. In 1863, Margaret Wallach of Culpeper, Virginia, was living at her childhood home, but her father William Wallach had been jailed in Washington, D.C., since the war began. Receiver Francis L. Smith petitioned Judge James Halyburton to sequester the imprisoned Wallach's real and personal estate because his "domicile" was outside of the Confederate states. Halyburton agreed and ordered Margaret Wallach evicted from the property. Soon after, Wallach's entire estate was sold at auction.[14]

Women weren't the only people turned out of house and home by the Confederate courts. Before the war, Peter Kemper was an employee of the WyKoff Gold Mining Company in Fauquier County, Virginia. The company was incorporated in the State of New York sometime in the 1850s. Kemper and his young family lived on the company's eight-hundred-acre property until October 1862, when Judge Halyburton declared the WyKoff Company an alien enemy and ordered the sheriff to evict the Kemper family. Like so many others ensnared in the sequestration frenzy, Peter Kemper was considered disloyal, arrested, and jailed for nearly a year because he had not been forthcoming with court officials about the gold mine's ownership.[15]

Even supporters of the Confederate cause weren't safe from the masters of sequestration. William Johnson of Scott County, Virginia, inherited five hundred acres of land from his parents upon their deaths many years before, and he and his younger brother Walter lived there up to the outbreak of war. William, who was a staunch supporter of the Confederate cause, was on a business trip to Indiana when the war began. Unable to return directly to his home in Virginia, William traveled to Confederate-controlled territory in Missouri and from there sought to return to Virginia. In March 1862, acting on false information provided by the local grand jury that William Johnson was an alien enemy, Archimedes Davis filed a petition for garnishment of property in Judge John Brockenbrough's court. Walter Johnson appeared before the judge several times to argue that he and his brother William were loyal Confederates and that William was in fact in Confederate-controlled territory in Missouri, trying to return to Virginia. Walter provided the court with several sworn statements from friends attesting to his and William's loyalty to the Confederacy. Brockenbrough, however, remained unconvinced and ordered Johnson's five hundred acres of land sequestered and sold at auction. William Johnson was branded an alien enemy simply by virtue of the fact that he was not in Virginia at the proper time. Until the war's end, Archimedes Davis and the grand jury harassed Walter Johnson with garnishments for alleged debts to alien enemies.[16]

In a similar case, J. B. Allen, a Wilmington, North Carolina, merchant who owned several storefronts in town, was accused by a neighbor, William Gordon, of being disloyal. In Gordon's petition to receiver Du Brutz Cutlar, he alleged that Allen, a native of New Hampshire, had gone over to the enemy. Cutlar seized Allen's storefronts and successfully petitioned Judge Asa Biggs to declare Allen an alien enemy. Allen's property went up for auction within days of Judge Biggs's decision, and accuser William Gordon purchased it at a rock-bottom price. About a month after the sale of his property, J. B. Allen returned home to Wilmington from behind enemy lines, where he had been trapped for several weeks, unable to return. Authorities promptly arrested him and hastily handed him over to military authorities to be punished for disloyalty.[17]

Slave property was particularly valuable, and court officials were eager to seize as much as possible. In Rockbridge County, Virginia, receiver Joseph Steele seized and sold the property of Cyrus McCormick, inventor of the mechanical reaper, who, after a violent confrontation with a grand jury member in his district, fled to Illinois for safety in October 1862. Among McCormick's property was an enslaved woman named Emily and her infant child, both of whom Steele "exposed to sale at public auction on the 5th day of January, 1863 in the town of Lexington." The highest bidder purchased them for $2,500.[18]

Slaves commanded high prices in the market even late into the war, and that fact fostered corruption among some court officials. One particular incident sheds light on the value of enslaved property and the risks court officers were willing to take to seize it. In the case of *Confederate States v. Fenton and Fern*, receiver Francis L. Smith filed a petition of garnishment for slave property against two attorneys who, in January 1863, were executors of the estate of Eden Carter of Albemarle County, Virginia. In his petition, Smith stated that the slaves in the defendants' possession were slated to become, by the terms of Carter's will, the property of Thomas Kent and Francis Carter, both longtime residents of Ohio. Smith named all eleven slaves in question and provided ages for most: Amistad (56); Hannah, his wife (40); and their children John (20), George (18), Jeff (16), Jenny (12), Gilmore (7), Hero, Bartley, Frank, and Susan-Jane. Judge Halyburton's response to Smith's petition was predictable. He determined that Thomas Kent and Francis Carter were indeed "alien enemies" living in Ohio and "that the said negro slaves" should rightfully "be sequestered and . . . delivered up . . . to Francis L. Smith Receiver for District No. 1."[19]

On November 18, 1863, Smith reported to Halyburton on the dispensation of most of the slaves. "After giving notice by advertisement in the *Richmond Dispatch* of the time, place, and terms of sale," the receiver had Amistad, Hannah, "and their children Hero, Bartley, Frank, Gilmore, Susan-Jane, and George" sold at "public auction," for a total of $16,555.00. Three other bondpeople from Smith's original petition—John, Jeff, and Jenny, all among the most valuable of the lot—were not part of this transaction. The court record is silent about their fates, leaving one to wonder if Halyburton and Smith somehow profited by clandestinely selling them.[20]

Sworn statements found in the case file indicate a profound irony lurking behind this incidence of sequestration. Thomas Kent and Francis Carter, who were to inherit Amistad, Hannah, and their children from Eden Carter but who had been declared alien enemies because they were residents of Ohio, were in fact residing in Albemarle County, Virginia, as late as November 1862. Both men were known critics of the district court and its officers presiding over sequestration and had drawn the ire of the local grand jury. Kent and Carter had fled to Ohio from their Virginia homes in an effort to save their lives.[21]

Seizing and selling the property of individuals accused of being alien enemies of the Confederacy, whether they were or not, proved a lucrative business. The potential for corruption was abundantly evident even as lawmakers drafted the Sequestration Act. To curb possible abuses of power, the authors of sequestration established fixed salaries for marshals, receivers, and bailiffs, but judges' salaries were set at an amount equal to those of their respective state Supreme Court justices, which varied widely among the states. Envy among some district judges toward their counterparts elsewhere in the Confederacy was palpable. As one historian observed: "It is not hard to imagine the dissatisfaction which was produced among the district judges by these unequal results. For example, the judge in North Carolina, Asa Biggs, found his salary was only $2,500, whereas to the north of him judges in Virginia got $3,000 and to the south of him the judge of South Carolina received $3,500. Yet the North Carolina judge had three divisions to preside over and his neighbors had only two divisions each."[22]

Perhaps then it's not surprising that the North Carolina district court saw some of the most egregious examples of corruption among court officials. David Schenck, receiver for the Western Piedmont district, is a prime example. At the outset of the war, Schenck was a struggling middle-class lawyer from Lincolnton, North Carolina. Judge Asa Biggs appointed him receiver of the district in June 1862 as a political favor. Both Schenck and Biggs were founding members of the Southern Rights Party, North Carolina's only prosecession political party. By September, Schenck recorded in his diary that he had sold $20,000 worth of confiscated real estate in his district. In the weeks that followed, Schenck went on a spending spree, purchasing an eighteen-year-old male slave named Charles for $1,225, a new lot in town, and an additional three acres of land on the outskirts of town. He was also purchasing materials to build a new house. What was the source of this newfound wealth? The receivers' ledger for the sequestration fund from the Confederate Treasury offers a clue. According to the ledger, which recorded all funds remitted to the treasury by each receiver every quarter, David Schenck's district remitted only $3,610.24 in the year 1862. It also shows that the district court paid Schenck $319.58 to cover the costs of expenses incurred while executing the duties of his office. There is no evidence, in other words, that the full $20,000 worth of confiscated real estate sold at auction in September was ever deposited in the sequestration fund in Richmond.[23]

In South Carolina, corruption among court officials was even more blatant. In September 1861, a district attorney indicted Charleston merchant Walter Hooey and charged him with being an alien enemy. Judge Andrew G. Magrath ordered all of Hooey's possessions "sequestered and deliver[ed] . . . into the custody . . . of John W. Caldwell, Receiver," who would hold the belongings pending "the further order of the bench." Meanwhile, Hooey, who was living in Charleston, mounted a vigorous defense and ultimately persuaded Magrath that he was in fact a loyal Confederate. Hooey's property, however, had not been delivered over to Caldwell but rather remained in the custody of the bailiff, Michael Maguire. One month later, after Hooey satisfied the court of his loyalty, Judge Magrath ordered Caldwell to return Hooey's property. To the judge's shock, it was never delivered into Hooey's custody. Further inquiry revealed that Michael Maguire, Magrath's bailiff, had "disregarded [the] process of the court" and instead sold Hooey's property, scoring a tidy profit for himself. An embarrassed Magrath responded with a bench order demanding that Maguire appear and "show cause . . . why for such conduct his office should not be vacated."[24]

In many instances, district courts allowed the Sequestration Act to facilitate covetousness in some communities. For example, in November 1861 in Galveston, Texas, the grand jury took the deposition of John H. Crossman, who alleged that J. Hawley, owner of a dredge boat docked in Galveston, "was an unsafe man in the South. That two years prior he overheard Hawley utter seditionary sentiments." He also informed the grand jury that Hawley owned land on the San Antonio River. On Crossman's testimony alone, Hawley was arrested, declared an alien enemy, and imprisoned. His dredge boat and his land on the San Antonio River were sequestered and sold. Moreover, as was true of so many others victimized by the corruption associated with the sequestration law, all of Hawley's property ended up in the hands of his accuser, John Crossman.[25] The Confederate District Court for the Eastern District of Texas was unusually active in seizing land and property. William Pitt Ballinger, the receiver for the district, personally orchestrated the sequestration and sale of hundreds of properties and took custody over hundreds more. Perhaps it was no coincidence that, after the war, Ballinger went into the real estate business.[26]

Few individuals found the courage to speak out against sequestration and the abuses committed by the district courts. Most who did were themselves accused of disloyalty, declared alien enemies, and suffered the full consequences of violating the sequestration law. Nevertheless, a small handful of objections to confiscation stand out. All opponents of sequestration stressed the law's unconstitutionality as an *ex post facto* writ of attainder. Unlike the northern confiscation law, which separated property for the lifetime of the individual from whom it was taken, sequestration was forever: A descendent or relative could never reclaim it. The condemnation of blood was arguably the most repugnant aspect of the Confederacy's sequestration law. One opponent of sequestration, writing under the pseudonym "Nemo," wrote: "The law should be repealed! It is effectually, and to all intents, an *ex post facto* law, and a law impairing the obligation of contracts." He further argued that "an act perfectly innocent, usual and universally recognized by civilized nations, as legal and honorable at the time is afterwards declared null, and punished with forfeiture."[27]

Nemo's objections spoke to the Confederate government's warping of the law to suit its own ends by rendering contracts, business transactions, and relationships, perfectly legal and honorable before the war, now illegal and condemnable. Richmond attorney John H. Gilmer's 1862 lawsuit against the Confederate government's policy of confiscation gave clarity to this point. Gilmer was served with a writ for property belonging to a prewar northern client. He refused to comply, so his case went before Judge James Halyburton. Although Gilmer offered a sound defense, arguing that the law was "a bill of ravishment" riddled with inconsistencies, Halyburton's response was rather doctrinaire. The judge wrote that "the Constitution was made for citizens and friends, and not for the benefits of aliens and enemies." He further argued the Confederate government was within its rights to "make war of any kind and in any shape which the discretion of the Congress would dictate." Halyburton's decision, in effect, was an open admission that the Confederate government preferred to ignore the means to achieve its ends, even if that meant calling evil good and good evil.[28]

When the sequestration law went into effect in August 1861, it was made retroactive to May 22. As might be expected, the first year that sequestration was enforced, large numbers of garnishments for real estate, property, and debts were recorded. By 1863, however, the number of garnishments for real estate and property began to decrease, while at the same time the number of garnishments for debts began to increase sharply. Indeed, the district court records for the Cape Fear District of North Carolina for the 1863 November term record no garnishments for property at all; only petitions for debts. By 1865, nearly 85 percent of all sequestration proceedings were for debts owed to alien enemies. This fact raises an important question: How were southerners increasingly becoming indebted to alien enemies? How would it be possible for common folks on the home front to get around the insurmountable barriers of battlefields, armies, and the war in general, either to borrow money or to purchase goods from sellers outside the Confederate States? The answer is simple: They couldn't. How, then, is the increase in garnishments for debts explained? The court records offer a clue. The districts that saw the sharpest increases in garnishments for debts as the war progressed were in southern and southeastern Virginia, the Piedmont and mountain districts of North Carolina, northern Alabama, east Tennessee, west Texas, and the German district near San Antonio. In each of these districts, a strong Unionist sentiment dominated before the war. Additionally, most of these districts sheltered large numbers of deserters. Many were epicenters for antiwar protests or peace movements. Using the powers granted by the Act of Sequestration, the Confederate courts sought to punish residents of these districts by depriving many of their land and property and by extorting money from many others.

It is deceiving to say, as the authors of the Act of Sequestration did, that the law dealt a blow to northern financial interests in the Confederate States. In fact, the law was unnecessary, as the war itself delivered the greatest blow to northern economic concerns in the South. Southerners were not paying debts owed to northern creditors. That was treasonous, and fraught with all manner of risks. The Act of Sequestration was meant to compensate "loyal Confederates" for losses resulting from Union confiscation, using proceeds from the sale of property or the collection of debts owed to northerners, but in reality this rarely, if ever, was how the law functioned. The great irony of the Act of Sequestration is that a law designed to punish "alien enemies" and northern creditors in the end punished only common folks on the southern home front.

Notes

1. "An Act to Confiscate Property Used for Insurrectionary Purposes," 12 Statutes at Large 319 (1861). See also Daniel W. Hamilton, *The Limits of Sovereignty: Property Confiscation in the Union and the Confederacy during the Civil War* (Chicago: University of Chicago Press, 2007). There are surprisingly few scholarly works that seek to examine the Confederate Act of Sequestration in its totality. Hamilton's *The Limits of Sovereignty* is a legal history of property confiscation during the Civil War that offers a thorough justification for confiscation and sequestration. All other existing works on Confederate sequestration approach the subject from oblique angles. For other works on the Confederate Act of Sequestration, see William W. Robinson, *Justice in Grey: A History of the Judicial System of the Confederate States of America* (New York: Russell & Russell, 1941); T. R. Havins, "Administration of the Sequestration Act in the Confederate District for the Western District of Texas, 1862–1865," *Southwestern Historical Quarterly* 43 (January 1940): 295–322; Brian R. Dirck, "Posterity's Blush: Civil Liberties, Property Rights, and Property Confiscation in the Confederacy," *Civil War History* 48 (September 2002): 237–56; Mark E. Neely, Jr., *Southern Rights: Political Prisoners and the Myth of Confederate Constitutionalism* (Charlottesville: University Press of Virginia, 1999); James G. Randall, "Captured and Confiscated Property during the Civil War," *American Historical Review* 28 (October 1913): 65–79; Thomas G. Dyer, *Secret Yankees: The Union Circle in Confederate Atlanta* (Baltimore: Johns Hopkins University Press, 1999); Rodney J. Steward, "Confederate Menace: Sequestration on the North Carolina Home Front," in *Weirding the War: Stories from the Civil War's Ragged Edges*, ed. Stephen Berry (Athens: University of Georgia Press, 2011), 54–70; Mark A. Weitz, *The Confederacy on Trial: The Piracy and Sequestration Cases on 1861* (Lawrence: University of Kansas Press, 2005); and Barton A. Myers, *Rebels against the Confederacy: North Carolina's Unionists* (New York: Cambridge University Press, 2014). Myers's *Rebels against the Confederacy* examines the treatment of Unionists in North Carolina at the hands of Confederate officials. The Sequestration Act deemed every person caught or suspected of having knowledge of liable property or debt as criminals and likely Unionists, whether they had true Unionist sympathies or not.

2. Dirck, "Posterity's Blush," 239; Havins, "Administration of the Sequestration Act," 5 (online); Thomas B. Alexander and Richard E. Barringer, *The Anatomy of the Confederate Congress* (Nashville, Tenn.: Vanderbilt University Press, 1972), 372. See also William C. Davis, *Look Away: A History of the Confederate States of America* (New York: Free Press, 2002), 166.

3. "An Act for the Sequestration of the Property of Alien Enemies," in *Confederate Imprints*, reel 2, no. 49 (hereinafter cited as "Act of Sequestration").

4. "Act of Sequestration." See Steward, "Confederate Menace," 56.

5. "Act of Sequestration"; Steward "Confederate Menace," 56–58; Davis, *Look Away*, 169. A thorough examination of the Confederate District Court Records found in Record Group 21 at the National Archives and Records Administration (hereinafter cited as NARA) and a search of the Confederate Congressional Record failed to locate any "Loyal Confederate" awarded an indemnity from the sequestration fund as a result of the loss of personal property due to federal confiscation. Articulating standards for citizenship and the naturalizing process proved to be a difficult task for

the Confederate government. The only legislation put forth addressing these matters in Congress sought to give individual states the right to set their own standards. President Jefferson Davis objected to this measure, however, arguing that the Confederate constitution gave that power exclusively to the national government.

6. "Act of Sequestration"; Dirck, "Posterity's Blush," 240.

7. See Myers, *Rebels against the Confederacy.*

8. Archimedes Davis to William Nash, March 1862, in Confederate District Court Records (hereinafter cited as CDCR), Western District of Virginia, NARA, Philadelphia.

9. Lipscomb Pomeroy to Archimedes Davis, December 16, 1861, Box 1, NARA, Philadelphia.

10. Pomeroy to Davis; "Act of Sequestration"; Dirck, "Posterity's Blush," 241; Francis L. Smith to Hon. Judge James Halyburton, October 1862, and T. N. Campbell to Judge Halyburton, October 1862, in CDCR, Eastern District of Virginia, Robert Alonzo Brock Collection, Reel #4604, Library of Virginia, Richmond (hereinafter cited as LVA).

11. Steward, "Confederate Menace," 57–58.

12. C. N. White to Asa Biggs, January 1862, Box 1, Folder 1, NARA, Atlanta.

13. Affidavit of Jacob Lynch to Archimedes Davis, January 1862, NARA, Philadelphia.

14. CDCR, Eastern District of Virginia, Brock Collection, Reel #4605, LVA.

15. Lynch to Davis, CDCR, Eastern District of Virginia, Brock Collection, Reel #4605, LVA.

16. Confederate States v. William Johnson (1862), Box 4, NARA, Philadelphia.

17. Petition of William Gordon, in Du Brutz Cutlar Papers, p. 89, Southern Historical Collection, Wilson Library, University of North Carolina, Chapel Hill; Steward, "Confederate Menace," 64.

18. Confederate States v. Mary Anderson, August 1862, CDCR, Western District of Virginia, NARA, Philadelphia.

19. Confederate States v. Mary Anderson; CDCR, Eastern District of Virginia, Brock Collection, Reel #4004, LVA.

20. CDCR, Eastern District of Virginia, Brock Collection, Reel #2608, LVA.

21. CDCR, Eastern District of Virginia, Brock Collection, Reel #2608, LVA.

22. Robinson, *Justice in Grey,* 158.

23. Steward, "Confederate Menace," 62.

24. District Court Ledger, September 19 and October 2, 1861, CDCR, District of South Carolina, NARA, Atlanta.

25. Testimony of John Crossman, November 29, 1861, Grand Jury Minutes for the Eastern District of Texas, Tucker Papers, Briscoe Center for American History, University of Texas at Austin (hereinafter cited as BCAH).

26. William Pitt Ballinger Papers, BCAH.

27. Steward, "Confederate Menace," 66.

28. Steward, "Confederate Menace," 66–67.

"Irresistibly Impelled toward Illegal Appropriation"

THE CIVIL WAR SCHEMES OF WILLIAM G. CHEENEY

JIMMY L. BRYAN JR.

In the fall of 1861, Allan Pinkerton heard rumors that engineers at the Tredegar Iron Works in Richmond, Virginia, were developing new, insidious marine technologies. As General George McClellan's chief of intelligence, Pinkerton sent an operative to the Confederate capital to investigate. Identified only as "Mrs. E. H. Baker," the spy witnessed the demonstration of a submarine apparatus on the James River. She reported the alarming news to Pinkerton, who alerted the commander of the Union blockading squadron. The spy master later claimed that his information foiled an attempt to sink the flagship USS *Minnesota* by this "infernal machine."[1]

Historians and buffs, drawn to the sensational and unsolved, find tantalizing the story of famed detective Pinkerton, his lady spy, and a submarine that may have predated by three years the *H. L. Hunley*, the first operable, wartime submarine. The elusive details led researchers to a few scattered records that identified an "Acting Master" William G. Cheeney as the supervisor in charge of constructing, if not designing, a human-powered, underwater vessel on the James River. In assessing the evidence, Milton F. Perry and Tom Chaffin find the claims inconclusive, but others like John M. Coski and Mark K. Ragan seem more willing to accept the circumstantial data. Coski asserts that Cheeney had served previously as an officer in the U.S. Navy and that "it is clear that the Confederates developed a submarine in Richmond in 1861–1862." Ragan further states that Cheeney had acquired expertise in underwater explosives and concludes that "enough documentation has been uncovered to sketch out its [the submarine's] obscure history with reasonable certainty."[2]

If these scholars had a better understanding of William G. Cheeney's personal history, they may have invested less credence in his story. Coski came the closest to realizing the character of the acting master on the James River. He notes that in the spring of 1862, the officer "became an embarrassment to the Confederate Navy" after he fled to the North and informed Union officials of his efforts to develop submarine technology.[3] In fact, Cheeney never served in the U.S. Navy. If he had experience with underwater explosives, he did not gain it until he arrived in Richmond just after the war began. Furthermore, the name "Cheeney" was an alias. Instead, the acting master formerly operated several printing concerns and, for a brief time, a lead mine. He was also a habitual thief, a credit dodger, and a schemer. His attempt to build a submarine may have been nothing more than a plot to defraud the Confederate navy of cash.

Historians have shown that, among the many social and cultural disorientations created by the market intensification of the antebellum period, the desire for personal independence and belief in the myth of upward mobility drove many toward reckless and sometimes deceitful quests for capital. As Edward J. Balleisen and Scott A. Sandage illustrate, the dream of becoming a "proprietor" or a "businessman" operated powerfully within the imaginations of the working and middle classes and often lured individuals toward failure and fraud.[4] Their stories marked the inherent vulnerabilities of an economic system that relied on "personal lending" or "relationship lending" conducted within a "world of strangers." As Jane Kamensky notes, confidence became the currency for early nineteenth-century capitalists, which led to an epidemic of what Ian Klaus terms "reputation contagion." Klaus explains that, "once reputational mechanisms became the primary vehicles of trust, they also became the targets and unwitting facilitators of fraud."[5] By 1849, the New York press identified these archetypical swindlers, sharpers, or humbugs as "confidence men"—most famously represented by P. T. Barnum. The scholarship, however, typically presents confidence men as literary tropes or as unfortunate obstacles to legitimate business practices.[6]

Although Cheeney did not achieve the level of notoriety of a P. T. Barnum, or an Andrew Dexter, or a George Appo, his story invites an examination of how one fraudster took advantage of the practice of relationship lending and the economy of personality to gain access to capital that he did not possess on his own.[7] Like the "counterfeit preachers" described in John Lindbeck's essay in this volume, Cheeney proved adept at assuming alternate identities. His experiences further show how he stoked the tribal loyalties of the secession crisis to ingratiate himself with those rising to power in the South or to draw upon their favor as a professed compatriot. He donned loyalty or disloyalty depending on his financial needs with the same facility as fellow New Yorkers William and Audley Britton, chronicled in Jeff Strickland's essay in this work. Cheeney played the confidence game with charisma and professions of expertise while he relied upon the anonymity of urban life and the turbulence of wartime to drift from one community to another, escape past debts, and search for new resources to exploit. Cheeney may have been sincere in his efforts to establish a printing career in Missouri, or build a submarine in Virginia, or dig up silver in Texas, but wherever he went, his dubious transactions and audacious promises defined him as a confidence man who maneuvered through the stresses and vulnerabilities evident in the early market system of the United States.

Early Life, Felonies, and a Big Fire

William G. Cheeney was born William C. Grummon (often Grummond) on September 20, 1829, at York, Livingston County, New York. He was the only child of Rebecca and Ebenezer Grummon, a poor couple who by 1830 moved to the outskirts of nearby Le Roy. The young "Bill" Grummon attended the Round House and Cooper Street schools, where his classmates recalled how he troubled the "gnarled face of Dr. Winsor," their teacher. Though Winsor "was a tyrant by nature, malicious, cruel and seemed rather to seek for excuses to apply the rod," Grummon "was too foxy for" the schoolmaster and managed to prank him. He "notched his [Winsor's] whips with his jackknife, so that they flew all to pieces." After fifty years, Grummon's friends recalled him as charming and quick-witted, but they remembered most his propensity to steal. He pilfered his classmates' desks and attained a talent for lock-picking—the "use of a crooked nail, or wire soon served the purpose of a key," student M. S. Elmore recalled.[8]

In 1844, when about fifteen years old, Grummon left school and took on an apprenticeship. He first worked for Edward Bliss at the *Le Roy Courier* as a printer's devil, but that firm only operated for about a year. He then joined Charles B. Thomson's *Le Roy Gazette*. Baxter L. Carlton also worked for Thomson and recalled that the editor "gave me much fatherly advice and extremely low wages." Grummon nevertheless learned the skills of a printer, if not a capacity for the publishing business, and he would rely upon that trade for most of his adult life.[9]

Whether dissatisfied with Thomson's advice or pay, or whether he struggled with the class reorientations of the market revolution, or whether he suffered from some emotional affliction, Bill Grummon pursued a brief but active career as a burglar.[10] In late 1846 or early 1847, he broke into numerous local businesses—taking cash, trifles, and in one instance about $150 of dress silks from the Mitchell and Royce store. Working at the *Gazette,* he typeset the reward message for his own capture. To cache his growing ill-gotten inventory, he fashioned a hideout within a haystack near his parents' home. By the spring of 1847, Grummon had amassed enough contraband that he quit his printer's job and traveled the region "peddling trinkets and fancy articles with hand trunks," as the *Gazette* later reported. He returned to Thomson's newspaper, but perhaps sensing his employer's distrust, he left Le Roy and hired on with the *Troy (N.Y.) Whig* as a compositor. During his two months in eastern New York, Grummon sent back generous amounts of money to his parents. The *Whig* also reported about $60 stolen from its office but did not immediately suspect the "quiet, smooth-spoken youth."[11]

During his return home, Grummon stopped at Brockport, a town on the Erie Canal north of Le Roy and west of Rochester. He broke into the post office and a retail store, but he lingered too long. The local constable discovered and very nearly caught the thief. Grummon stole a horse and rode for Le Roy, pursued by the lawman, but he managed to elude arrest by hiding in his haystack den. He remained inactive for several weeks, but on the night of December 20, 1847, he burglarized J. P. Darling's store before attempting to escape the region by boarding a train at Rochester. There, law enforcement caught up with the thief and arrested him.[12]

Grummon's apprehension and the revelation of his criminal career received a wide readership in western New York newspapers.[13] The community expressed surprise to learn that a young man of eighteen years had committed the audacious and sophisticated break-ins, often accomplished with employees sleeping in an adjacent room. The *Troy Whig* described Grummon's theft as "cleverly done." When the *Gazette* initially reported the Darling robbery, it suggested that a group of thieves had performed the crime. M. S. Elmore worked for Darling at the time and gave a detailed account of how Grummon used an augur on two doors to unlatch the bars that blocked entry from the inside. Elmore recalled, "There was much excitement and many theories regarding the burglar; as he had exhibited all the skill and deliberation of a professional."[14]

After his capture, Grummon confessed to his crimes. His former classmates Elmore, Carlton, and Elliott P. Halbert remembered him with bittersweet fondness. Elmore described him as a "gifted, though wayward youth." Carlton called him "the unfortunate Grummond," explaining that he "was by nature a kleptomaniac and often times mourned and wept over the fact that he seemed irresistibly impelled toward illegal appropriation of the property of others." His tears, however sincere, would not spare Bill Grummon from a jail term. At Albany on January 21, 1848, the federal court convicted and sentenced him to five years in Auburn Prison.[15]

By March 1853, William C. Grummon obtained his release from Auburn and returned to Le Roy. He publicly apologized to his community and attempted to rejoin it as a responsible citizen. His father died just before or soon after his arrival, leaving him to care for his mother and to assume the mortgage on his parents' property. He called upon his experience as a printer and in March 1854 established his own newspaper, the *Genesee Herald,* hiring old school friends Elliott Halbert and H. C. "Greely" Hollister. In the prospectus Grummon promised "to be neutral in politics," but he attended local meetings supporting temperance, the Missouri Compromise, the Know-Nothing Party, and the Western New York Editor's Association. He joined the Masonic Order and on December 20, 1854, married Ann Eliza Walker, daughter of a farming family from Pavilion, and moved into a house on Myrtle Street.[16]

Less than a month after Grummon's marriage, a fire consumed the business section of Le Roy. The conflagration originated in his newspaper's office. Halbert recalled that he and Hollister worked at the *Herald* late into the night before retiring to Grummon's home. They awoke the next morning, January 13, 1855, to an alarm ringing from the bell at the Eagle Hotel. They looked out the window and "saw the fire on the front and roof of the Herald office." The flames, spreading quickly through the mostly wooden buildings, overwhelmed the local fire crews, but the community rushed in to salvage what they could. After the devastation, the *Le Roy Gazette* estimated that twenty-five businesses suffered damages totaling more than $100,000.[17]

In his initial reporting, Charles B. Thomson of the *Gazette* suggested that the fire was the work of an arsonist and further implied that he suspected his former employee and current newspaper rival Grummon as the culprit. Elliott Halbert and Baxter Carlton defended their friend. Halbert attributed the accusations to Grummon's "unfortunate record" and Thomson's contempt of him, and Carlton reminded readers that Grummon "was conspicuous during its [the fire's] progress in assisting to stay its ravages."[18]

According to the *Gazette,* Grummon and the *Herald* lost about $700 in fire damage. He was insured, but the company did not want to pay out his claim. Carlton assisted with the efforts to restart the business. "I worked for him awhile shortly after the event and was cognizant of his strenuous efforts to get his paper again on a prosperous basis. He lost steadily," and his creditors called upon him. After his return from Auburn Prison, Grummon took on several mortgages and personal notes apparently to finance the *Herald.* In August 1856, the courts ruled against him in a suit claiming $375 and sold the family's two-acre town lot at a sheriff's auction. In July 1858, the courts issued a judgment against him for $1,200, but he had already left town. Grummon, with his wife, Ann Eliza; mother, Rebecca; and infant daughter, Ida Belle, had left Le Roy, changed their name to Cheeney, and relocated to Jefferson City, Missouri.[19]

Confederate Missouri

William C. Grummon—now William G. Cheeney—arrived in Jefferson City by September 1857, a time when the Missouri state capital seethed with deep political divisions over slavery. Roused by the August 1858 defeat of the proslavery Lecompton Constitution in Kansas, the Ultra Democrats in Missouri won a majority in the state legislature. Cheeney was acquainted with Claiborne F. Jackson, a leader of the state's proslavery Democrats, and the New Yorker found supporters within that group. In the few extant records, Cheeney expressed no overt sympathies toward slavery, but in New York, he had participated in functions endorsing the Know-Nothing Party and attended an Anti-Nebraska meeting. His allegiances to one faction or another, however, probably had less to do with his political tendencies and more to do with attaching himself to the party in ascendancy. Although he happily took money from anyone willing to provide it, Cheeney may have used the tribal mentality of the crisis years to procure the confidence of those eager to help a fellow adherent to a shared cause.[20]

At Jefferson City, Cheeney successfully restarted his printing career. He hired on as a foreman for Charles J. Corwin's *Jefferson Examiner,* and by November 1858, he had established the *Missouri Educator* with Dr. A. Peabody as editor. Cheeney cultivated a reputation and goodwill among his fellow printers. In an announcement regarding the new periodical, the *Weekly California News* of Moniteau, Missouri, evoked a familiar descriptor, characterizing "Mr. Cheeney" as "a good printer, and a very clever gentleman, and we wish him every success in his enterprise." In May 1859, Cheeney purchased the *Examiner* from Corwin. Although the new publisher pledged not to change the newspaper's political stance, an observer writing in the *Glasgow Weekly Times* hinted that Cheeney's affiliation with the proslavery Ultras of Missouri was stronger than the outgoing Corwin's. He commented that "Corwin was rather vulnerable on the leading point of nationalism—the nigger—and we suppose goes out under advisement. We know nothing of Mr. Cheeney's antecedents, but presume he is sound on the goose." The confidence man thrived in this lack of "antecedents" and the default presumptions of the community.[21]

When Corwin sold the *Examiner,* he also resigned as Missouri's public printer. Governor Robert M. Stewart, a pro-Union Democrat, appointed Cheeney to replace him. In that capacity between 1859 and 1861, he produced more than twenty books for the state and local patrons. On June 8, 1859, Cheeney actively participated in a convention of Missouri editors held at Jefferson City. He called the meeting to order, served as secretary pro tem, and contributed to several committees, including one charged with investigating "swindling agents." Within two years of arriving at the capital, he had positioned himself as one of the leading printers in the state.[22]

Cheeney also attempted lead mining. As historians have shown, the promise of wealth, the understanding of the need for large investment, and the central role of the promoter rendered the mining industry particularly vulnerable to fraud. Sincere businessmen and swindlers alike used the prospectus to generate interest from investors.[23] Cheeney published his in the summer of 1859 in the pages of the *Examiner.* He announced that he and a partner wanted to hire a small group of workers to prospect Cole and surrounding counties. He hoped that once they had demonstrated the mine's productivity, they could employ as many as two thousand men in the enterprise. Cheeney later claimed that he established a mine and a smelting furnace on the west side of the Osage River, perhaps in Maries County, south of Jefferson City. By July 1860 when the census taker arrived at his door, Cheeney claimed $11,000 in real estate and $15,850 in personal property. Despite the promising beginning, his printing and mining empires were short-lived.[24]

On January 17, 1861, the *Inquirer*—a rival newspaper—accused the legislature's Committee on Public Printing with mismanagement. Behind the charge lay the implication that Corwin and later Cheeney drastically overcharged the state government for their services. After a brief investigation, a special committee found that the "misunderstanding" derived from poor wording in the bookkeeping, but the findings did not satisfy a group of legislators led by Thomas L. Price. During the House session on January 23, he reported that together Corwin and Cheeney had received more than $120,000 from their contracts and claimed that he had received bids from other printers who would save the government up to 30 percent off that amount.[25]

The concern over the public printer may have originated with financial issues, but it evolved into a political fight. In the aftermath of Abraham Lincoln's November 1860 election and as other slave states seceded from the Union, Claiborne F. Jackson assumed the governorship of Missouri. In his inauguration speech on January 3, 1861, two weeks before the legislature took up the issue over the public printer, Jackson declared his support for Missouri's "sister slave-holding States." Thomas Price, who originally introduced the question about the public printer, remained a pro-Union Democrat, and the proslavery Ultras in the House interpreted the move as an obvious effort to subvert the state press. Thomas W. Freeman and Thomas A. Harris, both of whom would later represent Missouri in the Confederate Congress, ardently defended Cheeney as the current printer. In his support, Freeman vowed, "We won't permit the election of a Black Republican printer," and Harris protested the proposal as "not worthy of the slaveholders we represent. . . . It would be one step in the establishment of a machine-shop that would strike its poisoned dagger, not only at the institutions of this State, but at the heart of the country itself."[26]

The legislature eventually decided to hold a special election for public printer, but before the prescribed date, seven southern states had seceded from the Union and formed the Confederate States of America at Montgomery, Alabama. That new reality may have led to a cooling of enthusiasm for the hard-line Ultras. On February 18, Missouri voters overwhelmingly sent moderates to the state's secession convention, which met on February 28 at Jefferson City. On March 13, the legislature met in a joint session to vote for public printer. The record does not show to what degree the political climate or the suspicions of malfeasance influenced the choice, but Cheeney lost his contract, placing second (45 votes) to the more moderate Democrat Joseph P. Ament (76 votes). On March 19, the secession convention, by then reconvened in St. Louis, voted 98 to 1 to keep Missouri in the Union.[27]

Although he may have miscalculated secession sentiment in February, Governor Jackson still favored Missouri's withdrawal. He gained further leverage in April after Confederate troops fired on Fort Sumter, after Abraham Lincoln called for volunteers, and after Virginia, North Carolina, Arkansas, and Tennessee joined the Confederacy. By May, opposing militias had formed in Missouri, and on April 10, units defending the Union captured secessionist troops at Camp Jackson near St. Louis. At midnight, with rumors that loyalist soldiers intended to march on the capital, a group of pro-Jackson militia attempted to destroy the nearly quarter-mile-long railroad bridge that spanned the Osage River and connected Jefferson City with St. Louis. Later, U.S. authorities accused Cheeney of participating in that illegal action, but he denied it. He claimed instead that he watched the flames from his lead-smelting works.[28]

By the end of May, Cheeney sold the *Examiner* to Ament, who had succeeded him as public printer, and soon after left the state. Any loyalty he might have shown to Jackson and the secessionist Democrats did not supersede his desire to avoid his creditors. In order to build his Missouri printing and mining enterprises, Cheeney took advantage of the nineteenth-century financial system that relied on personal lending.[29] On May 12, 1859, when he purchased the *Examiner* from Charles J. Corwin, he opened a line of credit with Henry B. Graham, and for the next two years, he charged more than $2,500 for paper and ink. He later used a $312.50 promissory note from Corwin to obtain bookbinding services provided by E. F. Dietz and John Walde. In June, launching his mining enterprise, Cheeney acquired $349.50 in lumber and the use of a flatboat on credit secured from Richard A. Wells, and later took on a mortgage of

$713.14 for lands in Moniteau County from Thomas L. Price, the same legislator who had pushed for a new public printer.[30]

Cheeney was not alone in incurring debt within the antebellum capitalist system, but he apparently never intended on repaying these obligations. Further, he used the informal credit system to delay, shift, and hide his financial dealings. Corwin, for example, endorsed his $312.50 note as security, but when Cheeney signed it over to Dietz and Walde, he implied that Corwin would share in the debt, creating what Corwin's attorneys later described as a "material variance" in the legality of the note. In another case, Jacob Colvin gave a promissory note to Cheeney for $811.90, but Colvin claimed that he only received $75. Cheeney, in turn, signed that note over to merchants Henry Burger and William Dean, apparently for a line of credit. In defending himself from a suit brought by Burger and Dean, Colvin concluded that Cheeney had deliberately manipulated the circumstances "to obtain an undue advantage—that it [the note] was procured on the false & fraudulent pretense that he had money to lend . . . when in truth and in fact said Cheeney, as this respondent afterwards learned, was and is still insolvent."[31]

In early 1861, with the legislature debating his future as public printer, with the Jackson governorship under pressure, and with his debts increasing, Cheeney borrowed more. He obtained cash from promissory notes on Edmond H. Linsenbard as well as Burger and Dean. He secured the last note on June 10. Within nineteen days, Linsenbard became the first to file suit against the wayward printer and lead miner, and on July 2, the Cole County Circuit Court issued its first summons. By that time, Cheeney had already fled Jefferson City. In his wake, he left at least six suits in the courts, claiming debts totaling $5,340.18.[32]

Cheeney's Infernal Apparatus

In the summer of 1861, Richmond, Virginia, bustled with preparations for war. The Confederacy had relocated its capital there in April, about the same time that U.S. president Abraham Lincoln announced his plans to blockade southern ports. As the two sides marched troops toward their first major engagement at Bull Run, Maryland, they also scrambled to cobble together their respective naval assets. William G. Cheeney later claimed that when he first arrived at

Richmond, he intended to pursue his trade as a printer. At a new locale where no one knew of his financial indiscretions back in Le Roy or Jefferson City, he looked for fresh sources of cash to exploit. He donned a new identity—perhaps as a former U.S. naval officer—and found a new sponsor with the Confederate Navy Department.[33]

The circumstances of Cheeney's employment with the Confederate navy remain undocumented and vague. The degree to which he initiated or joined a preexisting conversation about submarine technologies remains equally so. On June 21, 1861, a correspondent writing under the pseudonym Argus reported to the *Charleston Mercury* from Richmond. He observed: "War brings out talent and genius. Some individuals here are endeavoring to establish the efficacy of a marine infernal machine." He continued to describe the design by which men in a submersible could attach an explosive device to the underside of enemy ships, maneuver to a safe distance, and detonate the charge. Cheeney was likely a part of this group. By August, he had submitted a similar plan to Matthew F. Maury, who had taken charge of the Confederate navy's effort to develop torpedo and mine technology. Maury gave the plans to his able lieutenant John M. Brooke, who recorded in his diary on August 17 that he had recommended the "plan proposed by Mr. Wm G. Cheeney for the destruction of blockading ships. The plan I believe practical and effective." Based on Brooke's endorsement, the Confederate secretary of the navy commissioned Cheeney as an "acting master," gave him charge of a crew, and granted him access to resources available at Richmond's Tredegar Iron Works.[34]

Between September 1861 and May 1862, Cheeney led a group of workers to construct the first operable military submarine. Several accounts suggested that he may have succeeded. Apparently after hearing rumors about the project, U.S. intelligence officer Allan Pinkerton dispatched a female spy— "Mrs. E. H. Baker"—to Richmond. In November 1861, she witnessed a demonstration of a manned submarine in the James River that successfully destroyed a small target. Pinkerton described "a terrific explosion, and the scow seemed lifted bodily out of the water and thrown high into the air," alarming Mrs. Baker about the craft's devastating potential. Pinkerton alerted the U.S. secretary of the navy, apparently just in time—assuming that the intelligence officer had misremembered the November date. Louis M. Goldsborough, the U.S. flag officer of the James River fleet, reported that on October 9 "an attempt, no doubt, was had by the insurgents to get an infernal machine among our shipping here, but it was happily foiled." According to his information, the Confederate submersible had targeted his own flagship, the USS *Minnesota*. On December 15, Michael Martin, a Union man employed in Richmond, managed to return to New York City, where he reported to the *Herald* that the Confederates attempted to develop at the Tredegar Iron Works "a machine intended to act against the blockading vessels." He described it as an iron, cigar-shaped craft as long as fifty feet, "propelled by air, manned by six persons. . . . It was considered by the people of Richmond to be a very formidable apparatus, and great things were expected of it." These accounts imply that by the end of 1861, Cheeney had designed and overseen the construction of a submarine that performed a successful demonstration and undertook at least one, albeit thwarted, operation against the U.S. Navy.[35]

The authors of these reports, however, received their information from hearsay. Pinkerton wrote his account twenty years after the events, based on the observations of a person unconfirmed in the historical record, and written within a self-serving autobiography meant to credit him with saving the Union with his network of spies. "The efficient manner in which this work was performed," Pinkerton wrote of the submarine episode, "was of great service to the nation, and sustained the reputation of the Secret Service Department, as being an important adjunct in aiding the government in its efforts to suppress the rebellion." Goldsborough obtained his information from a Confederate deserter who had surrendered at Fortress Monroe, and in his account, Martin never claimed that he personally observed the submarine or witnessed its operation.[36]

The only direct evidence of Cheeney's efforts came from several requisitions drawn on Tredegar and the correspondence and journal entries of Lieutenant Brooke. These documents tell a different story. For one, developing new submarine technology was an expensive enterprise. The records from Tredegar show that between October 1861 and May 1862 Cheeney spent in excess of $8,000 for equipment, supplies, and labor.[37] For another, Brooke's journal entries implied that the submarine never became operational. On November 8, a month after the reputed attempt on the USS *Minnesota*, the lieutenant noted that "Cheeny [sic] will be ready to start on his submarine expedition soon." Brooke repeated the same observation on December 21. As late as February 13,

1862, the lieutenant recorded: "Mr. Cheeney's boat is not ready yet. He pro-
poses to go down on a preliminary trip in a row boat to try and blow something
up." Naval historian Mark Ragan suggests that after the *Minnesota* incident,
Cheeney began construction on a second machine. Even so, the inaction reported by Brooke indicated that this new technology remained unproven.[38]

Cheeney's letters to Brooke, however, revealed tension between the two
naval engineers over the lack of progress and hinted at the acting master's ulterior agenda. Writing from Norfolk on March 12, 1862, Cheeney informed the
lieutenant: "I have not yet made any attempt against the enemy's vessels. . . .
I have not yet overcome all troubles and hindrances occasioned by Military
regulations, Martial Law &c. I had great trouble in obtaining any kind of boat
to suit my purposes." He expressed his desire to make his first test against the
USS *Monitor,* "the only enemy our noble 'Virginia' [formerly the *Merrimack*]
has to fear," and he hoped to "return to Richmond and get my sub-marine boat
in order." In the meantime, he admonished Brooke, "Do not get impatient—I
assure you that if I am slow at the same time persevering and doubt not that I
will yet fully succeed." By May 2, Cheeney claimed to have "made several trials
with my apparatus, but as yet have not made any attempt upon the enemy's
vessels. . . . My apparatus worked well, except that in water rough or rolling."
He promised to deploy his submarine in the near future but continued to defend his lack of results. "I cannot explain all the causes which have delayed
me so long," Cheeney insisted. "I am doing what in my judgement seems best,
and I only ask that the confidence which has been so generously accorded me
heretofore may not yet be withdrawn. . . . Like all first trials it has some defects
which may be very much improved upon."[39]

Although the reports of submarine activity in the James River originated
from hearsay, Brooke's personal records and receipts from Tredegar confirmed
that Cheeney led a team of developers to construct an operable submersible.
His efforts may have been sincere, if not earnest. In creating a new technology, he no doubt encountered delays and unfulfilled expectations, but coupled
with his history of embezzlement, his letters to Brooke suggested that Cheeney
may have been happy to continue to delay his progress in order to maintain
a cash source from the Confederate navy. The comments that Argus made in
June 1861 to the *Charleston Mercury* further echoed the kinds of schemes that
Cheney attempted back in Missouri and later in Texas. The correspondent

noted that the developers of the "marine infernal machine" in Richmond were eager "to test its powers as soon as a company of capitalists can be formed who will *guarantee* a sufficient sum to put the exterminator [submarine] in operation." Argus observed that such private investment was unlikely because of the dubious nature of the project. "The appeal of the inventor to the patriotism of capitalists is well enough, but there are very few persons who are willing to invest their money without ocular proof of the efficiency of the invention."[40]

Acting Master Cheeney likely never developed a functioning submarine, but he nevertheless served the Confederate navy in its mission against the United States. He performed reconnaissance and constructed battery-powered torpedoes and underwater mines along the James River and Hampton Roads. Lieutenant Brooke was one of the leading designers who transformed the steamship *Merrimack* into the ironclad CSS *Virginia*. After its retrofit, Cheeney described it as an "an anomalous monster." He witnessed the *Virginia's* March 8, 1861, destruction of the USS *Congress*. "She continued to burn until long into the night, shedding a lurid glare upon all around," he recalled. "I was watching the burning vessel, when suddenly a column of fire shot up to the clouds, scattering spars, timbers and debris in all directions, accompanied with a noise and quaking of the earth simply terrific." The next day, he watched the battle between the *Virginia* and the *Monitor* "that lay upon the water like a cheese box. . . . I then had no knowledge that such a craft as the Monitor had ever been planned." The battle "was one of great wonder and speculation."[41]

The circumstances under which Cheeney decided to leave the Confederate service remain as murky as his joining. Apparently, the Navy Department ceased its sponsorship of his experiments by June 1862, and the acting master fled Richmond under a new alias, "William L. Walker." He claimed that he traveled to the White House in order to offer President Lincoln "information . . . of great importance"—perhaps referring to his work in developing submarine technology for the South. He left a note with the porter and continued on his return to his former home in western New York. By January 1863, using his birth name Grummon as an alias for his Cheeney alias, he found work as a printer in Albany and later in New York City, employed by the *New York World* and *Harper's Weekly*. Unfortunately for Cheeney, his Missouri offenses caught up to him. On November 25, U.S. authorities arrested the printer in New York City and transported him to Gatriot Street Prison in St. Louis.[42]

Gatriot Limbo

Cheeney did not know with which crime the United States had charged him. He and his attorney could only surmise that it stemmed from the attempted destruction of the Osage River Bridge in support of embattled governor Claiborne F. Jackson. Cheeney denied any participation in that action, and if his creditors in Jefferson City had learned of his incarceration, the court records do not show it. Without a trial or conviction, he remained in prison for almost a year. During that time, he found himself playing a small part in uncovering a national conspiracy—or at least perpetuating rumors of its existence.[43]

Sometime in May 1864, or so Cheeney claimed, fellow prisoner Charles E. Dunn inducted him into a secret society. Dunn served as "deputy grand commander" of the Order of American Knights, a group of northerners who opposed the war and planned on, among other things, assassinating Abraham Lincoln and fomenting guerilla war behind Union lines. When John P. Sanderson took over as provost marshall general for Missouri, he launched an investigation that led to an interview with Cheeney at the Gatriot Street Prison. The inmate confessed that Dunn had "initiated him into the mysteries of the first degree" of the order that boasted a membership of forty thousand within Missouri. Sanderson deemed Cheeney's information "of a most important and conclusive character," further assessing, "Of the truthfulness of Cheeney there can be no question." Sanderson, as some historians have concluded, was an especially eager and ambitious conspiracy theorist. Although the Order of American Knights may not have presented a serious threat, the Republican press used the fears generated from Sanderson's report to help solidify support for Lincoln's reelection later in the year.[44]

As a northerner with southern sympathies, Cheeney's outward political views conform to the reputed mission adopted by the Order of American Knights. In Jefferson City, he had aligned himself with the proslavery Democratic Ultras, and in Richmond, he led efforts to develop new technologies for the Confederate navy. In his interview with Sanderson, Cheeney admitted that "he believed the action of the Southern States in seceding was warrantable and just, but upon becoming thoroughly acquainted with their objects and motives saw the mistake made." He later hired St. Louis attorney John N. Straat to help resolve his case. According to his lawyer, Cheeney admitted to making "a great ass of himself in going South." Straat added, "I do not think he was ever a genuine rebel." Although these words reflect a prisoner's desire for release, the comments also show Cheeney's fluid loyalties. He may have sincerely believed in the southern cause, but he also used these sentiments to form close associations with idealists, whose avid dedication to their own crusades might have distracted them from his ulterior purposes.[45]

Cheeney spent nine months' incarceration in the Gatriot Street Prison. For much of that time, he remained in the hospital ward. Straat attempted to arrange for his trial, but U.S. authorities made no formal charges. In the meantime, the facility, formerly McDowell College, had achieved a reputation as being less than secure. A local newspaper described it as an "old rattle-trap" and lamented: "The title of *prison* is of questionable application to the edifice. A great many people are shoved in at the front door, who shove themselves out the back door." Tired of waiting for a legal resolution, Cheeney took advantage of these deficiencies. On October 6, 1864, he and two others escaped by scrambling up through a hole in the hospital ceiling. The local reports presumed that the fugitives would head for the Confederates at Jefferson City.[46]

A year later, the Civil War concluded, and Straat continued his efforts to resolve Cheeney's criminal charges. Writing to Joseph Holt, the U.S. judge advocate general, Straat explained that he took Cheeney's case pro bono "because of former acquaintance," because he believed in his client's sincerity and harmlessness, and because of Cheeney's financial straits. Straat wrote that Cheeney "is not a person of any political or social influence or consequence. He is simply a practical printer without money & without friends." He emphasized that his client was eager to accept Lincoln's amnesty and added that "if all the big rebels in the South are to be forgiven . . . , I can't see why a little rebel shouldn't be forgiven also." In his endorsement on the letter, however, Judge Holt identified the legal limbo that trapped Cheeney. His charges were civil, not military, so he was not eligible for the "executive clemency." Somehow unknown to them, on October 14, 1864, eight days after Cheeney had escaped, U.S. Assistant Adjutant General Edward D. Townsend issued special orders to release the prisoner "upon his taking the oath of allegiance."[47]

Apparently, U.S. authorities did not pursue the case or the fugitive. Cheeney returned to Jefferson City in November 1865 and sold his Maries County lead mining operation to a group of investors from western New York. For a time after, he relied upon his printing skills. In 1868, he moved his family to Cincinnati, working for the *Commercial,* and in 1870 to Indianapolis, employed by the *Journal.* Between 1872 and 1875, he resided in Memphis, where he operated his own printing shop and worked as a supervisor at another firm. In Memphis, his daughter Ida Belle married James H. Cole, a tinsmith, and gave birth to Cheeney's first grandchild. During this period, he seemed to have avoided incurring any debts that resulted in lawsuits, but he also failed to obtain the wealth or distinction he had pursued earlier in his life. He soon looked to Texas for one last chance.[48]

Texas Mineralogist

In June 1875, William G. Cheeney arrived in Austin with big plans. Months before, he had prospected the counties to the immediate west of the Texas state capital and offered an optimistic report about the potential mineral wealth there. The *Austin Evening News* happily spread the word for the newly styled mineralogist and assayer: "There is in our city at the present time a gentleman, Mr. W. G. Cheeney, who for some years before coming to this State, was engaged in the business of lead and coal mining and has a definite and practiced knowledge of the work from actual personal experience." Cheeney focused his efforts on Llano County, but he faced the same problems that hindered his earlier ventures. He had little of his own capital, and he needed investors. The writer for the *Evening News* remarked, "We trust that some of our practical business men will turn their attention to the subject of mining and we know that if they will but place themselves in communication with Mr. Cheeney he will cheerfully furnish them with much practical information upon the subject." The suggestion that Cheeney called for investors mirrored similar tactics that he had employed in Le Roy, Jefferson City, and Richmond. That is, he relied on a measure of charisma and selective use of his personal history to convince others that he was an expert whose authority presented potential investors and business partners opportunities for grand enterprise.[49]

In generating interest in his Texas ventures, Cheeney adapted strategies that he had used in Missouri, but he also relied upon financing techniques established during mining booms decades earlier. In examining the Colorado mining industry of the 1850s, historian Joseph E. King demonstrates the crucial role of the promoter who coupled eastern capital with western enterprise. The prospectus, a key tool in the promoter's kit, became ubiquitous in mining districts, and a few cagey boosters also created "bureaus" to clothe their enterprises within the reassurance of disinterested agents of scientific objectivity. Fraud thrived in such environments and led to the emergence of professional engineers both to assess potential ore-bearing ground and to oversee increasingly sophisticated and expensive operations. Genuine expertise and experience proved scarce, but individuals with charisma and audacity could mask those deficiencies and pass themselves as engineers. When he arrived in Austin, Cheeney presented himself as promoter, bureau, and engineer.[50]

Cheeney had so convinced the Austin community of his expertise and of the ready opportunities for profit that the *Weekly Democratic Statesman* provided him with the extraordinary venue of the entire first page of its November 11, 1875, issue. The eight-column article entitled "Mineral Resources of Western Texas" functioned as his prospectus, in which he attempted to debunk previous geological surveys that found Llano County and vicinity wanting in exploitable resources. He cataloged his own findings and made his pitch to potential investors.[51]

"Mineral Resources" documented Cheeney's particular method of financing, if not scheming. "I hope to convince the business men and capitalists of Austin that they have a deep interest in the speedy development of the immense stores of mineral wealth almost at their doors," Cheeney opened. He thus set the bait, stoking personal greed and civic pride attainable with only modest risk. "In my candid opinion there is no other interest—no other enterprise—the development of which will so surely give prosperity and wealth to Austin, as well as to those who may have the courage and enterprise to embark a little of their money in the undertaking." He established the reasonableness of his venture by acknowledging that previous accounts of tremendous mineral riches were exaggerated, but he promised that his personal observations—filled with impressive technical jargon—confirmed the potential for profits. He solidified his credentials as an expert by citing numerous books on geology and history. Cheeney further positioned himself as the sober scientist and engineer in contrast to the wild-eyed promoter by reassuring his readers that he was not looking for outrageous $250,000 investments for massive operations: "I want nothing to do with any mines of that character. . . . The experienced miner will go to work in the most economical manner. He will not put up expensive machinery and furnaces until he has found mineral and placed a sufficient quantity of it above ground to fully warrant the further necessary expenditures." Instead, Cheeney advocated smaller mines with a $1,000 investment for each, and he inserted the final stipulation that would preserve him from charges of fraud. He reminded his audience that he could not guarantee success, adding, "there is, of course, some uncertainty attending initiatory explorations in any country."[52]

Cheeney managed to attract a modest number of investors. He set up an assayer's office—his "bureau," as King would call it—in Austin and established a base in Burnet. After selling a few shares or entering into agreements on percentages with local landowners, he opened a mine at Packsaddle Mountain, ostensibly digging for silver. In September 1876, Adam R. Johnson, former Confederate general and longtime resident of Burnet County, visited Cheeney's operation. The local newspaper reported that Johnson, who also had interests in mining, was "much encouraged with the prospects of the Cheeney mines, and he thinks before many months Llano county will be the center of attraction on account of her mines." Such mineral wealth, however, did not exist in the region. By March 1879, Cheeney was quarrying soapstone for use in carving grave markers, but he would continue to work his Packsaddle Mountain outfit until his death.[53]

The venture that Cheeney outlined in his *Statesman* article was not illegal, and he apparently incurred no civil suits from spurned creditors in Texas, but before his death, he would abet one last act of malfeasance that would devastate his daughter's family. His son-in-law, James H. Cole, operated a dry goods store in Florence, Texas. In September 1883, Cole acquired on credit an inventory of stoves and equipment from Wilson and Austin, a firm in nearby Belton. Cole claimed that he passed the notes along to Cheeney, who likely had instigated the scheme. When Cole and Cheeney failed to pay or return the goods, Wilson and Austin filed a complaint. Cole attempted to flee to Mexico, but Texas authorities apprehended him in Laredo and returned him to Belton, where the courts convicted him of embezzlement and sentenced him to three years in prison. In August 1884, en route to the Huntsville penitentiary, Cole escaped, and his family never heard from him again.[54]

Conclusion

On February 19, 1891, Cheeney died in Burnet, Texas. The *Austin American Statesman,* which helped launch his mining ventures in Texas, confirmed that he passed having never settled the disquiet that persistently bedeviled him: "He was a scientific mineralogist, and though he opened mines that may some day prove valuable, he was called from his labors before he had realized the fortune prospectors always have in anticipation." In 1905, after the *Le Roy Gazette* published a story commemorating the devastating fire of 1855, several of his former friends recalled Bill Grummon fondly as intelligent and charismatic and wistfully regretted the personal afflictions that led him to steal and cheat his neighbors. "It seemed, indeed, a great pity that natural endowments such as Grummond certainly possessed," M. S. Elmore recalled, "had not been directed in channels to have distinguished him in a different order of achievements." The nostalgia that germinated after fifty years softened the memories that former classmates recalled about Grummon. For them, he entered the realm of the literary confidence man that occupied a contradictory space between culprit and antihero.[55]

Historians would not have noticed Cheeney if he had not inserted himself into the Confederate navy's effort to develop submarines on the James River, and even then, those scholars were more interested in the phantom machine than the elusive man. He did not enjoy a successful business or criminal career. He lived most of his life under false identities, but wherever he went, Cheeney made quick friends and trusting associates, and they would remember him— some fondly, some bitterly. Although the record does not reveal what emotional or cultural forces motivated Cheeney, perhaps the question calls for a simple answer. He desired wealth but did not have any of his own. When his "natural endowments" and his personal labor could not secure it, Cheeney took advantage of the vulnerable credit system of the early nineteenth century and the turmoil of Civil War to appropriate it illegally from others.

Although the record on William G. Cheeney, formerly William C. Grummon, remains incomplete, it shows a consistent pattern of scheming and at times fraud. It shows a pattern of a nineteenth-century man dissatisfied with his place in a disorienting world—a pattern of an ambitious man with no capital of his own convincing others to part with theirs. In an economic environment that relied on personal lending, Cheeney possessed charm and intelligence—evident since his school days—that could beguile newfound business partners. He obtained their confidence with his self-educated expertise and with visions of grand enterprise. At a time of intense partisanship, he exploited the tribalism forged between members blinded by an avid cause, and took advantage of the disruptions of war that made it easier for him to move to new locales and escape his histories of financial irregularities.

Notes

1. Allan Pinkerton, *The Spy of the Rebellion* (New York: G. W. Carleton & Co., 1883), 394–403. The author is a direct descendent of William G. Cheeney. He thanks family historians Gloria Clark and Paige Walk, who first confirmed Cheeney as William C. Grummon and who generously shared their own research.

2. Milton F. Perry, *Infernal Machines: The Story of Confederate Submarine and Mine Warfare* (Baton Rouge: Louisiana State University Press, 1965), 92–94; Tom Chaffin, *The H. L. Hunley: The Secret Hope of the Confederacy* (New York: Hill and Wang, 2008), 60–63; John M. Coski, *Capital Navy: The Men, Ships, and Operations of the James River Squadron* (Campbell, Calif.: Savas, 1996), 117–20, 137; Mark K. Ragan, *Submarine Warfare in the Civil War* (1999; repr., Boston: De Capo, 2002), 18–19. See also Raimondo Luraghi, *A History of the Confederate Navy*, trans. Paolo E. Coletta (Annapolis, Md.: Naval Institute Press, 1996), 252; Robert P. Broadwater, *Civil War Special Forces: The Elite and Distinct Fighting Units of the Union and Confederate Armies* (Santa Barbara, Calif: Praeger, 2014), 182–83.

3. Coski, *Capital Navy*, 120–21.

4. Edward J. Balleisen, *Navigating Failure: Bankruptcy and Commercial Society in Antebellum America* (Chapel Hill: University of North Carolina Press, 2001), 2, 14–16; Scott A. Sandage, *Born Losers: A History of Failure in America* (Cambridge, Mass.: Harvard University Press, 2005), 72–98.

5. Balleisen, *Navigating Failure*, 2, 17, 26–41; Sandage, *Born Losers*, 75–79; Lyn Lofland, *A World of Strangers: Order and Action in Urban Public Space* (New York: Basic, 1973); Jane Kamensky, *The Exchange Artist: A Tale of High-Flying Speculation and America's First Banking Collapse* (New York: Viking, 2008), 32–34; Ian Klaus, *Forging Capitalism: Rogues, Swindlers, Frauds, and the Rise of Modern Finance* (New Haven, Conn.: Yale University Press, 2014), 110–28. See also Mary O'Sullivan, "A Fine Failure: Relationship Lending, Moses Taylor, and the Joliet Iron & Steel Company, 1869–1888," *Business History Review* 88 (Winter 2014): 650–51, 676; and Matt Seybold, "Destroyer of Confidence: James Gordon Bennett, Jacksonian Paranoia, and the Original Confidence Man," *American Studies* 56 (June 2018): 97. Stephen Mihm and Sharon Ann Murphy focus on the vulnerabilities of institutional lending (Mihm, *A Nation of Counterfeiters: Capitalists, Con Men, and the Making of the United States* [Cambridge, Mass.: Harvard University Press, 2007]; Murphy, *Other People's Money: How Banking Works in the Early American Republic* [Baltimore: Johns Hopkins Uni-

versity Press, 2017]). For criminality from a microhistorical view of the urban poor, see Timothy J. Gilfoyle, *A Pickpocket's Tale: The Underworld of Nineteenth-Century New York* (New York: Norton, 2006).

6. James Gordon Bennett may have coined the term "confidence man" in 1849 during the *New York Herald's* coverage of swindler William Thompson. For the literary confidence man, see Warwick Wadlington, *The Confidence Game in American Literature* (Princeton, N.J.: Princeton University Press, 1975); Gary Lindberg, *The Confidence Man in American Literature* (New York: Oxford University Press, 1982); William E. Lenz, *Fast Talk & Flush Times: The Confidence Man as a Literary Convention* (Columbia: University of Missouri Press, 1985); Johannes Dietrich Bergmann, "The Original Confidence Man," *American Quarterly* 21 (Autumn 1969): 560–77; and Seybold, "Destroyer of Confidence," 84–97. Karen Halttunen, *Confidence Men and Painted Women: A Study of Middle-Class Culture in America, 1830–1870* (New Haven, Conn.: Yale University Press, 1982), focuses on advice manuals. For P. T. Barnum as confidence man archetype, see Wadlington, *Confidence Game*, 12; Lindberg, *Confidence Man*, 6–12; Lenz, *Fast Talk*, 23–28; Halttunen, *Confidence Men and Painted Women*, 30; Balleisen, *Navigating Failure*, 183–84; and Sandage, *Born Losers*, 75–76.

7. For Andrew Dexter, see Kamensky, *The Exchange Artist*. For George Appo, see Gilfoyle, *A Pickpocket's Tale*.

8. The *Burnet Bulletin*, reprinted in *Dallas Morning News*, March 6, 1891; M. S. Elmore, including "Early Le Roy Burglaries" and "The Cooper Street School," *Le Roy (N.Y.) Gazette* (hereinafter cited as *LRG*), March 1, 1905, and December 5, 1906; E. P. Halbert, "Dr. E. P. Halbert Notes down a Few of His Recollections of School Days," *LRG*, December 26, 1906. See also "Historic Spot Changes Hands," *LRG*, July 24, 1906. The 1850 census listed Ebenezer Grummon as a fifty-six-year-old laborer with no real estate (Manuscript Census Returns, Seventh Census of the United States, 1850, Genesee County, New York, Schedule 1, Free Population, National Archives Microfilm Series [NAMS] M-432, roll 507, p. 82).

9. Elmore, "Early Le Roy Burglaries"; B. L. Carlton, "A Former Le Royan Recalls the Fire of Fifty Years Ago and Incidents Connected with It," *LRG*, March 15, 1905; S. N. D. North, *The Newspaper and Periodical Press* (Washington, D.C.: Census Office, Department of the Interior, 1884), 393.

10. For the impact of the market revolution on western New York, see Paul E. Johnson, *A Shopkeeper's Millennium: Society and Revivals in Rochester, New York, 1815–1837* (New York: Hill and Wang, 1978); Mary P. Ryan, *Cradle of the Middle Class: The Family in Oneida County, New York, 1790–1865* (New York: Cambridge University Press, 1981); Charles E. Brooks, *Frontier Settlement and Market Revolution: The Holland Land Purchase* (Ithaca, N.Y.: Cornell University Press, 1996); Carol Sheriff, *The Artificial River: The Erie Canal and the Paradox of Progress, 1817–1862* (New York: Hill and Wang, 1996); and Thomas Rasmussen, *Ox Cart to Automobile: Social Change in Western New York* (New York: University Press of America, 2009).

11. *LRG*, reprinted in *Rochester Republican*, January 11, 1848; Elmore, "Early Le Roy Burglaries"; *Troy Whig*, reprinted in *Buffalo Daily Courier*, January 11, 1848.

12. *LRG*, reprinted in *Rochester Republican;* Elmore, "Early Le Roy Burglaries"; "Burglary," and "Stolen Goods Found," *LRG*, December 22 and 29, 1847.

13. The *Le Roy Gazette* originally published an account of Grummon's history of theft, probably in a January 5, 1848, number that has not survived. Several newspapers in the area reprinted the *Gazette*'s article. See *Buffalo Daily Courier*, January 11, 1848; *Rochester Republican*, January 11, 1848; *New York Commercial Advertiser*, January 13, 1848; *Springville (N.Y.) Express*, January 22, 1848; *Utica Daily Gazette*, January 13, 1848.

14. *Troy Whig*, reprinted in *Buffalo Daily Courier*; "Burglary," *LRG*; Elmore, "Early Le Roy Burglaries."

15. Elmore, "Early Le Roy Burglaries"; Carlton, "A Former Le Royan"; Halbert, "His Recollections"; "Sentence of Wm. C. Grummond," *LRG*, January 26, 1848.

16. "Proceedings," "Freedom of Territories," and "Anti-Nebraska Meeting," *LRG*, March 23, 1853, April 19, and July 19, 1854; Carlton, "A Former Le Royan"; William C. and Ruby Grummon mortgage, February 9, 1854, Genesee County, New York, Mortgages, 43:17; "Genesee Weekly Herald," *Bath (N.Y.) Advocate*, March 29, 1854; Halbert, "More about the Big Fire," *LRG*, February 1, 1905; "Meeting of the Western New York Editor's Association" and "American Celebration," *Spirit of the Times* (Batavia, N.Y.), June 23 and December 8, 1855; marriage notice, *LRG*, December 27, 1854.

17. Halbert, "Big Fire"; "Destructive Fire in Le Roy," *LRG*, January 17, 1855. See also Elmore, "The Fire of Fifty-Five," *LRG*, January 25, 1905.

18. "Destructive Fire in Le Roy," *LRG*; Halbert, "Big Fire"; Carlton, "A Former Le Royan." On the fiftieth anniversary of the fire, the *Le Roy Gazette* ran a story reflecting on it, which noted that out of the destruction came rebirth. After the wooden structures burned, Le Roy businesses replaced them with three-story brick buildings. The publication also inspired M. S. Elmore, Elliott Halbert, and Baxter Carlton to submit their recollections of the fire and of William C. Grummon. "Le Roy's Big Fire," *LRG*, January 18, 1905

19. See Genesee County, New York, Mortgages, 43:17, 345; Genesee County, New York, Deeds, 91:294–95, 95:198, 102:60–61; undated clipping, *Batavia Republican*, ca. 1856; *Buffalo Commercial*, April 14, 1858; W. G. Cheeney to C. F. Jackson, September 24, 1857, John S. Sappington Papers, State Historical Society of Missouri, Columbia. "Cheeney" may have been William C. Grummon's middle name or his mother's maiden name, but family historians have not confirmed Rebecca Grummon's origins.

20. Cheeney to Jackson, September 24, 1857, Sappington Papers. His attorney later noted that Cheeney was "politically identified with the Claib Jackson party" (Jno. N. Straat to Joseph Holt, St. Louis, October 5, 1865, Letters Received by the Adjutant General, 1861–1870, NAMS M-619, file M2056, roll 385, n.p.). Christopher Phillips, *Missouri's Confederate: Claiborne Fox Jackson and the Creation of Southern Identity in the Border West* (Columbia: University of Missouri Press, 2000), 217n6, 219–24.

21. Cheeney to Jackson, September 24, 1857, Sappington Papers; *Weekly California News* (Moniteau, Mo.), November 20, 1858; *Daily Missouri Republican* (St. Louis), November 28, 1858; *Glasgow (Mo.) Weekly Times*, May 19, 1859. Cheeney sold the *Missouri Educator* in December 1860. *Rolla (Mo.) Express*, December 17, 1860.

22. *Randolph Citizen* (Huntsville, Mo.), June 17, 1859; *Glasgow Weekly Times*, June 16, 1859.

23. Joseph E. King, *A Mine to Make a Mine: Financing the Colorado Mining Industry, 1859–1902* (College Station: Texas A&M University Press, 1977), 14–20, 27–28, 39–55; Jeremy Mouat, "Looking for Mr. Wright: A Tale of Mining Finance from the Late Nineteenth Century," *Mining History Journal* 10 (2003): 7–8, 14; Sarah E. M. Grossman, "Mining Engineers and Fraud: The U.S.-Mexico Borderlands, 1860–1910," *Technology and Culture* 55 (October 2014): 821–49.

24. *Examiner*, reprinted in *Weekly California News*, October 8, 1859; *Missouri State Times* (Jefferson City), November 17, 1865; William G. Cheeney deposition, ca. June 1864, *War of the Rebellion: A Compilation of the Official Records of the Union and Confederate Armies*, ser. 2, vol. 7 (Washington, D.C.: U.S. Government Printing Office, 1899), 343; Manuscript Census Returns, Eighth Census of the United States, 1860, Jefferson City, Cole County, Missouri, Schedule 1, Free Population, NAMS M-653, roll 615, p. 355.

25. *Journal of the House of Representatives of the State of Missouri at the First Session of the Twenty-first General Assembly* (Jefferson City: W. G. Cheeney, 1861), 105, 108; *Journal of the Senate of Missouri at the First Session of the Twenty-First General Assembly* (Jefferson City: W. G. Cheeney, 1861), 106–7; *Missouri Daily Republican* (St. Louis), January 24, 1861. The *Inquirer* reported that Corwin resigned the post of public printer in 1859 "to save exposure for over-charging the State." *Glasgow Weekly Times*, May 26, 1859.

26. Claiborne F. Jackson, inaugural speech, January 3, 1861, *Journal of the Senate of Missouri* (1861), 50; *Missouri Daily Republican* (St. Louis), January 25, 1861; *Journal of the House* (1861), 441, 559, 563–64; Phillips, *Missouri's Confederate*, 232–37; Ezra J. Warner and W. Buck Yearns, *Biographical Register of the Confederate Congress* (Baton Rouge: Louisiana State University Press, 1975), 90–91, 109–10. As public printer, Cheeney also published a separate pamphlet of Jackson's speech: *Inaugural Address of Governor C. F. Jackson, to the General Assembly of the State of Missouri. January 3, 1861* (Jefferson City: W. G. Cheeney, 1861). See also Dennis K. Boman, *Lincoln and Citizens' Rights in Civil War Missouri: Balancing Freedom and Security* (Baton Rouge: Louisiana State University Press, 2011), 21; and Gary R. Kremer, "'We Are Living in Very Stirring Times': The Civil War in Jefferson City, Missouri," *Missouri Historical Review* 106 (January 2012): 61–74.

27. *Journal of the House* (1861), 559, 563–64; *Journal and Proceedings of the Missouri State Convention, Held at Jefferson City and St. Louis, March 1861* (St. Louis: George Knapp & Co., 1861), 9–10, 18; Phillips, *Missouri's Confederate*, 237–40; William E. Parrish, *A History of Missouri*, vol. 3, *1860–1875* (1973; repr., Columbia: University of Missouri Press, 2001), 1–10; Ralph Gregory, "Joseph P. Ament—Master-Printer to Sam Clemens," *Mark Twain Journal* 18 (1976): 1–2.

28. Cheeney deposition, 343; Correspondence of the *Missouri Democrat*, Jefferson City, September 22, 1861, *Philadelphia Inquirer*, September 26, 1861; Phillips, *Missouri's Confederate*, 245–55; Parrish, *History of Missouri*, 6–16; Boman, *Lincoln and Citizens' Rights*, 22–23.

29. See Balleisen, *Navigating Failure*, 17, 26–32; O'Sullivan, "Fine Failure," 650–51, 676; and Murphy, *Other People's Money*, 40–42.

30. *Columbia (Mo.) Statesman*, May 17, 1861; Richard A. Wells v. Cheeney (case no. 2509), Henry B. Graham v. Cheeney (case no. 2460), and E. F. Dietz and John Walde v. Cheeney (case no. 2476), Cole County Circuit Court Cases, Missouri State Archives, Jefferson City; *Weekly California News*, July 18, 1863.

31. Dietz and Walde v. Cheeney; Jacob Colvin deposition, June 9, 1863, in Wells v. Cheeney; Balleisen, *Navigating Failure*, 25–48.

32. Wells v. Cheeney, Graham v. Cheeney, Dietz and Walde v. Cheeney, Edmond H. Linsenbard v. Cheeney (case no. 2459), and Jacob Colvin v. Cheeney (case no. 2673), Cole County Circuit Court Cases; *Weekly California News*, July 18, 1863; Cheeney deposition, 343. By one measure, $5340.18 in 1861 is equivalent to about $162,000 in 2020 (MeasuringWorth.com).

33. Cheeney deposition, 343. Coski states that Cheeney was a former officer in the U.S. Navy. Although that claim is consistent with Cheeney's tactics, Coski does not specify from where he obtained that information (Coski, *Capital Navy*, 117).

34. Argus to *Mercury*, Richmond, June 21, 1861, *Charleston Mercury*, June 24, 1861; John M. Brooke journal, in *Ironclads and Big Guns of the Confederacy: The Journal and Letters of John M. Brooke*, ed. George M. Brooke, Jr. (Columbia: University of South Carolina Press, 2002), 30; Confederate Navy Subject File, N Personnel, NAMS M-1091, USNA, roll 16, p. 133; Note confirming George C. Stedman's employment with Cheeney, E. M. Tidball, Richmond, March 18, 1892, in Kurt F. Leidecker, "Amid the Strife: Further Correspondence of George Clinton Stedman," *Register of the Kentucky Historical Society* 51 (July 1953): 207; Perry, *Infernal Machines*, 5–6; Ragan, *Submarine Warfare*, 18–20, 278.

35. Pinkerton, *Spy of the Rebellion*, 395, 401; L. M. Goldsborough to Secretary of the Navy, Hampton Roads, Va., October 17, 1861, *Official Records of the Union and Confederate Navies in the War of the Rebellion*, ser. 1, vol. 6 (Washington, D.C.: U.S. Government Printing Office, 1896), 334; *New York Herald*, December 23, 1861. Ragan provides the best documentation on Cheeney's project (Ragan, *Submarine Warfare*, 18–26, 61–67). See also Perry, *Infernal Machines*, 92–94; Coski, *Capital Navy*, 117–118; and Luraghi, *Confederate Navy*, 252.

36. Pinkerton, *Spy of the Rebellion*, 403; *New York Herald*, December 23, 1861. The *Herald* interviewed the deserter and published his account, widely circulated in the U.S. press. Reprinting the *Herald* story, *Harper's* included an engraving of an artist's concept of the supposed submarine (*New York Herald*, October 15, 1861; "A Rebel Infernal Machine," *Harper's Weekly* 5 [November 2, 1861], 701). Another report suggested that the attempt on the *Minnesota* damaged the apparatus and that the Confederates abandoned it on a nearby beach (*New York Times*, October 25, 1861). Ragan emphasizes the countermeasures against submarines that Captain William Smith developed as well as his reference to the *Minnesota* incident as further evidence of Cheeney's success. Smith, however, likely received the information about the attack from Goldsborough rather than from personal observation (Ragan, *Submarine Warfare*, 34–33; see also Coski, *Capital Navy*, 118–20).

37. Confederate Navy Subject File, B Ordinance, Roll 12; receipts reproduced in Ragan, *Submarine Warfare*, 24, 34, 62.

38. Brooke journal, in Brooke, *Ironclads and Big Guns*, 54, 66; Ragan, *Submarine Warfare*, 36–37.

39. Cheeney to Brooke, Norfolk, Va., March 12 and May 2, 1862, in Brooke, *Ironclads and Big Guns*, 78, 89–90.

40. Argus to *Mercury*, *Charleston Mercury*, June 24, 1861.

41. M. F. Maury to Sir, Richmond, Va., June 19, 1862, *Official Records . . . Navies*, ser. 1, vol.

7, 544–46; Cheeney's recollection in *St. Louis Republican*, reprinted in *Minneapolis Star Tribune*, July 5, 1885; Cheeney to Brooke, May 2, 1862, in Brooke, *Ironclads and Big Guns*, 237–38; Maurice Melton, *The Confederate Ironclads* (New York: Thomas Yoseloff, 1968), 30–51; Coski, *Capital Navy*, 122; Ragan, *Submarine Warfare*, 66; Luraghi, *Confederate Navy*, 94–96, 137–45.

42. Cheeney deposition, 343; Robt. Nugent to [John] Schofield, New York City, November 25, 1863, Union Provost Marshals' File of Papers Relating to Two or More Civilians, NAMS M-416, roll 14, n.p. In October 1862, a Rochester newspaper reported "Wm. C. Grummon brought in for drunkenness" (*Rochester Evening Express*, October 11, 1862).

43. Cheeney deposition, 343; *Cape Girardeau (Mo.) Weekly Argus*, January 7, 1864.

44. Cheeney deposition, 343; J. P. Sanderson to W.S. Rosecrans, St. Louis, June 22, 1864, *War of the Rebellion*, ser. 2, vol. 7, 316; Frank L. Klement, *Dark Lanterns: Secret Political Societies, Conspiracies, and Treason Trials in the Civil War* (Baton Rouge: Louisiana University Press, 1984), 64–90; Louis S. Gerteis, "'An Outrage on Humanity': Martial Law and Military Prisons in St. Louis during the Civil War," *Missouri Historical Review* 96 (July 2002): 302–22; Boman, *Lincoln and Citizens' Rights*, 252–55.

45. Cheeney deposition, 343. Straat also inaccurately claimed that Cheeney never served in the Confederate military (Straat to Holt, October 5, 1865).

46. Straat to Holt, October 5, 1865; *Daily Missouri Democrat* (St. Louis), October 7, 1864.

47. Straat to Holt, including Holt endorsement, October 5, 1865; E. D. Townsend, S.O. No. 347, October 14, 1864, and Straat to William T. Sherman, St. Louis, September 16, 1865, Union Provost Marshal's File of Papers Relating to Individual Civilians, NAMS M-345, roll 50, n.p. In April 1865, a report circulated that Cheeney rode with a group of "bushwhackers" and was killed near Big Gravois, although the *State Times* correctly predicted, "The statement that it was Cheeney may prove to be a mistake" (*Missouri State Times* [Jefferson City], April 29, 1865).

48. *Missouri State Times*, November 17, 1865; *Williams' Cincinnati Directory* (Cincinnati: Williams & Co., 1868), 126; *Hutchinson's Indianapolis City Directory* (Indianapolis: Sentinel Steam Printing Establishment, 1870), 46; *Swartz & Tedrowe's Indianapolis Directory, 1872–73* (Indianapolis: Indianapolis Sentinel Printers, 1872), 67; *Boyle & Chapman's Memphis City Directory*, vol. 1 (Memphis: Boyle & Chapman, 1872), 75; *Edwards Memphis Census Report and Improved Director* [sic], *1874* (n.p.), 147; *Memphis Daily Appeal*, December 4, 1872; Marriage and Birth Records, Shelby County, Tenn. At Memphis, Cheeney printed at least two books: *Digest of the Charters and Ordinances of the City of Memphis* (Memphis: W. G. Cheeney, 1873); and Joseph S. Williams, *Old Times in West Tennessee* (Memphis: W. G. Cheeney, 1873).

49. *Austin Evening News*, June 14, 1875.

50. King, *Mine to Make a Mine*, 14–17, 21, 27–28, 33–34, 39–55, 129–30; Mouat, "Looking for Mr. Wright," 7–8, 14; Grossman, "Mining Engineers and Fraud," 821–49.

51. Cheeney, "Mineral Resources of Western Texas," *Weekly Democratic Statesman* (Austin), November 11, 1875.

52. Cheeney, "Mineral Resources."

53. Advertisement for "W. G. Cheeney, Practical Mineralogist and Assayer"; *Weekly Democratic Statesman*, June 15, 1876; *Burnet (Tex.) Bulletin*, August 18, September 1, 1876, and March

12, 1879; *The Handbook of Texas,* https://tshaonline.org/handbook (accessed May 13, 2019). See also Ray Bachman, "More Light on the Lost San Saba Mine," *Burnet Bulletin,* March 29, 1923.

54. A. M. Jackson and A. M. Jackson, Jr., *Report of Cases Argued and Adjudged in the Court of Appeals of Texas during the Austin Term, 1884* (Austin: E. W. Swindells, 1885), 461–70; *Georgetown (Tex.) Sun,* May 8, 1884; Convict Record Ledgers, 1849–1954, 240, and Convict and Conduct Registers, Texas State Penitentiary, 730, Archives Division, Texas State Library, Austin.

55. *Austin Statesman,* February 24, 1891; *Galveston Daily News,* February 21, 1891; *Burnet Bulletin,* reprinted in *Dallas Morning News,* March 6, 1891; Elmore, "Early Le Roy Burglaries." For the confidence man as literary antihero, see Wadlington, *Confidence Game,* 9–15; Lenz, *Fast Talk,* 57–65; Seybold, "Confidence Man," 84–85; Bergman, "Original Confidence Man," 565, 570.

Das Kapital on Tchoupitoulas Street

THE MARKETING OF STOLEN GOODS AND THE RESERVE ARMY
OF LABOR IN RECONSTRUCTION-ERA NEW ORLEANS

BRUCE E. BAKER

In 1866, a year before Karl Marx published the first volume of *Das Kapital*, an unidentified member of the New Orleans lumpenproletariat (locally known as "levee rats") eased his skiff underneath the wharf near the foot of Gravier Street. Positioning himself directly under his target, he quietly bored through the planks of the wharf with an auger, through the bottom of a cask, and began removing the contents as the waterfront echoed with its typical midday melee. One, two, eventually all dozen hams were safely deposited in the boat and covered with a tarpaulin. As quietly as he had entered, his skiff drifted under the wharf, eventually emerging into the Mississippi and, with the loot, disappearing among the steamships, luggers, and general chaos.[1]

As the gratuitous mention of Marx might suggest, this essay seeks to understand the informal economy of stolen goods in New Orleans during the first years of Reconstruction as part of a larger economic system and, indeed, as a key underpinning of the reproduction of the labor force upon which the Louisiana port depended. The focus is less on the levee rat in the opening episode and more on the hams—what became of them? How was the market for stolen goods configured in New Orleans, and how did it sustain the laboring poor of the Crescent City? To fully understand the structure of the labor force that kept the vessels moving in and out of the port—the foundation of the city's formal economy—we must look beyond the formal economy. It was the underground economy as much as the formal economy, "the appropriation by the poor of the means of living," that made the very continuation of that labor force, and hence the formal economy its sweat and strain created, possible.[2] In fact, we might even question the usual distinction between a legitimate or formal economy and an informal or illegitimate economy. Rather, the entire economy of New Orleans existed on a spectrum of legality, none of it, like the muddy waters of the Mississippi, entirely clean.

❦

The liberation of New Orleans by Union forces in spring 1862 makes a fairly logical starting point for this study. While sources suggest that some of the activity of fences was just a continuation of antebellum practices, as were many aspects of the day-to-day work of the waterfront, the war had brought significant changes. The port's regular patterns of trade, and the business relationships that underpinned them, had been completely disrupted, and the restoration of trade, halting as it was, was a sort of reset. More significantly, the influx of freedpeople from the countryside set in motion a demographic change in the personnel of the waterfront, transitioning from a situation in which immigrant whites (mostly Irish and German) dominated the longshoreman jobs to one in which African Americans controlled a substantial share of the work.[3]

The financial chaos of the immediate postwar period, when artificially high cotton prices swiftly spiraled downward and the city was awash in refugees who could not support themselves, makes this an opportune moment to examine property crime. From 1866 to 1867, arrests for burglaries increased from 46 to 96, and for robberies from 155 to 316, suggesting either better detection and record keeping or a significant assault on the property of New Orleans residents, visitors, and businesses.[4] While one of the main items stolen was cash, this essay will not consider that aspect of theft since the focus is more on the circulation of goods and the various networks by which commodities were either exchanged or converted into cash. It is worth bearing in mind just how little material wealth most people had in this period, something which made the relative value of stolen goods greater but also made it harder to conceal them. As Susan Strasser points out, "Most people had little by today's standards until well into the twentieth century."[5] In an environment where the movement of goods in the waterfront economy provided many opportunities for theft, thieves needed actors and networks who could take what they had acquired and get it to someone who wanted it: a fence.

The main reason that thieves needed fences was the danger of getting caught with stolen goods. As an 1873 newspaper article summarized, "A thief cannot afford to keep stolen property, because if found in his possession it will convict, and because what he obtains for nothing he can dispose of for a mere nominal value, and the risk of detection is much lessened by its being in the hands of a third party."[6] One option was to find a place to store the stolen goods temporarily. A coffee-shop owner allowed thieves to use a house with a courtyard on the corner of St. Peter and Levee to store goods stolen from the steamship landing before they were shifted elsewhere, but this was probably unusual.[7] Sometimes thieves would carry "stolen goods to the lower part of the city, to groceries which had no neighborhoods or customers to keep them in existence" or take them over the river to a hideout in Algiers, where the delay involved in getting a warrant would give them time to move the goods again.[8] The danger here, though, was that these havens could always be raided by police, and they also created another layer of accomplices, increasing the thieves' vulnerability. Better was to rapidly convert the stolen goods into something the thief actually needed, such as cash.

In many cases, thieves could dispose of stolen goods themselves, without recourse to a fence. Probably much of this activity took the form of an informal barter system, where the thief who had stolen something he did not need swapped it to someone for what he did need. Such barter left only scattered and sidelong evidence in the documentary record. A newspaper article was probably not exaggerating when it gave one such example, describing Elephant Johnny's barrelhouse as "the cheapest lodging house in town, where one can get a roosting place and a drink for five cents, or in the absence of five cents an old shoe, or antiquated hat."[9] The newspapers of the period were full of notices of the arrest of individuals who were in possession of stolen goods with no mention of theft or of selling the goods, suggesting that they may have acquired the stolen goods for use through barter or purchase. Sometimes stolen goods could serve as wages for labor. When Billy McDonnell had the contract "to clean the stalls at Poydras Market," he "employed two colored men, whom he paid in stolen meat."[10]

Some things that were stolen could be used or consumed immediately by the thief or his household. This was especially the case for food items. The waterfront provided many opportunities for cashless self-provisioning. Sugar was frequently stolen, usually in small quantities that may have been consumed directly.[11] People often deliberately knocked over sacks of corn in order to spill and steal a few handfuls. Sacks of coffee were equally vulnerable.[12] Hams, smoked or salted and shipped in barrels, supplied more substantial fare.[13] Not one to pass up the finer things, Charles Clarke got a section of cane to use as a straw and followed the gaugers around as they sampled wine barrels in order to make sure the appropriate tax had been paid. Clarke double-checked the quality of each barrel until overcome by his efforts and arrested by the police.[14] Greater necessity inspired thefts of fuel. Stealing coal was fairly uncommon, but stolen firewood regularly warmed New Orleans residents during the winter months.[15]

The markets of New Orleans also provided a place where food could be pilfered. The woman who stole potatoes from Poydras Market in November 1860 almost certainly did so out of desperation, and the same could be said of the woman two years later arrested for stealing cabbage.[16] Drunken soldiers stole apples, but those who took fish, sausages, beef, and chickens probably did so to put food on the table at home.[17]

Other food was stolen for resale. In 1863, the regular supply of livestock from the countryside to the city's butchers had been disrupted by the fact that the city was now in Union hands, whereas much of the countryside remained in the control of the Confederates. Thieves began stealing cattle and selling them at a discount to butchers. The first case that seems to have come to public attention was in February, when three men from New Orleans hired a pair of African Americans to break down a plantation fence and drive a herd of cattle down to the city, where they were sold at half price to a couple of butchers.[18] In the summer, a more extensive scheme was uncovered. Two butchers stole cattle or bought stolen cattle from Plaquemines Parish, slaughtered them in the woods, then brought the meat into town in carts covered in tarpaulins and hay, selling it on to other butchers in various markets. Eventually, the hauling got to be too much trouble, so they hired a slave to drive the cattle at night to their slaughterhouses, but the business fell apart in late July 1863.[19] Later the same summer, other thieves followed suit, selling stolen livestock to butchers, who could easily and safely dispose of it.[20] Boardinghouse keepers who used large quantities of food seem to have been another reliable market.[21] In 1866, John McKnight made off with five barrels of pork, and stallholders in Poydras Market took five barrels of eggs in 1867. More ambitious thieves in 1869 forged a paper in order to steal five hundred dozen eggs from the levee after they had been unloaded.[22]

Some items were easier to resell than others because they were very difficult to trace and could be "sold to the end user of that item."[23] That could certainly be said of stolen meat (and, presumably, eggs), but it also applied to many other items. A businessman complained in 1866 of people repeatedly stealing his tarpaulins from the levee; these were probably covering other goods elsewhere within hours of being taken.[24] When a sailmaker was offered suspicious canvas for purchase, he had no easy way to determine if it was stolen, but he did ask the seller which wholesaler he represented.[25]

Probably the most widespread item stolen and easily resold was cotton. Picked up by the handful when it legitimately fell off the bale as a natural result of handling or purloined from the bales by passersby or samplers, considerable quantities of the staple were sold to junk shops, which in turn sold it to cotton pickeries that took apart, sorted, and rebaled damaged cotton, thus returning it to the mainstream of the trade.[26] In addition, in the nineteenth century, many people, especially craftsmen or small retailers, "could not avoid purchasing stolen property as part of their everyday business."[27] Many industrial and productive processes used postconsumer goods as inputs. As Susan Strasser puts it, "Materials cycled between households and factories, creating a *two-way* relationship between manufacturers and consumers."[28] Much of this material would have been subject to legitimate trade, but a portion must also have been stolen.

There was a substantial gray area in the fencing of stolen goods since some people who bought (and perhaps used or resold) stolen goods might not actually know they were stolen, or at least be able to make a plausible argument that they did not. As we see in the essays by John Lindbeck and Jimmy L. Bryan, Jr., in this volume, much hinged on self-presentation and the ability to give an account of oneself that others would believe. When someone stopped by to sell canvas to a sailmaker named Cassidy, the targeted buyer was immediately suspicious. Cassidy, who would presumably know all the merchants who regularly sold canvas, asked "what house [the canvas] came from." But the young man deflected the query, claiming "he had taken it for debt."[29] To allay suspicions, the seller asked for market price, rather than knocking the price down, which could be another sign the goods were stolen.[30] Still, it was often easy enough to avoid being charged with buying stolen goods. Someone caught with stolen goods could always say, "We purchased them from a peddler without knowing they were stolen."[31]

Certain kinds of businesses that could be run entirely honestly nonetheless had a reputation as fronts for fences. Not all fences were "low and mean, with a haggard, bleared look of bad whiskey, misery and crime"; many were "in general appearance equal to any one you will meet in our crowded thorough-fares."[32] Jewelers were particularly obvious in this regard. Much jewelry that came in to jeweler-fences was immediately broken down, gems removed, and sometimes shipped to New York or Europe, where they would fetch a better price, the gold or silver melted down for use in new items. Watches, in particular, were quickly taken to pieces, the workings set aside and sold, the case polished and reengraved to avoid detection.[33] In 1873, a New Orleans jeweler was arrested after a stolen piece of jewelry, "a golden eagle with a diamond in its breast," was recognized; the jeweler claimed to have made it himself, but it became clear he had only added a pin to it.[34] Fences might have long-standing relationships with particular thieves. This seems to have been the case when an African American thief named William Toney testified against three Italians who "always purchased his stolen wares, though at rates far more profitable to themselves than him."[35] Some fences of low-weight, high-value items such as jewelry appear to have been part of a regional network. Police finally caught up with George Ritter, one of the city's best-known jeweler-fences, in 1873 when they were tipped off that a watch stolen in Mobile had been sent to him.[36]

As historian Matt Neale observes of Bristol, England, "a vibrant realm of economic activity existed in which the shop was by no means the only location of trade, and in which second-hand goods could be traded as vigorously as new ones." This is demonstrated nowhere better than in the trade in secondhand clothing.[37] New Orleans seems to have had a number of secondhand clothing dealers. In the early 1870s, Antoine Girod had a shop at 101 Toulouse Street. P. Volney, a tailor, also dealt in secondhand clothing as well as offering cleaning, dying, and repairing services.[38] John Mullan sold used apparel at auction every Saturday and Monday, along with other items, though his emphasis was on clothing.[39] Then there were the other secondhand clothing dealers, the ones like Julius Mania, "who keeps a sort of second-hand clothing store or 'fence' on Crossman street." He was arrested in 1874 for selling clothing obtained from burglaries, including "a shawl belonging to the mother of one of the detectives."[40] Or Philip Roquet, whose secondhand clothing shop on Toulouse Street was busted for selling a stolen overcoat.[41] As in that case, when someone stole clothing from a prostitute and sold it to a shop on St. Philip Street, or when a waiter sold clothing he had stolen to a shop at Burgundy and St. Louis, there is no way to know whether the dealers realized the goods they purchased for resale were hot.[42]

Perhaps the most significant outlets for marketing general stolen goods in New Orleans were the junk shops that clustered "on the streets near the river and basins."[43] Some junk dealers went right to the river's edge or onto the river itself to purchase things. One, it was said, "habitually makes all kinds of purchases on the levee," and "thieves who operate on the river, are nearly always provided with licenses to buy 'junk,' and . . . that has been decided to include cotton in sacks and bags, or almost anything else which they can pick up on board of a ship."[44] Some dealers went right to the source, operating "junk boats" on the river.[45] Along with lots of cotton, junk shops bought a bit of everything, even, in one case, a dozen stolen Bibles.[46] One of the key things junk shops bought was metal of various kinds. From brass pipe pilfered from the levee, to brass fittings for gas lamps, to several thousand dollars' worth of lead and copper pipe taken from a candle factory, it all wound up in junk shops, and from there probably was sent on to metal brokers in northern cities.[47]

Police had a hard time dealing with the flow of stolen goods through the junk shops of New Orleans. On the face of it, they did have the powers they needed. The 1868 act that created the Metropolitan Police who patrolled the city gave them the power to exercise "general police supervision and inspection . . . over all licensed and unlicensed pawnbrokers, vendors, junk-shop keepers, junk boatmen, cart, cab and hackmen, dealers in second hand merchandise, cotton pickeries, intelligence office keepers and auctioneers" and to inspect the premises and books of any such enterprises.[48] Of course, many in New Orleans suspected such powers were limited because proprietors could afford to "pay the police for casting only a very lenient eye in their direction."[49] But even determined police found it difficult to gather solid evidence for a successful prosecution. Unless they got lucky tracing a particular theft, police often had to wait a long time to act on their suspicions about a junk shop that was operating as a fence.[50] Sometimes public health measures could be used to push junk shops out of business, but what eventually made a difference was changes to how cotton was handled in the mid-1870s, which limited the supply of loose cotton that kept many of the junk shops running.[51]

Pawnbrokers, who had a long-standing role in the economy of the poor, often dealt in stolen goods, whether they realized it or not.[52] Pickpockets took watches and other small valuables to the pawnshop and pledged them, getting a quarter or a third of the value, and then destroyed the pawn ticket, leaving no evidence of the crime but the money in their pockets. The pawnbrokers, on the other hand, "never inquire who the customers really are, where they live or how they came into possession of the article to be pledged."[53] Pawnbrokers in New Orleans seem to have been very difficult to catch fencing goods, judging from the coverage in the newspapers. Otto Schwaner, who was running a junk shop in 1864, was convicted of "buying stolen property knowing it to be stolen" but appealed on the grounds that it was not proven that he had guilty intent.[54] He dissolved his business in 1865 but around 1870 began working at the St. Charles Loan Office, a pawnshop on Baronne Street, and by 1875 he had made enough money to take a long trip to Europe.[55] (He might have made all the money honestly, of course.) The other pawnbroker who came to the attention of the police in this period was S. Jacobs, whose pawnshop was on the corner of St. Charles and Poydras.[56]

All cities, and many rural areas, would have had a network of individuals who disposed of stolen goods, with the assumption that greater populations would presumably increase the property available to steal, the number of potential thieves, and the number of people to buy the goods. Equally, the structure of this network would necessarily vary according to the availability of goods to steal and, crucially, the needs of potential buyers. Chicago, for example, presumably had little in the way of a system for fencing loose cotton.

For reasons related to the particular features of the Mississippi River, trade patterns, and its infrastructure, the port of New Orleans was highly reliant on casual labor for keeping goods moving in and out of the city, and the decade after the Civil War both exacerbated this need and, especially in the first few years, saw a dramatic increase in the labor force available for waterfront work. Unusually, New Orleans was a port that could service oceangoing ships, but it sat a hundred miles from the sea near the bottom of the continent's greatest river system. It was, as Harold Sinclair points out, very much a river town, connecting an extensive river traffic conducted via low-draft New Orleans packets, barges, and a few anachronistic flatboats with a domestic and international maritime trade carried on aboard a promiscuous mix of sail and steam vessels.[57] The river's course, and especially its edges, were ever-changing, and this, along with French-derived riverine rights, impeded the development of a modern port infrastructure. Instead, well past the time frame covered in this essay, much of the work on the New Orleans waterfront had not really changed technologically in centuries. It was black and white muscle that unloaded and loaded the vast commerce of the Crescent City. The problem of supplying and sustaining all that muscle required links with the underground economy of which the market in stolen goods was an important component.

Given the mix of an extensive river traffic and coastwise and oceangoing trading, shipping in New Orleans was more complexly structured and varied than might have been the case in many other ports. Steamboats, and later barges pulled by tugs, brought a wide variety of goods downriver to New Orleans for transshipment, most notably cotton and grain, but including nearly anything produced in the Mississippi River basin. These boats also served to carry imported goods upriver for distribution or reshipment to other destinations. An important distinction in shipping was whether vessels were engaged in the coastwise trade, in which case they were protected by legislation and required to have American-owned boats and American crews, or whether they were involved in foreign trade, in which case they would have to clear customs. A final distinction that was becoming increasingly important in the years following the Civil War was in the motive power—sail or steam.[58]

Labor on any waterfront was always divided into a number of disparate categories that varied according to how the waterfront was organized and controlled, the nature of the cargoes handled, and other factors, and New Orleans was no exception to this rule. At the top were the stevedores, who exercised more power in this "middle-man's city" than their equivalents in many ports. While dock companies in some ports owned and managed particular parts of the waterfront, making durable capital improvements, the New Orleans waterfront was managed by Eager, Ellerman & Co. but remained publicly owned.[59] Rather than a dock company dealing with shipmasters and ordering an employed stevedore to load or unload a certain vessel, in New Orleans the lack of central control and ownership meant that shipmasters dealt directly with stevedores to contract for unloading or loading. The stevedore then hired and paid his crew and was responsible for overseeing their labor and completing the task. It behooved stevedores to build enduring relationships with ship agents who might provide jobs for them and their crews, but it was also to the advantage of ship agents who needed to know they could get ships loaded and unloaded expeditiously when they needed. Of course, to keep these relationships functioning smoothly, a certain degree of lubrication was required.[60]

Next down the hierarchy, and specific to New Orleans and other cotton ports, were the screwmen, experts at using jackscrews and a hard-won understanding of practical physics to fit as many bales of cotton in the hold of a ship as possible. This was a highly skilled role, and it paid well. The screwmen were essential to maximizing the profit on any journey, since their expertise and precise knowledge of a ship's hold could free up space for more bales or other cargo. Repeated working with specific vessels only enhanced this quality, so continuity and stability of employment made a screwman even more valuable to the stevedores who hired him and the shipmasters or ship agents who contracted with the stevedore. As a result of this strong position, screwmen were the first branch of waterfront labor in New Orleans to organize, forming the Screwmen's Benevolent Association as early as 1850 to control entry and defend wages and privileges.[61] Screwmen and stevedores did not have steady employment as such, but they suffered the least from the casual structure of waterfront labor in New Orleans.

Longshoremen and the rest of the New Orleans waterfront labor force did suffer the effects of casualization. While this structure had always been present, the shift to steam exacerbated it. According to E. L. Taplin, "the spread of steamships intensified the casual nature of dock work" because "the capital investment in a steamship was far greater than in a sailing ship and hence the pressure to reduce the period of time a vessel was idle in port."[62] In New Orleans, longshoremen "received the cotton over the side of the steamboat from the screwmen" and "unloaded all sugar, molasses, and other shipments themselves."[63] While experience counted to ensure efficiency and safety, long-shoremen lacked the very specialized skills of screwmen, and their ability to get work depended on maintaining a relationship with a stevedore and remaining available for labor. Still, work was inconstant at best for longshoremen. An observer in 1873 explained that while longshoremen earned four dollars a day, they "seldom work more than four days in the week, often much less, and of course uncertainty and carelessness come in as a general drawback, and make him no better in pocket than the average man employed in general job-work about the city."[64] The distinction between a longshoreman waiting for a chance to be of use to a stevedore and thus earn a day's wages and a loafer cluttering up the wharves was a fine one not often made by more comfortably placed observers. Draymen and teamsters who hauled various kinds of goods to and from the riverfront were in similar positions in terms of the casual nature of their employment.

At the bottom of the waterfront hierarchy were the men who would later be known on the New York docks as "shenangoes." While that term seems to date from the years just before World War I, the sort of worker it described had a longer pedigree. Describing dockers in London, John Lovell explains: "Outside the class of regular port workers there existed a broad class of complete casuals. The services of this class were required by the industry to meet the very widest fluctuations in business, but it did not constitute part of the regular labour force. It was composed of two distinct elements. On the one hand were the unemployed from other trades, and on the other were the men demoralised by irregular work in the port or some other industry."[65] "Shenangoes" were often those who, "though partly wrecked by drink, can find odd jobs along the waterfront and still be classed as a longshoreman," those dock laborers who "continue to slip down the industrial scale until they" become "down-and-out longshoremen who finally become burdens on charity."[66] But even dissipated, broken-down men, the ones whom years of casual work and hard living had destroyed, had their uses in extremis. When a pair of horses fell off a Brooklyn pier in 1915, a quick-thinking employee "took in the situation, and calling a half-dozen 'shenangoes' to his aid," managed to rescue one of them.[67] In an emergency situation, such as a ship on fire, the shenangoes of New Orleans might be drafted into service.

Roustabouts, on the other hand, were a completely separate category. As Harold Sinclair points out, steamboat work on the river was very different from ocean sailing, and there was little or no crossover of the men involved in each.[68] Roustabouts were almost entirely African American rural workers, hired from the plantation hinterlands served by the steamboats, who did the hard work on the journey of loading and unloading cargo and wood.[69] When these men from the plantations reached New Orleans, they were perceived as particularly exotic, wild, and brutish.[70] One newspaper sketch described them as "rough— and dumb," wearing ragged clothes and doing nothing but the most dangerous and hardest work: "pulling, hauling, rolling, tumbling, heaving, launching."[71] Since roustabouts did not handle cargo in New Orleans, they were effectively loafers until they went back upriver.[72]

One of the main reasons that New Orleans had such a fluctuating need for waterfront labor was the poor state of its infrastructure. By the mid-nineteenth century, some of the more advanced ports had permanent docks set off from the main harbor or river and equipped with hard quays. This was the case for London, which had begun a program of expansion and improvement in the first years of the century, and it was already the case for Hull and Liverpool as well. These docks and accompanying infrastructure, such as warehouses, required investment, which tended to be under the control of a dock company that often hired the labor required at that dock. The capacity of such docks was stable, and depending on the winds, it was possible to make berthing of vessels reasonably predictable.[73]

Such stability was not possible for a port that sat alongside a river with the third-largest drainage basin in the world. The fundamental problem was that the Mississippi River moves, constantly eroding and reforming its shores. As it moves, it deposits silt on the inside of curves where the current slows, creating new land called the batture.[74] In the early nineteenth century, steamboats moored alongside Tchoupitoulas Street, but by the 1830s, the shoreline had moved, and eventually Tchoupitoulas was a couple of blocks way.[75] It was, after all, the river that had created the natural levee that was the reason for siting New Orleans where it was. The city's French legal heritage protected the public's right to access the riverbanks in a way unusual elsewhere in the United States.[76] From the origins of the city, that public space had been used for recreation but also for important commercial purposes, loading and unloading goods from vessels, buying and selling, all in a confused melee.[77] But aside from the legal status of the riverbank and the consequent chaos, the continuing problem with the infrastructure of the New Orleans waterfront was the river itself and the massive floods that came as the snow upstream melted and spring storms raised the many rivers that fed into the Mississippi. Each year at the end of the spring, the river would rise and wash away many of the wooden wharves that extended into the river from the levee. The work of the summer was to rebuild them to be ready for the beginning of cotton season in the autumn. A further consequence of this annual cycle was that the wharves were never maintained as well as they would have been had they been permanent. Collapses were common, putting sections of the waterfront out of commission.[78] The river itself made it impossible to have a regular demand for waterfront labor.

The demand for waterfront labor remained seasonal due to infrastructure but also because of the nature of the trade that dominated the port. As Eric Arnesen has noted, "For much of the nineteenth century through to the mid-twentieth century, commerce in the port of New Orleans remained highly seasonal, dependent upon the arrival and processing of agricultural staples, particularly cotton, and to a lesser extent, sugar."[79] The season for cotton generally began in earnest in late September and continued until March. This was just as well, with a substantial and varying portion of the wharves washing away or being made unusable with the spring floods. In response to this seasonal shift in labor demand, some men, mostly those who were young and unmarried and more footloose, left for summer work as far away as Canada. Others found temporary work in breweries.[80] However, neither of these possibilities is likely to have diminished substantially the overall pool of casual labor.

Another feature of the Mississippi River provided an even more significant obstacle to the creation of a regular shipping schedule and a steady demand for labor: the ever-shifting sandbar at the mouth of the river. As the tonnage of vessels increased steadily, "by 1830 the bar had become of such proportions that the newest, largest, and fastest ocean vessels, those which would naturally have carried the vast and valuable cargo of New Orleans, were actually unable to reach the city. New Orleans' ocean cargo was being carried in bottoms that were second and third class in capacity and speed."[81] In addition to giving rise to a long-standing tugboat cartel, the sandbar restricted the depth of the river to fifteen or maybe eighteen feet until 1875, when jetties finally removed the problem for good.[82] This was too shallow for the new class of steamships that were the backbone of the shipping lines that "adhered to set schedules and relied on speed in turn-around time in port."[83] New Orleans was mostly left to tramp shipping, in which vessels followed no set schedule or itinerary, until the 1890s.

The shipping business in New Orleans, including the cotton handling business, needed considerable numbers of laborers to keep it viable but did not need them all the time or on any predictable schedule. It was reluctant to—probably, to be fair, unable to—pay them enough when they did work to sustain them when they did not. What the shipping business wanted was precisely what Karl Marx described as a "disposable industrial reserve army" of labor, "a condition of existence of the capitalist mode of production."[84] The background for Marx's formulation was a world of factories and mines whose heavily capitalized equipment needed to be continually in use to maximize profits, and the availability and cost of labor was a factor limiting profit. An excess supply of labor drove down wages, leaving more profit. In a port city such as New Orleans, where the winds and sandbars made the regular scheduling of work a mere pipe dream, the main function of the reserve army of labor was less to drive down wages (though it probably had that effect to a small extent, limited by the specialized division of labor on the waterfront that meant that many workers were not very interchangeable) and more to guarantee that the maximum number of workers would be available on those occasions when they were needed, ensuring that no ship stood waiting at the levee for lack of men to unload and load cargo.

The New Orleans waterfront was a world filled with loafers and idlers.[85] Most recruitment happened through a complex system of middlemen rather than through the classic pattern of the twentieth century, in which a foreman chose men to work out of an assembled group of hopefuls each day. In this period, only screwmen, the elite of the waterfront, had a union that could allocate work to its members. The rest of the waterfront laborers maintained relationships with the men who might hire them, knowing to frequent certain coffee shops (taverns) where deals might be done. Whether they stuck with one employer or drifted around, men needed to be near the waterfront to get whatever work was available.[86] The impression of a chaotic waterfront full of loafers was also exacerbated by the fact that New Orleans had no enclosed dock yard as some other ports did. Anyone could and did come and go from the waterfront, making it feel more continuous with the rest of the city.

The necessity of having a waterfront stocked with men who alternated between long periods of back-breaking work and periods of waiting for work to become available exacerbated the problem of the reconfiguration of vagrancy by emancipation. Former slaves sought opportunity along the riverbank, but the first summer after the Civil War concluded, "Certain black persons around the wharves were sent away, after being advised to go work on the plantations, instead of waiting for chance jobs of an hour or two."[87] John K. Bardes has argued that efforts to police vagrancy in New Orleans "reflected elite social-control anxieties, all revolving around constantly evolving conceptions of people—predominantly, but not exclusively, freedpeople—whose incomplete market integration and perceived social deviance marked them as dangerous, unaffiliated, and uncontrollable."[88] This created great conflicts when it came to a labor system where much of the work was "seasonal, short-term, and un-contracted."[89] Longshoremen, especially African Americans, were increasingly vulnerable to being rounded up and charged with vagrancy, despite their protests that they were employed, as happened in a series of raids in July 1865.[90] If the city authorities wanted "constant employ from the laboring classes," then they were doomed to disappointment, since there was simply not the constant work to provide this, whatever the workers' desires. As Eric Arnesen has noted, seasonal unemployment continued to be a problem through the early twentieth century, and "the workingmen between seasons did anything they could to eke out a living."[91] What is being described here is what economic anthropologists such as Rhoda Halperin describe as "multiple livelihood strategies," where "people [are] performing many kinds of work tasks in a given day, week, season, and lifetime." They "participate in a mix of economic institutions" which, taken together, provide a livelihood.[92] It is something easier to describe through fieldwork than by examining historical sources, but while we cannot rebuild the sorts of elaborate pictures that anthropologists have provided for Latin America or Kentucky in the 1970s and 1980s, we have no reason not to think that workers on the margins in earlier times and places were not using similar strategies.[93]

The challenge was sustaining, or in Marxian terms "reproducing," this pool of casual labor for the waterfront.[94] To some extent, in the years after the Civil War, the ebb and flow of population into and out of the city helped regulate the labor supply. With the capture of New Orleans by Union forces in spring 1862 and the later collapse of slavery in 1865 and the subsequent reign of terror in the countryside, as many as thirty thousand African Americans streamed into the city.[95] When necessary, some of this excess labor was captured in the city or siphoned off back to the countryside. From January 1863, General Nathaniel P. Banks ran a system of rounding up African Americans in the city and sending them to plantations where labor was needed. The vagrancy laws in New Orleans were tightened, and many out-of-work men were employed, whether they wanted to be or not, on public works projects.[96]

Still, these drains on the casual labor pool did not really keep up with the increases, as the city's black population grew by thirty thousand and the white population by fourteen thousand between 1860 and 1880.[97] All these people had to survive somehow, and they had to do so in an economy disrupted by the damage the Civil War had done to the city's trade patterns and financial infrastructure.

In an economy with a shortage of money and uneven opportunities for steady work, but a concurrent need to sustain a reserve army of labor, the underground economy, including the market for stolen goods, became important to reproducing the labor force that New Orleans needed. Like the slave traders whom Alexandra J. Finley and Jeff Forret discuss in this volume, fences in New Orleans may have been distasteful and disreputable, but they were necessary to the economic system that kept their betters in luxury. Among the many economic effects the Civil War had on New Orleans, one of the most pressing was a serious decrease in the amount of money in circulation. During the war, New Orleans bankers had refrained from suspending specie payment, but they eventually shipped out most of their specie to the Confederate government in May 1862, losing it. By the end of the war, money was in extremely short supply in New Orleans, as it was across the entire South.[98] This lack of money had an effect on all the daily exchanges in the city, pushing prices higher, at least when goods were paid for in cash. The supply of stolen goods, however, had a number of effects that made it easier for the poor to sustain themselves. First, with the informal bartering system for stolen food and other consumables, the poor had a means of provisioning themselves that did not require cash and altogether sidestepped inflated cash prices. Second, if stolen goods were offered for sale, at least to those who did not mind that they were stolen, they could be sold at a discount on the normal price, which could tend to pull down market prices somewhat.[99] To some extent, a market in stolen goods could operate in parallel with the regular economy, but it could also interface with it in complex ways.

Considering the underground economy as a fundamental part of the structure that maintained the labor force necessary to carry on the business of the port efficiently, especially in a port where shipping and port facilities had not yet fully modernized, pushes us to reconsider the nature of port cities and life on the waterfront. Traditionally, there was a strongly held view that port cities had vibrant underground economies based on functions such as drinking, prostitution, and gambling because these were the services that sailors, long at sea and with money in their pockets, demanded when they came ashore. However, this view of a demand-driven underground economy in port cities has been challenged by more recent scholarship that rethinks the nature of the social lives of sailors ashore. Robert Lee argues that "Such a one-dimensional representation of the urban world of seafarers is problematic and misleading" and that "seafarers often remained embedded within family and kin networks and were not invariably a source of trouble in ports."[100] Perhaps instead of looking at port cities' underground economies as existing primarily to service seafarers, we should focus more on their role in provisioning the waterfront labor needed to handle the ships those sailors came in on.

For that matter, the relationship between the market for stolen goods in New Orleans and its casualized waterfront labor force might require us to rethink the distinction between formal and underground economies in general. As Kenneth Lipartito and Lisa Jacobson have recently argued, "no natural or present border exists between the formal, legal, or visible market and the spaces where the hidden, obscured, and illegal market activity occur." Rather than examining capitalism as simply the history of markets, we need a new "social history of capitalism [that] offers a way to think about how diverse actors— from capitalist elites and petty entrepreneurs to scavengers, home workers, and consumers of illicit goods—have created varied markets, generated new sources or profit, and cobbled together a living." Building on the insights of

Karl Polanyi about how markets were themselves embedded in cultures and institutions, and not easily, either, Lipartito and Jacobson call for the study of a "capitalist ecosystem" that sits within economies conceptualized not simply as markets but, as Dave Elder-Vass suggests, "collections of diverse appropriative practices . . . socially and normatively structured interactions among people that influence who gets what."[101] Capitalism, in a port city anyway, required crime to survive.

Notes

1. "River Police," *New Orleans Times-Democrat*, June 20, 1866, 6; "Levee Thieves under the Hams," *New Orleans Daily Picayune*, May 8, 1875, 8.

2. Peter Linebaugh, *The London Hanged: Crime and Civil Society in the Eighteenth Century*, 2nd ed. (London: Verso, 2003), xxiii.

3. Eric Arnesen, "Race and Labour in a Southern US Port: New Orleans, 1860–1930," in *Dock Workers: International Explorations in Comparative Labour History, 1790–1970*, vol. 1, ed. Sam Davies, Colin J. Davis, David de Vries, Lex Heerma van Voss, Lidewij Hesselink, and Klaus Weinhauer (Aldershot, U.K.: Ashgate, 2000), 41.

4. "Comparative Arrests by the Police in 1866 and 1867," *Daily Picayune*, April 4, 1868, 1.

5. Susan Strasser, *Waste and Want: A Social History of Trash* (New York: Metropolitan Books, 1999), 21–22.

6. "In the Byways: Fences," *Daily Picayune*, June 1, 1873, 6.

7. "The Robberies on the Steamship Landing," *New Orleans Times*, March 31, 1870, 10.

8. "Smaller Piracies and Other Depredations upon the River—How the Stolen Property Is Disposed Of," *New Orleans Crescent*, November 10, 1866, 1.

9. "John Cowen to the Front," *New Orleans Times*, January 30, 1874, 6.

10. "Stolen Beef to Pay Employees," *New Orleans Republican*, October 9, 1868, 3.

11. "Provost Court," *New Orleans Daily True Delta*, July 8, 1863, 4.

12. "Sugar," *Daily Picayune*, January 24, 1863, 1; "Where Are the River Police?," *Daily Picayune*, July 28, 1866, 1; "New Orleans Correspondent," *Louisiana Democrat* (Alexandria), April 11, 1866, 2; "River Intelligence," *Times-Democrat*, December 18, 1863, 4; "River Police," *Times-Democrat*, June 20, 1866, 6.

13. "Gone Down for Trial," *New Orleans Republican*, August 25, 1871, 5.

14. "Wine Bibber," *New Orleans Republican*, April 3, 1868, 3.

15. "Third District," *Daily Picayune*, December 11, 1866, 4; "Larceny," *Daily Picayune*, January 18, 1874, 6; "Second District Recorder's Court," *Daily True Delta*, January 22, 1864, 3; "Recorder Campbell's Court," *Daily Picayune*, December 2, 1865, 2; "Recorder Ahern's Court," *Daily Picayune*, January 8, 1867, 2.

16. "Recorder Emerson's Court," *New Orleans Crescent*, November 15, 1860, 1; "Stealing Cabbage," *New Orleans Daily Delta*, December 4, 1862, 1.

17. "Military Provost Court," *Daily True Delta*, September 8, 1863, 3; "Recorder Ahern's Court," *New Orleans Crescent*, April 4, 1866, 1; "Larcenies, Etc.," *Daily Picayune*, March 19, 1872, 2; "Provost Court," *Daily Picayune*, April 6, 1864, 2.

18. "Provost Court," *Daily Picayune*, February 15, 1863, 1.

19. "Provost Court," *Daily Picayune*, July 22, 1863, 2; "That Cow-Stealing Case," *Daily True Delta*, July 2, 1863, 3; "The Cow-Stealing Case," *Daily True Delta*, July 30, 1863, 3; "The Cattle Stealing Case," *Daily Picayune*, July 31, 1863, 2.

20. "Cow Stealing," *Daily True Delta*, August 8, 1863, 3.

21. "The Cow-Stealing Case," *Daily True Delta*, July 30, 1863, 3.

22. "Local Intelligence," *New Orleans Times*, May 13, 1866, 18; "Recorder Ahern's Court," *Daily Picayune*, January 31, 1867, 8; "Five Hundred Dozen Eggs Stolen," *New Orleans Crescent*, April 8, 1869, 3.

23. Matt Neale, "Making Crime Pay in Late Eighteenth-Century Bristol: Stolen Goods, the Informal Economy and the Negotiation of Risk," *Continuity and Change* 26, no. 3 (2011): 443.

24. "Fifty Dollars Reward," *Daily Picayune*, May 9, 1866, 7.

25. "To the Editors of The Picayune," *Daily Picayune*, October 10, 1868, 2 (quotations); "The Junk Shop Raid," *Daily Picayune*, October 9, 1868, 2.

26. For a fuller account, see Bruce E. Baker, "The Loose Cotton Economy of the New Orleans Waterfront in the Late Nineteenth Century," in *Capitalism's Hidden Worlds*, ed. Kenneth Lipartito and Lisa Jacobson (Philadelphia: University of Pennsylvania Press, 2019), 67–80.

27. Neale, "Making Crime Pay," 443.

28. Strasser, *Waste and Want*, 73, italics in original.

29. "To the Editors of The Picayune," *Daily Picayune*, October 10, 1868, 2 (quotations); "The Junk Shop Raid," *Daily Picayune*, October 9, 1868, 2.

30. Neale, "Making Crime Pay," 444.

31. "Stolen Property—The Way Burglars Dispose of Their Gains," *Daily Picayune*, November 20, 1870, 2.

32. "In the Byways: Fences," *Daily Picayune*, June 1, 1873, 6.

33. "In the Byways: Fences," *Daily Picayune*, June 1, 1873, 6; "Stolen Property—The Way Burglars Dispose of Their Gains," *Daily Picayune*, November 20, 1870, 2.

34. "A Fence," *Daily Picayune*, February 21, 1873, 2.

35. "Receivers of Stolen Goods," *Daily Picayune*, February 18, 1864, 4.

36. "A Well Known Fence Arrested at Last," *Daily Picayune*, February 27, 1873, 8.

37. Neale, "Making Crime Pay," 444.

38. "Fire on Toulouse Street," *New Orleans Republican*, December 8, 1872, 5; advertisement, *Daily Picayune*, June 13, 1871, 5.

39. Advertisement, *New Orleans Morning Star and Catholic Messenger*, January 18, 1874, 5.

40. "Raid on a 'Fence' Shop," *Daily Picayune*, February 6, 1874, 8.

41. "Who Does It Belong To?" *New Orleans Bulletin*, September 25, 1875, 8.

42. "Stolen Property Recovered," *New Orleans Times,* October 9, 1875, 6; "Valuables Sold at Advantageous Price," *Daily Picayune,* May 6, 1877, 10.

43. "In the Byways: Fences," *Daily Picayune,* June 1, 1873, 6 (quotation); "Stolen Property—The Way Burglars Dispose of Their Gains," *Daily Picayune,* November 20, 1870, 2.

44. "How Cotton Bales Are Stolen," *New Orleans Republican,* December 29, 1870, 5; "Smaller Piracies and Other Depredations upon the River—How the Stolen Property Is Disposed Of," *New Orleans Crescent,* November 10, 1866, 1.

45. "Capture of a Junk Boat," *New Orleans Times,* July 16, 1867, 2.

46. "First District Court," *New Orleans Times,* July 8, 1869, 2; "The Recent Burglaries," *New Orleans Times,* December 18, 1868, 2; "Tobacco," *New Orleans Republican,* January 30, 1872, 5.

47. "Brass Pipes," *New Orleans Republican,* September 23, 1871, 5; "Stolen Property," *Daily Picayune,* January 7, 1868, 8; "Examination on a Charge of Receiving Stolen Goods," *New Orleans Times,* March 17, 1864, 5.

48. "Laws of the State of Louisiana," *New Orleans Republican,* September 22, 1868, 4.

49. "In the Byways: Fences," *Daily Picayune,* June 1, 1873, 6; "Stolen Property—The Way Burglars Dispose of Their Gains," *Daily Picayune,* November 20, 1870, 2.

50. "The Junk Shop Raid," *Daily Picayune,* October 8, 1868, 1.

51. "More War upon Junk Stores," *New Orleans Republican,* August 5, 1868, 3; Baker, "The Loose Cotton Economy," 77–78.

52. Wendy A. Woloson, "In Hock: Pawning in Early America," *Journal of the Early Republic* 27 (Spring 2007): 35–81.

53. "In the Byways: Fences," *Daily Picayune,* June 1, 1873, 6.

54. "Examination on a Charge of Receiving Stolen Goods," *New Orleans Times,* March 17, 1864, 5; "First District Court," *Daily Picayune,* May 22, 1864, 8.

55 "Dissolution," *Daily Picayune,* January 22, 1865, 5; *Edwards' New Orleans Directory* (New Orleans: Southern Publishing Co., 1870), 540; "The Loan Office, No. 17 Baronne Street," *New Orleans Republican,* June 7, 1873, 3; "Personal," *New Orleans Times,* October 24, 1875, 12.

56. S. Jacobs, "Recorder Long's Court," *Daily Delta,* July 30, 1858, 2; "Recorder Vennard's Court," *New Orleans Times,* April 1, 1865, 3.

57. Harold Sinclair, *The Port of New Orleans* (Garden City, N.J.: Doubleday, Doran, 1942), 202.

58. Sinclair, *Port of New Orleans*; John B. Hutchins, *The American Maritime Industries and Public Policy, 1789–1914* (Cambridge, Mass.: Harvard University Press, 1941), 542–44.

59. John Smith Kendall, *The History of New Orleans* (Chicago: Lewis, 1922), 600.

60. Arnesen, "Race and Labour in a Southern US Port," 42. For a taste of the corruption endemic to the shipping business in New Orleans, see Albany de Grenier de Fonblanque to Marquess of Salisbury, June 21, 1880, FO 5/1734, National Archives, Kew, England. On corruption more generally, see Paula Baker, Mary Berry, Daniel Czitrom, Barbara Hahn, James Kloppenberg, Naomi Lamoreaux, and David Witwer, "Interchange: Corruption Has a History," *Journal of American History* 105 (March 2019): 912–38.

61. Eric Arnesen, *Waterfront Workers of New Orleans: Race, Class, and Politics, 1863–1923* (Ur-

bana: University of Illinois Press, 1994), 21, 39; Colin J. Davis, *Waterfront Revolts: New York and London Dockworkers, 1946–61* (Urbana: University of Illinois Press, 2003), 38.

62. E. L. Taplin, *Liverpool Dockers and Seamen, 1870–1890* (Hull: University of Hull Publications, 1974), 3.

63. Arnesen, *Waterfront Workers of New Orleans*, 39.

64. "Humanity in Our City: Our Poor White People. Among Mechanics, Longshoremen, and Laborers—At Their Firesides, with Their Wives, Sons and Daughters. Hard Times—Grocery Credit and the Wonders of Daily Life," *New Orleans Times*, February 23, 1873, 5.

65. John Lovell, *Stevedores and Dockers: A Study of Trade Unionism in the Port of London, 1870–1914* (London: Macmillan, 1969), 31.

66. "The Longshoreman of New York," *Greensboro (N.C.) Daily News*, February 13, 1916, 27; Rene Bache, "Unskilled Workers Grow Old More Quickly Than Well to Do People," *El Paso Herald*, July 1, 1916, 29.

67. "Rescue Horse from Water," *Brooklyn Daily Eagle*, January 28, 1915, 11.

68. Sinclair, *Port of New Orleans*, 166.

69. Arnesen, "Race and Labour in a Southern US Port," 43.

70. "The Roustabout," *Richmond Beacon* (Rayville, La.), July 28, 1877, 2.

71. "In Re Roustabouts," *New Orleans Crescent*, January 3, 1869, 4.

72. *Roustabouts*, in *Every Saturday* (Boston), September 2, 1871, 233.

73. Lovell, *Stevedores and Dockers*, 11–29.

74. Ari Kelman, *A River and Its City: The Nature of Landscape in New Orleans* (Berkeley: University of California Press, 2003), 22–23.

75. Sinclair, *Port of New Orleans*, 168.

76. Kelman, *A River and Its City*, 24.

77. Kelman, *A River and Its City*, 19–28; Sinclair, *Port of New Orleans*, 168.

78. Kendall, *History of New Orleans*, 600.

79. Arnesen, "Race and Labour in a Southern US Port," 41.

80. Arnesen, "Race and Labour in a Southern US Port," 42.

81. Sinclair, *Port of New Orleans*, 173.

82. Christopher Morris, *The Big Muddy: An Environmental History of the Mississippi and Its Peoples, from Hernando de Soto to Hurricane Katrina* (New York: Oxford University Press, 2012), 156–58.

83. Arnesen, "Race and Labour in a Southern US Port," 45.

84. Karl Marx, *Capital: An Abridged Edition*, ed. David McLellan (Oxford: Oxford University Press, 1995), 352.

85. Joe Gray Taylor, *Louisiana Reconstructed, 1863–1877* (Baton Rouge: Louisiana State University Press, 1974), 322, 326.

86. In London, where the work was controlled by dock companies that ran particular docks, longshoremen tended to stick with a particular employer rather than going elsewhere, even if it meant waiting for work. With the employers in New Orleans being the stevedores, since the wa-

terfront was more open, regular laborers focused instead on them (Lovell, *Stevedores and Dockers,* 32–33).

87. "Recorder Vennard's Court," *Daily Picayune,* July 21, 1865, 8.

88. John K. Bardes, "Redefining Vagrancy: Policing Freedom and Disorder in Reconstruction New Orleans, 1862–1868," *Journal of Southern History* 84 (February 2018): 70.

89. Bardes, "Redefining Vagrancy," 73 (quotation), 88.

90. Bardes, "Redefining Vagrancy," 69, 85.

91. Arnesen, *Waterfront Workers,* 271–72n24.

92. Rhoda Halperin, *The Livelihood of Kin: Making Ends Meet "the Kentucky Way"* (Austin: University of Texas Press, 1990), 19.

93. Rhoda Halperin and James Dow, eds., *Peasant Livelihood: Studies in Economic Anthropology and Cultural Ecology* (New York: St. Martin's, 1977). For further methodological discussion, see Colin Murray, "Livelihoods Research: Transcending Boundaries of Time and Space," *Journal of Southern African Studies* 28 (September 2002): 489–509.

94. Marx, *Capital,* 317–23.

95. Bardes, "Redefining Vagrancy," 70; John W. Blassingame, *Black New Orleans, 1860–1880* (Chicago: University of Chicago Press, 1973), 1.

96. Bardes, "Redefining Vagrancy," 77–84.

97. Blassingame, *Black New Orleans,* 1.

98. Scott P. Marler, *The Merchants' Capital: New Orleans and the Political Economy of the Nineteenth-Century South* (New York: Cambridge University Press, 2013), 187–88.

99. Ted Roselius and Douglas Benton, "Marketing Theory and the Fencing of Stolen Goods," *Denver Law Journal* 50, no. 2 (1973): 192–94.

100. Robert Lee, "The Seafarers' Urban World: A Critical Review," *International Journal of Maritime History* 25 (June 2013): 26–27.

101. Kenneth Lipartito and Lisa Jacobson, "Introduction: Mapping the Shadowlands of Capitalism," in *Capitalism's Hidden Worlds,* ed. Lipartito and Jacobson (Philadelphia: University of Pennsylvania Press, 2019), 6, 8, 10–11.

The Violent Lives of
William Faucett

ELAINE S. FRANTZ

The Civil War era was one of the most violent times in U.S. history. In its distribution, that violence skewed to the South, but even within the South, certain areas stood out as particularly violent. Union County, South Carolina, was one such place. President Ulysses S. Grant considered it so violent that it was one of nine counties he placed under martial law in the fall of 1871. Even within that county, however, only a minority took advantage of the chaotic place and time by living lives of violence. Among these, one man stands out: William Faucett. Too predictably short of capital to be called a capitalist, and never even close to respectable enough to hold an office, William Faucett nevertheless played a crucial role in the deeply corrupt economic and political life of Civil War–era Union County. While he was extraordinary in his prolific use of violence, he was a recognizable type in the mid-nineteenth-century South—a bully who made himself strong enough and useful enough to be feared, tolerated, and, at times, embraced, by economic and political elites. The extractive capitalism that characterized the region required the constant and pervasive use of violence against enslaved people and anyone else whose interests conflicted with those of local elites, but it also shaped a system in which middling and poor men and women regularly used and suffered violence as they navigated their own political, economic, and social relationships. Faucett's life reveals the continuity of the economic and political violence central to the chaotic capitalist system of the rural South. Criminal violence, violence against women, the violence of personal masculine competition, and white-on-black violence all afflicted his home county in the nineteenth century.

Historians often depict the Reconstruction-era Ku Klux Klan as sprouting from seed sewn in southern soil during the Civil War. But the life of William

Faucett—a man for whom the label "scoundrel" is too generous—reveals that, while Klan terrorism took its own form, it was radically nourished by structures of status oppression in place well before the war's disruptions.

The William Faucett who is the subject of this essay had a cousin in Union County, also named William Faucett (I will call him "Pinkney William Faucett" here), who will appear briefly as his foil, modeling a life William Faucett might have lived had he been less extraordinarily committed to violence. Both William Faucetts were born in South Carolina around 1810: white, illiterate, and economically marginal men.[1] Both appear to be from Pinkney District, fifteen miles east of the county seat of Unionville, and situated along the Broad River, where York and Chester Counties bordered Union County, home of the Faucett clan since before the census of 1790. Pinkney was the whitest district in Union County. The county's population was majority black, with 8,718 white and 10,530 black residents in 1870. In contrast, Pinkney District was predominantly white, presumably because its land had not been ideal for plantation slavery. In 1870, it had 1,451 white and 962 black or mulatto residents.[2]

Both William Faucetts were examples of what Keri Leigh Merritt has described as "masterless men": marginal, illiterate white men with unstable lives who existed in frequent tension with elites. Both were usually without property, though their fortunes varied over their lives. The fact of their poverty, and the poverty of many of those, black and white, with whom they interacted, keeps receding to the background of the narrative, only because it was a gnawing constant in their lives. These two men, the women and children who were forced to depend upon them for food, shelter, and physical safety, and most of the people they variously allied with and attacked, owned nothing and had no safety net beyond their family and neighbors. When they did interact with local elites, those interactions were always informed by the urgency of their need and by elites' understanding of their own precarious position in this always unstable economic structure. The violence that "masterless men" like William Faucett engaged in so frequently absolutely must be understood in the context of an immediate, pressing struggle for survival.[3]

Brothers Samuel and Richard Faucett appear to have been the fathers of the two William Faucetts.[4] The William Faucett who was Richard's son, who will not be the focus of this essay, seems to have lived his entire life in Pinkney.[5] In the 1850 census, he appears as a thirty-nine-year-old laborer living in a propertyless household headed by forty-seven-year-old Rebecca Hampton and including sixteen-year-old Mary Hampton and six-year-old Nancy Hampton.[6] In 1860, Rebecca Hampton continued to head the still-propertyless household. Mary and Nancy were still at home, along with William, who was now listed as a "farmer." Both Rebecca and William aged slowly. He was listed as forty-five and she as fifty-five.[7] Around fifty years old when the Civil War started, William joined Capt. James M. Gadberry's company of the first regiment of South Carolina volunteers in January 1861.[8] By 1870, a purportedly sixty-year-old William Faucett headed a household boasting a modest $200 in real property, containing Rebecca Faucett (allegedly sixty years old), thirty-five-year-old Mary Faucett, and a three-year-old boy named Vernon Faucett. William, apparently, had finally married his longtime companion and been promoted to household head, and they had somehow acquired a child.[9] In 1880, Pinkney William Faucett was on his own again, a sixty-eight-year-old widower, boarding with a middle-aged woman named Sarah Floyed and her two children in Unionville.[10]

Pinkney William Faucett's life was neither easy nor peaceful but was perhaps standard for a man of his time and station. Union County was a place in which people felt the struggle for survival, and he, too, seemed to have navigated his share of conflict. He periodically gave bond for his neighbors, and even once for Rebecca and Mary, when they became involved in disputes that grew to the level where they involved the courthouse.[11] And no one in the county was far from the everyday violence white citizens used to keep their black neighbors down. One election day in 1869, Faucett walked through the streets with another middle-aged man, Charles Garner. As they approached a group of black children who were wrestling each other in the street, Garner singled out fifteen-year-old Billy Gist, engaged him in banter, and then surprised him by swinging his deerhorn-tipped cane at him, hitting his head with a cracking sound heard by those nearby, knocking him to the ground, and causing blood to flow down his face. Billy reported himself still "addled" at the later trial. All witnesses, white and black, attested to the friendly response Billy had given Garner's banter and vividly described the blow Billy absorbed. Faucett, in contrast, defended his friend in court. He alone had heard Billy taunting Garner and had not noticed Garner's blow.[12]

It seems likely that Pinkney Faucett maintained some connections to his more violent cousin, the other William Faucett, though it is striking that they never appear together in any records. They had been raised close to one another, and their adult social groups overlapped. Still, we must consider Pinkney William Faucett personally peaceful by the standards of that time and place. If he engaged in any violence himself, those conflicts were resolved without bringing in the local government.

The William Faucett who was Samuel's son was another matter. He had moved from Pinkney across the county by the time he was young man, and by 1840 had a farm near Cedar Bluff plantation on the far side of Unionville. He was not a complete stranger there. A close neighbor in Cedar Bluff, Samuel Sumner, was named in his uncle's will back in Pinkney. William Faucett's domestic structure was even less conventional than his cousin's. In the 1840 census he headed a household with an adult woman and two small children. In 1850, he appeared, apparently in the same place, as a forty-year-old illiterate "planter" worth $1,200, owning fifty-six improved and ninety-four unimproved acres of land, with some cows, horses, and cattle, growing cotton, wheat, Indian corn, oats, and sweet potatoes. His household included Penelope Faucett; their sons Isaac Faucett, fifteen, and John Faucett, thirteen; and two girls— nine-year-old Jane Sumner and seven-year-old Minerva Sumner.[13]

By the 1860 census, the Sumner girls had disappeared, Faucett's now-adult sons had left home, and Faucett had lost both his farm and his wife. He appeared as a fifty-two-year-old laborer heading a propertyless household in Unionville. Keeping house for him was a twenty-five-year-old woman named Elizabeth ("Lizzie") Willard. Also in the home was an older woman named Narcissus ("Narcissa") Willard and a four-year-old boy named William Willard. When the war came, Faucett enlisted in the Confederate army, mustering in on December 17, 1861, eleven months after his cousin had done so. He joined Company B of South Carolina's Eighteenth Infantry regiment. After only five weeks, he was listed as absent without leave.[14]

In 1870, the last census in which he appears, Faucett was recorded as a sixty-year-old with $125 in personal property living in Unionville, with twenty-nine-year-old Victoria Faucett keeping house. Also in his household was a twenty-nine-year-old black woman named Jane Faucett, a twenty-year-old black woman named Emlie ("Emily") Jeter, three white children listed as "Nancy Faucett (4)," "Sallie Faucett (3)" and "Th[omas] Faucett (1)," and a seven-year-old black child named "Mary Faucett."[15]

William Faucett's life was defined by an array of conflicts. The first and most pervasive were his competitive conflicts with white male neighbors and companions. He frequently fought with his neighbors over large things and small. We cannot know how many of his conflicts were resolved informally, but we should assume that the ones that made it to the courthouse were the tip of the iceberg. Between 1852 and 1878, Faucett played a role in more criminal indictments in the county than did any other person with the exception of one man who served as a sort of professional bondsman. In 1853, for instance, Faucett accused a neighbor of stealing his axe.[16] In August 1855, Leonard Fowler charged Faucett with drawing a knife and threatening to kill him. The following month, Faucett claimed that Leonard, together with two relatives, attacked him with a stick.[17]

In 1858, Faucett jumped into a new round of conflicts, posting bond for a man who accused another man of assaulting him on a public highway.[18] When a circus came to town a week later, and his friend Samuel Sumner got into a fight there with three men, "drawing pistols and clubs," Faucett posted Sumner's bond.[19] A few weeks later, Faucett himself got into a brawl in front of the county courthouse with a man involved in the earlier fight on the public highway. Thomas Jackson, the man whom Faucett fought, was also a familiar face at the courthouse and had recently been convicted, fined, and imprisoned for trading with an enslaved man. Nevertheless, the sheriff may have indicated his partisanship in the quarrel when he personally posted Jackson's bond.[20]

The records tell us little about Faucett's conflicts during the war. Having deserted, he may well have been at home, and surely it was a particularly violent time, but the courthouse hardly functioned during the war and early Reconstruction, and, quite simply, no one in wartime Union County was likely in a position to arrest him. Union army officers attempting to keep order in the county after the war named a close friend of his, but not him, a troublemaker. As indictments in Union County ramped back up in the late 1860s, however, Faucett comes back into focus, still fighting with his poor white neighbors. In February 1869, for instance, he got into a fight in his own yard with a small man disabled by a bad foot. When the man tried to run away, Faucett hit him with a wooden rail, then called for someone to bring him an axe. The man, presumably desperate, stabbed Faucett six times. The court found him not guilty of the assault charge Faucett brought. Four months later, in June, another man stabbed Faucett in the arm. In 1872, still another anxious white neighbor requested a peace warrant against Faucett.[21]

In addition to continuing to fight with white male neighbors, Faucett after the war seems to have been spending more time socializing and drinking with a group of particularly bellicose men. The conditions of war and Reconstruction may have drawn these unusually violent men together. In early July 1869, Faucett's sometime-friend Tom Hughes stabbed him in the throat, marking the third time Faucett was stabbed in a six-month period. A few weeks later, a serious fight broke out in a barroom involving Faucett's close associate T. Jefferson Greer. The quarrel ended with another man getting shot. Faucett witnessed the fight and testified at the ensuing trial. Two years later, when Tom Hughes shot Jefferson Greer with a shotgun, Faucett witnessed that as well.[22]

Faucett's relentless brawling tells us both about him and about everyday life in Union County. While his more pacific cousin was sometimes drawn into ugly conflict, violence was a routine part of this William Faucett's life. Any man interacting with him would have been wise to bear the possibility of violence in mind. This violence was not organized around feuding. Faucett could ally with a man at one moment and fight with him at another. But simply because many of Faucett's confrontations were barroom fights or fights among acquaintances does not mean that they were playful. Jeff Forret's reference to the "shadowy subculture of conviviality and violence" seems apt here. Faucett's violent encounters, and those that swirled around him, could be truly dangerous, with combatants often threatening to kill each other and using deadly weapons. The fights seemed to emerge from quarrels, and to be competitions for limited resources and for status which, as Forret has discussed, can be read as a poor white variant of "honor culture."[23] Faucett lived within a particularly chaotic corner of a more generally chaotic system in which some men regularly felt required to engage in mortally perilous conflict. Given the dire situation families found themselves in when male breadwinners were killed or incapacitated, these were desperate struggles indeed.

While Faucett almost exclusively used violence against other marginal men, elites often had more than a passing interest in these fights. It was prudent to keep a wary eye on power relationships among even their meaner neighbors. Occasionally elites were pulled more directly into Faucett's sphere. Particularly before the war, Faucett sometimes involved himself in conflicts that involved local elites—challenging them or trying to win their favor. In 1855, on the same day that Faucett alleged that Leonard Fowler and his relatives had beaten him with a stick, he also alleged that another neighbor, a wealthy planter in his sixties, had thrown a rock at him.[24] In April 1856, a man named William James, likely a thirty-five-year-old overseer, accused Faucett's by-then-adult son Isaac of hitting him with his fist, wielding a knife, and threatening to cut his throat.[25] A few months later, Faucett confronted James about the accusation levied against Isaac. James claimed that William Faucett called him a damned liar, hit him a severe blow, and grabbed a rock, forcing James to draw his gun. According to Faucett's account, James had tried to convince him to have Isaac implicate a member of the wealthy Bogan clan, also named Isaac, in the earlier assault. When Faucett refused, James called him a damn liar and drew a pistol. Both Faucett and James were convicted, but the judge apparently felt that Faucett bore most of the blame. He fined James a hefty $50, but fined Faucett $100 and sentenced him to ten months in jail.[26] Faucett was by no means chastened by his incarceration. At some point before February 12, 1858, he failed to appear in court in a matter related to the James assault charge, causing his bondsmen, his good friend Samuel Sumner and Charles Bogan (a wealthy planter who lived next to Isaac Bogan and was perhaps his father) to default.[27]

Like many marginal southern whites, William Faucett's antebellum economic and social interests often conflicted with those of elites, as they attempted to maintain their positions in a society where a few men dominated most of the capital and used the government to protect their interests. Jeff Forret and others have explored the many ways that marginal whites like Faucett interacted with enslaved men and women, particularly by trading, drinking, and gambling together. Elites used their control over the local government to punish such interactions between those they enslaved and men like Faucett, but poor whites and enslaved people, out of affinity, self-interest, or necessity, often chose to engage in business (and pleasure) together. Faucett stood behind his friends when their dealings with enslaved people got them in trouble with elites. He gave bond in 1854 for a young, illiterate man who was convicted of trading with a slave. In 1857, he did the same for another man accused of gambling with a slave owned by future governor William H. Gist.[28]

At least some of Faucett's conflicts with both poor men and elites were tied to his entrepreneurial efforts to make a living illegally. As a marginal man accustomed to violence, Faucett quite visibly lived outside of the law, and elites understood that he would make it difficult to subject him to their rules. And despite his many visits to the courthouse, the law generally appears to have given him wide berth. A planter once accused him, along with his son Isaac and two other young men, of cattle stealing, alleging that he had received seven cattle stolen by his son and two friends. Charges against both Faucetts were thrown out (as charges against Faucett often were), but the other two young men were found guilty.[29] That was the only time Faucett was indicted for a property crime. He was never himself indicted for a vice charge, though he was closely connected to Union County's illegal economy both before and after the war. Faucett posted bond for two neighbors in 1856 on a charge of retailing without a license. A Samuel Faucett, likely a brother or cousin running a grocery in Pinkney, was indicted for distilling without a license during the war, and William Faucett's son John was indicted in 1873 on the same charge. And Faucett himself was closely connected to a group of men who allegedly illegally transported whiskey, which had been distilled either in North Carolina or perhaps closer to home, into Unionville barrooms.[30]

Faucett's capacity to use violence, and elites' reluctance to stop him, opened up other opportunities as well. Throughout his life, he surrounded himself with troubled, stigmatized, and vulnerable women. As a young man with a family, he had provided a home to two young Sumner girls. When Nancy White, a former neighbor of Faucett's, in her fifties, was accused of running through the neighborhood committing depredations against her neighbors' property in 1867, he posted her bond.[31] No one's behavior is simple, and perhaps in these instances Faucett was extending patriarchal protection in a nonexploitative way to girls and women not otherwise connected to a male guardian. If he mistreated these vulnerable females, no one brought it to the attention of the court.

But there was more going on in this violent man's affinity for marginal girls and women than paternalistic protection. Take Lizzie Willard, who was keeping house for him in 1860, living with him along with her older female relative Narcissa and the four-year-old William Willard. Lizzie had brought a bastardy case against Monroe Sumner in 1857, so the boy was presumably her child by him. Lizzie seems to have struggled. Not only was she the mother of a bastard child, but she had also been formally charged in 1858 with "Raising a Fuss/ Affray." The fact that the court stepped in to discipline her rather than deferring to a male relative to do so speaks volumes, but also, "Raising a Fuss" appears nowhere else in the county's criminal docket. It was a tailor-made criminal charge, suggesting that the county's powers-that-be were reaching for ways to deal with her. That same year, she accused two women and a man of assaulting her. They consisted of a married couple and a woman named Emiline who shared the Willard surname. The court found the man guilty but recommended him to mercy. One of Victoria Bynum's "deviant" and "unruly" women, Lizzie appeared in court records as immoral, unprotected, and more fundamentally out of control.[32]

We cannot be certain why Faucett chose to live with Lizzie, her son, and her older female relative in 1860. Perhaps this was an act of charity. William Willard was likely the grandson of Faucett's friend Samuel Sumner. Or Faucett may have been romantically attached to Lizzie. (Narcissa is closer to his age, but Lizzie is listed as keeping house.) He may, like his namesake cousin, simply have needed a place to live, though the fact that he was listed as head of household suggests that the census-taker perceived the house to be his. Whatever its purpose, this arrangement did not endure. Lizzie brought another bastardy charge against another man in December 1860. In July 1861, Faucett, with two male friends, went to Lizzie's home, which was apparently by then not also his own, and he "did beat her in a most barbarous manner" as his companions urged him on. Faucett later explained that he had been forced to beat Lizzie because she had thrown stones at his wife. (A lot had changed since the 1860 census.) Lizzie's outrageous behavior, he claimed, "compell[ed] him to use means not common or proper to protect his wife's life."[33]

Two houses away from Faucett and Lizzie in 1860 lived twenty-five-year-old Sarah Vanderford, who headed a household consisting of herself, a thirty-nine-year-old woman, a twenty-one-year-old woman, and a four-year-old child.[34] Like Lizzie Willard, Sarah Vanderford must have been quite marginal. In 1854, at nineteen, she had been indicted for disturbing a Methodist church meeting by "passing through the congregation and cursing and swearing and attempted to take by force a child from Mrs. Mary McDaniel [preacher Lemuel McDaniel's wife] in an insulting manner." In 1857, twenty-two-year-old Sarah was charged, along with a man named James Fowler, with keeping a disorderly house and selling liquor without a license. While the charge of keeping a disorderly house did not necessarily imply prostitution, it is almost certain that when Vanderford's household of three adult women and a fatherless child was called a "disorderly house," prostitution was implied.[35] From 1852 to 1874, there were seventy-two charges for illegal liquor sales and thirty-two for gambling in Union County, but no one at all was indicted for prostitution or keeping a bawdy house. There were, however, six charges of "keeping a disorderly house." The county was either remarkably moral sexually or quite tolerant of prostitution. In either case, it was likely that it used this less-pointed charge on the rare occasions when it decided to confront it. When Sarah Vanderford found herself in trouble with the law, William Faucett posted bond for her.[36] Sarah and Faucett shared enemies as well. In 1859, she had a dispute with Jackson Powell, a longtime enemy of Faucett, which led to a slew of peace warrants.[37]

Emily Jeter—the black woman found in 1870 living with William Faucett, two other women in their twenties, and several fatherless children—had a life that resembled those of Sarah Vanderford and Lizzie Willard. In the summer of 1871, she was accused of assaulting a woman. In 1872, she, in turn, accused a man of striking her with a stick.[38] In 1876, another man apparently assaulted her, using threatening language and drawing a pistol.[39] Even in the violent context of Union County, physical aggression was heavily gendered male. It was unusual for a woman to be involved in one, much less multiple, acts of violence that came to the attention of the court, but like Vanderford and Willard, Jeter lacked the family and reputation that might normally keep a woman safe from public violence. Somehow, in 1870, however, she found a home with William Faucett.

Twinned with Faucett's many connections with marginal women, and particularly marginal women in their twenties, was his close relationship to violence against women. Lizzie Willard was the only woman to bring an assault charge against Faucett, when he claimed to discipline her through a barbarous beating in 1861. We can assume that the vast majority of sexual crimes and domestic violence went unreported in this place and time, as in others. When they could, girls and women relied on other men to protect them from male violence. But violence against women swirled around Faucett. As Freedmen's Bureau agents were trying ineffectively to protect freedpeople in Union County, the local agent reported his unhappiness with his inability to intervene effectively in a telling incident. One Saturday night in 1868, Tom Hughes, a close friend and drinking companion of Faucett, came banging on the door of a black family, searching for a seventeen-year-old black girl who seems to have been hiding from him. When the woman of the house told him the girl was not there, he threatened her with a knife.[40] Faucett reached out a hand to men accused of such violence. He posted bond for a neighbor when an unrelated woman requested a peace warrant against him. The neighbor apparently violated the bond conditions in 1864, presumably by attacking the woman. A few years later, Faucett also posted bond for another man accused of attacking an unrelated young woman with a knife and an iron rod.[41]

Faucett's tendency to surround himself with troubled and disreputable women, together with his immersion in a world of violence, including violence against women, suggests that the rotating cast of marginal young women he lived with and near were engaged in prostitution, as he exploited and controlled them. His own households, as recorded in the 1860 and 1870 censuses, were never formally labeled disorderly houses but were certainly disorderly. In 1860, he lived with two women unrelated to him, two doors down from Sarah Vanderford's disorderly house. In 1870 he lived with three women in their twenties, one white and called his wife, the other two black, one of whom was also listed as bearing his name (though she cannot be found under that name in subsequent censuses). Most tellingly, Lizzie and Narcissa Willard reappear after the war. After Faucett beat Lizzie, she remained embroiled in other troubles. Two women took out a peace warrant against her in 1862. In 1867, Lizzie took out her own peace warrant against a Mary Ann Willard. The court paperwork indicated that the warrant had been rendered unnecessary, since Mary Ann was "imprisoned." In 1868, when a white woman claimed that a black man "seized her in the dark and tried to kiss her," Lizzie served as a witness. Four years later, she witnessed a man assaulting a woman, probably his wife, by beating and kicking her.[42]

Depressingly, the 1870 census found Lizzie living just a few households away from Faucett. She was heading a household that still included Narcissa and her son, and now also three younger, apparently fatherless, children. When the court filed one of Lizzie's many indictments, in 1867, they filed it together with an apparently unrelated one of Faucett's.[43]

Although Faucett had many enemies, both among other marginal whites and among elites, and was often indicted, he was rarely convicted of or punished for his assaults or other criminal actions. The substantial fine and five months in jail for his affray with William W. James was atypical. We cannot know how often Faucett committed offenses for which no one bothered or dared to charge him, but we do know that charges against him often tailed off into a no bill or a dismissal (*nolle pros*). This was common in nineteenth-century courtrooms: prosecutors and defendants even in cases involving violent assault often were expected to come to agreements outside of the court structure. But it could also suggest either that Faucett was often falsely accused, or, more likely, that those who attempted to bring him to justice came to think the better of it. And while Faucett was willing to bring his neighbors before the court, he also seemed to have had substantial contempt for the usually elite-controlled judicial process. He failed to appear for a court date. He fought with a man who had brought formal charges against his son, publicly suggesting that people were sometimes bribed or coerced into bringing false charges. He had a brawl on the street in front of the courthouse, presumably while coming to or going from one of the many cases he was involved in at that time. For that matter, his drinking friends often brawled over who had brought court cases against whom, to the extent that the drinking affrays served as a sort of para-courtroom. It seems likely that Faucett did not make it easy to arrest him. One of his drinking companions once resisted arrest, telling the sheriff that "he was as much a peace officer" as him.[44] Perhaps it took more courage than accusers and trial justices usually had to punish Faucett for his constant criminal behavior. And some elites in power in Union County took advantage of or profited from Faucett's criminal enterprises. The sheriff, for instance, sometimes drank with Faucett's friends and appears to have been a business partner with William Steen, who ran the hotel and barroom in town, which, though licensed, apparently made use of the illegal liquor transportation services of Faucett and his friends.[45]

In some ways Faucett's violent behavior remained constant from the pre- to the postwar years. He continued to fight competitively with white men, to participate in commercial vice, to live with and in close proximity to young women of ill repute, and to dwell in a culture of violence against women. But the war's results, which transferred power over local institutions like the courts from white elites to a new class of Republicans, and notably former slaves, made Faucett's ease with living outside the law, facility with violence, and connections with others who shared the same skills and aptitudes, particularly valuable to the county's white elites and allowed him to reinvent himself and gain their more active support.

Because enslaved people did not have access to the courts and antebellum free black people likely did not expect justice from them, we cannot know whether or how much Faucett had used violence against black people before the war. After the war, however, Faucett aimed much of his personal aggression toward black Union Countians. Many of the incidents tell stories of freedpeople's most basic struggle for existence in (and outside) the new economic system. In 1866, Faucett served as a witness to testify that a freedman had stolen cotton from a person or persons unknown. In the summer of 1868, he brought an indictment against another freedman for stealing bread and beef from him. By the time the case came to trial, the man had died of causes unknown, though we must wonder if starvation was a factor. Faucett also brought a charge of theft against a thirty-eight-year-old black laborer, whom he accused of stealing fifty nails. The laborer claimed it had been a misunderstanding. In 1869, a middle-aged black farmer brought a peace warrant, claiming that Faucett had shot two of his cows and that he feared further aggression from him. That same year, Faucett apparently stabbed another freedman in the arm.[46]

Faucett would have had two reasons to be displeased with the political emergence of black leaders in Union County during the Reconstruction era. The first was racial solidarity. Despite, or perhaps because of, the fact that Faucett had a pronounced tendency to interact across the color line both before and after the war, he was deeply invested in white dominance, aware of the potential economic value of his whiteness, and cognizant of the dangers of black competition for limited resources. The second was that the black men who emerged as leaders of the town seem to have quickly understood that one of their first tasks was to bring men like Faucett and his friends under control. When Ellison Scott, a leader in Unionville's black community, witnessed Faucett stab freedman Joseph Nix in the arm, he may well have convinced Nix to bring an indictment. In any case, he posted bond for Nix to appear at the trial.[47] Consider also Faucett's relationship to Junius Mobley, a mulatto man and a local Republican leader who would soon be elected to serve as a state representative. Two weeks after Mobley was appointed a commissioner of elections, and a few days before the 1868 presidential election, Mobley took out a peace warrant, claiming that he had reason to fear that Faucett would attack him.[48] A month later, presumably as a calculated and retaliatory insult, Faucett took out a peace warrant against Mobley's wife, Amy.[49]

Faucett's contentious relationship with J. Alexander (Alex) Walker proved more fateful. Walker, a highly literate black man, was twenty-three years old in 1870, living in Unionville with his wife, Laura, and their three sons. He was a schoolteacher, elected school trustee, and captain of one of the two colored militia companies in Union County. Calling for a cautious approach to the new political era, he was a voice of reason and moderation with the ear of Governor Robert Kingston Scott, who appointed him as one of Union County's trial justices in the spring of 1870.[50] Walker was determined to control the illegal behavior of men like William Faucett. In July 1870, Faucett threatened a fifty-two-year-old black man named Solomon Hobson with a knife. Walker, likely aware that his authority as trial justice would be challenged, made the unusual choice of bringing in a clerk to take a transcript of Hobson's testimony. Apparently, Faucett had surprised Hobson in his wagon, grabbing his arm, pulling out a knife and threatening to kill him. Hobson jumped from the wagon to defend himself, well aware that Faucett was a "darn old raskall." At that, either Hobson or Faucett said he would give the other "hell." Democratic Sheriff J. Rice Rogers posted Faucett's bail, signaling to the Republican-controlled courts that Union County elites stood behind Faucett. Despite this, and despite Faucett's defense that Hobson had also threatened to "cut my damned life out," Justice Alex Walker found the troublesome white man guilty. Rather than *nolle pros* him, as Walker's white predecessors had customarily done, the black justice sentenced him to serve twenty days in the county jail.[51]

The three-part struggle between the county's disorderly underclass, its old white elite, and its newly established black leadership continued. A few months later, a close associate of Faucett, a drayman and one-armed Confederate veteran named Mat Stevens, was accused of assaulting sheriff's deputy B. Frank Gregory. Gregory responded by demanding peace warrants not only from Stevens but also from his brother-in-law, a notorious brawler named Tom Hughes. Gregory was white, and almost certainly a Democrat, but elite whites chose to support Hughes. Despite the facts that Hughes was one of the most violent men in Union County and had assaulted Deputy Gregory, Sheriff J. Rice Rogers personally posted Hughes's bond. Faucett also signed Hughes's bond, even though Hughes had recently stabbed him in the neck and, on another occasion, had shot his friend.[52]

It is at this moment and in this context of white solidarity against freedpeople that the Ku Klux Klan emerged with remarkable speed and force in Union County. The Klan had no membership roll, and we cannot know with certainty who was involved in it, but William Faucett and his friends had their fingerprints all over it. Klan groups made their first brief but menacing appearance in Union County at the time of the 1868 elections, when they approached and threatened active Republicans, focusing particularly upon political candidates. Meanwhile, armed whites in broad daylight threatened potential voters, stuffed ballot boxes, and assaulted people bringing Republican ballots to polling places. One of the three polling stations where the level of violence successfully prevented Republicans from delivering ballots at all in 1868 was Faucett's old neighborhood of Cedar Bluff.[53] It was only a few days before that election that black political leader Junius Mobley took out a peace warrant against Faucett. Although we have no evidence that Faucett did in fact attack Mobley, we do know that a masked group of the Klan made the rounds in the county one night before the election, proclaiming that if they found Mobley they intended to kill him.[54] Mobley, apparently, was well aware of the living men behind the masks.

The Klan disappeared in Union County for two years after that, returning in the fall of 1870, just after a set of elections disappointing to local Democrats. Andrew McNeace, a prominent Pinkney grocer (and purveyor of illegal liquor), along with two other prominent Democrats, in September alleged that they had fortuitously come upon a circular someone had dropped in front of Steen's hotel in Unionville. The circular outlined a plan, as terrifying as it was implausible, in which Republicans called for Republican martyrs to volunteer to be killed in order to frame Democrats for the crime.[55] It was at this time that Klan groups began moving around at night, attacking Republicans in their homes. On November 8, the Klan killed its first victim: trial justice A. B. Owens, a white Republican leader who lived in Gowdeysville, near Pinkney. A large group of costumed men surrounded his house and threatened to set it ablaze unless he came out. When he did, they killed him.[56]

Union County's Republicans apparently attempted to meet this escalating threat in kind. Five nights later, on November 13, unknown people threw rocks at the homes of Faucett and Tom Hughes. Faucett "made his escape," but the group allegedly approached the house and threatened that they would burn it down if he were within. Within the next month, Klan groups violently assaulted prominent Republicans Drury Going and Giles White in Pinkney, severely wounding them both. This was the moment when the foot soldiers of white supremacy were most decisively mobilized, and we may perhaps see another glimpse of Faucett's relatively more pacific cousin, Pinkney William Faucett. Giles White, a black man who had named a son after Abraham Lincoln, lived only a few houses away from Faucett's friend Charles Garner, owner of the deerhorn-tipped cane. We cannot know, but it is easy to imagine that Pinkney William Faucett played his role in the Pinkney Ku Klux Klan.[57]

An event on New Year's Eve 1870 served as the catalyst to the two most deadly acts of Klan violence in Union County. Two companies of black militiamen had informally gathered within Unionville, near Duck Pond Church, having heard that white terrorists were intending to kill Junius Mobley and white Republican W. F. M. "Bud" Williams. Alex Walker, the leader of one of the militias and always a force of moderation and compromise, was away. One can only imagine their distress over the racial violence that had consumed the county over the past several weeks, as whites had picked off black leaders with seeming impunity. The companies laid in wait along the road until a wagon approached. Honest, well-intentioned people did not drive wagons down roads late at night in the days before pavement and streetlights, so the militiamen would have been on high alert.

The wagon was revealed to contain one-armed Confederate veteran Mat Stevens and Ben Robinson, both neighbors and close associates of the more violent William Faucett, who claimed to be transporting whiskey to Steen's hotel. The militiamen would hardly have been inclined to apologize and wave them along. In fact, these were likely precisely the people they were hoping to intercept. Stevens started talking fast. He was simply on a whiskey run. The black militiamen demanded to see the whiskey. Stevens refused, saying it was in the back of the cart but did not belong to him. If they wanted whiskey, though, he offered to share the personal bottle he had purchased at Robert Greer's grocery. The militiamen did not accept this excuse, and Ben Robinson decided it would be best to make their getaway, whipping the horses forward. Someone shot after the wagon, disabling it, and Robinson and Stevens bolted in different directions. The militiamen caught Stevens, and, after serious arguments among the members, three men took him to a field and shot and killed him, laying his coat over his body and placing his hat over his face.[58]

Meanwhile, Ben Robinson ran to Tom Hughes's house, where, at the late hour of 11:00 p.m., he may well already have known he would find Hughes, Faucett, and a man named William Powell. They immediately headed out to rescue Stevens, only to discover his lifeless body. We have no evidence that any of the militia ever checked the cart to see if Stevens had, indeed, been carrying whiskey. We have to take the word of Robinson, and of Faucett, who claimed to have measured the remaining whiskey and found that only fifteen gallons remained of the original forty-five. Tom Hughes claimed to have found the bottle from which Stevens had been drinking hidden at black leader Ellison Scott's house. He could positively identify it by its particular taste. Grocer (and friend of Faucett) Robert Greer identified the bottle as his own.[59]

If, as it appears, the militia had in fact successfully thwarted a planned Klan raid for that evening, their killing of this marginal white man provoked Union County's whites, rallied local white elites, and lent them justification for a massacre. The white press immediately reinvented Stevens as a harmless drayman, a gentle one-armed veteran, just trying to make a living when his life was cruelly cut short by armed black men in search of liquor. Whites in town mobilized, searching black homes, confiscating guns, and rounding up and arresting dozens of militia members as accessories to Stevens's killing. When residents of one household, living in a home owned by prominent black leader Silas Hawkins, who was not then present, refused to surrender to a party of whites, a standoff and gunfight ensued that left one white searcher dead, further fueling the fire of white retribution. In two massive costumed raids of the jail on January 5 and February 12, 1871, dozens of Klan terrorists killed, respectively, two and ten of the incarcerated men, arriving at the jail each time with a list of names of the doomed. Survivors of the first raid fingered both Tom Hughes and Robert Greer as having been among their costumed attackers, noting that there was also a man dressed as a ghostly Mat Stevens. Since the second raid left no survivors, we know even less about who was involved in it. While we cannot be certain who all of these masked men were, we know from their horses and pricey costumes that many of them were elites. Contemporaries agreed that many of them had come over the Broad River, perhaps via Pinkney.[60]

Whoever was wearing these terrible costumes, their actions smartly served not only elite and marginal whites' purpose of suppressing black efforts to gain political and economic power but also the specific goals of William Faucett and his friends. It is telling that the very first man the Klan killed in these raids was trial judge and militia leader Alex Walker. Walker was universally acknowledged not to have been present at the shooting of Stevens, but he definitely had made life difficult for men like Faucett. White men had arrested him as an accessory to Stevens's murder. Another raid victim was Ellison Scott, the freedman who had testified against William Faucett in 1869 after the stabbing of freedman Joseph Nix, and at whose home Faucett's friends had "found" an incriminating bottle. A third, Joe Vanlew, had had a physical altercation with Tom Hughes in late October 1870, in which Hughes had accused him of putting his hand on his collar.[61]

One consequence of the extraordinary violence of the Klan in Union County during the winter of 1870–71 was that the state and federal government finally took notice and responded in a meaningful way, sending teams of investigators and a military unit. Although countless people spent countless hours testifying about the events in Union County, somehow William Faucett's name never came up. Federal investigators ultimately indicted forty-four men in the jail raids, including close Faucett associates Jefferson Greer, Robert Greer, and Tom Hughes, but not Faucett himself. Perhaps they simply had information we do not, which pointed suspicion away from him. But there is reason to think that, just as Faucett was particularly proficient at avoiding incarceration, Unionville elites deliberately threw federal investigators off Faucett's track. When a congressional committee visited Unionville and grilled a prominent lawyer thoroughly acquainted with Faucett about events leading up to the Klan attack, the attorney vividly recalled that militiamen had attacked the home of Tom Hughes after the murder of A. B. Owens. Somehow, he neglected to mention the second home they had attacked that night (the one more prominently featured in press coverage at the time), which belonged to William Faucett. Faucett was hardly an easy man to forget, but somehow he seems to have evaded arrest in the massive roundup that followed.[62]

Despite his advanced age and good fortune, the "elderly gentleman" William Faucett, now in his sixties, by no means ceased to fight with his neighbors as the forces of Reconstruction receded. On the evening of December 30, 1873, he had a conflict with a twenty-nine-year-old black man from Bogansville, who accused Faucett of striking and threatening to kill him.[63] And on January 6, 1874, Faucett got into his last fight. He squared off against a younger man named George W. Fowler outside of Andy McNeace's bar. There were many witnesses, so we have many details. The most thorough account is the testimony of A. J. Gibbs, who

> saw William Faucett thrust George Fowler backwards against the window of the house now occupied by Smith and Gregory. Faucett had his hand on the breast or near the throat of George Fowler, who while in this position opened his mouth as if choked. The next thing heard were these words of William Faucett, "Oh you've got your knife out have you?" At that moment deponent [Gibbs] saw a common-size pocket knife fall to the ground and saw George Fowler while in a half-bent position and William Faucett in the same position bent over him, Fowler make two or three grabs to get the knife, as soon as he had done so he rose straight up and commenced cutting William Faucett (having opened the knife while in said half-bent position). That William Faucett and George Fowler were standing or rather walking around most of the time they were fighting. Towards the last of the fight however George Fowler either fell or was pushed down on his back and William Faucett fell on Fowler with his face downward, his (Faucett's) head being above Fowler's breast. The cutting was not stopped while in this position nor until John Bevis by force pulled Fowler away. William Faucett was a large man, physically much superior to George Fowler, and was a quarrelsome [illegible] man.[64]

Faucett was "badly cut in twelve or thirteen places" and died a few weeks later.[65] Among those who served as witnesses in Fowler's murder trial was an untraceable "Ms. Eliza Faucett," possibly the same "Lizzie Willard" who had long been so entangled in Faucett's violent life.[66]

Stories of the Reconstruction-era South rarely have a happy ending, and neither does this one. John Faucett seems to have taken up his father's mantle. Two years after William's killing, John Faucett and Andrew McNease's son Daniel, living in Unionville, were indicted for selling liquor together. The prosecutor was Silas Hawkins, and one of the witnesses another prominent black figure, suggesting that black community leaders were still attempting to clean up Union County's underground economy.[67] John was his father's son in other ways as well. Less than a year after Faucett's death, John was indicted for assaulting a thirty-seven-year-old white woman named Mary Shell by "[taking] hold of her," forcing "her to [a] private room [and trying] to make her take her clothes off." He "drew his stick upon her swearing he would strike her."[68]

Meanwhile, the solidarity the Klan had brought between elite and marginal whites remained vital. In 1873, not long before William Faucett's demise, John, while serving as town marshal, had become involved in a "stabbing affray" with several of his father's freedman enemies and political leaders of black Union County: Silas Hawkins, Rock Johnson, Junius Mobley, and Elijah Meng. Faucett's old ally Robert Greer, by then deputy sheriff, reportedly intervened. In a richly symbolic act, Greer wielded Faucett's town marshal's (presumably ceremonial) mace as a weapon against the freedpeople.[69] The Klan was hardly necessary once Faucett's son and Robert Greer held legitimate power. Weaving together criminal, gendered, and racial violence to uphold a deeply abusive system of economic and political relations, another Faucett was making his way through the world.

Notes

1. I did not notice the duplicate William Faucetts when I wrote *Ku-Klux: The Birth of the Klan during Reconstruction* (Chapel Hill: University of North Carolina Press, 2016), because of the less developed state of search engines at the time I was researching, together with variants in the name's spelling. It is sometimes rendered "Fancett," "Fossitt," or "Fancette." Formal documents usually do not distinguish between the two William Faucetts, but occasionally the more violent William Faucett is referred to as "William W. Faucett."

2. *Ninth Census of the United States. Statistics of Population* (Washington, D.C.: U.S. Government Printing Office, 1872), 60, 260.

3. Keri Leigh Merritt, *Masterless Men: Poor Whites and Slavery in the Antebellum South* (New York: Cambridge University Press), 2017.

4. Fourth Census of the United States, 1820, Union County, South Carolina, National Archives Microfilm Series (hereinafter cited as NAMS) M-33, reel 121, p. 153.

5. Manuscript Census Returns, Ninth Census of the United States, 1870, Union County, South Carolina, Schedule 1, General Population, NAMS M-593, reel 1510, p. 547B.

6. Seventh Census of the United States, 1850, Union County, South Carolina, NAMS M-432, reel 859, p. 92B.

7. Eighth Census of the United States, 1860, Union County, South Carolina, NAMS M-653, reel 1227, p. 224.

8. Carded Records Showing Military Service of Soldiers Who Fought in Confederate Organizations, 1903–1927, Roll 0145, South Carolina, "F," 1st South Carolina, RG 109: War Department Collection of Confederate Records, 1825–1927, National Archives.

9. 1870 U.S. Census, Union County, S.C., NAMS M-593, reel 1510, p. 506B. It is suggestive that in 1867, a Hortense Painter brought a bastardy suit against John Faucett, likely the same John Faucett who was the son of the other Faucett. Perhaps John's uncle's family took in the child (State v. John Faucet [May 12, 1866], Box 36, Case 3609, L44158 Union County Court, General Sessions Indictments, South Carolina Department of Archives and History, Columbia [hereinafter cited as UCCI]).

10. Manuscript Census Returns, Tenth Census of the United States, 1880, Union Township, Union County, South Carolina, NAMS T-9, reel 1242, p. 407C.

11. State v. Lemuel Porter (October 11, 1852), Box 34, Case 2659, UCCI; State v. James McCreight, David C. McCreight, Jos. C. McCreight, and T. A. McCreight (December 4, 1857), Box 34, Case 3028, UCCI; State v. Eugenia Farr (May 20, 1871), Box 36, Case 4068, UCCI; State v. J. F. J. G Farr (May 20, 1871), Box 36, Case 4069, UCCI; State v. Rebecca Faucett (May 13, 1871), Box 36, Case 4070, UCCI; State v. Anderson Harris (May 20, 1871), Box 37, Case 4083, UCCI; State v. Mary J. Hampton (May 24, 1871), Box 37, Case 4085, UCCI.

12. State v. Charles Garner (April 13, 1869), Box 37, Case 4433, UCCI.

13. Manuscript Census Returns, Sixth Census of the United States, 1840, Union County, South Carolina, NAMS M-19, reel 516, pp. 200, 199; 1850 U.S. Census, Union County, S.C., NAMS M-432, reel 859, p. 29B.

14. 1860 U.S. Census, Union County, S.C., NAMS M-653, reel 1227, p. 249; Carded Records Showing Military Service of Soldiers Who Fought in Confederate Organizations, Roll 0298, South Carolina, "F," Company B, 18th Regiment, South Carolina Infantry. Narcissa is listed as thirty-five years old in 1860 but was also thirty-five years old, and living with Lizzie, in the 1850 census. She is perhaps either Lizzie's mother or much older sister (1850 U.S. Census, Union County, S.C., NAMS M-432, reel 859, p. 42A).

15. 1870 U.S. Census, Union County, S.C., NAMS M-593, reel 1510, p. 547B.

16. State v. Daniel Worthy (December 31, 1953), Box 34, Case 2986, UCCI.

17. State v. William Faucett (September 25, 1853), Box 34, Case 2799, UCCI; State v. William Faucett, August 15, 1855, Box 34, Case 2867, UCCI; State v. Leonard, G. W., and James Fowler (September 5, 1855), Box 34, Case 2859, UCCI.

18. State v. Thomas Jackson (August 15, 1858), Box 35, Case 3160, UCCI.

19. State v. Benjamin Scott (August 21, 1858), Box 35, Case 3080, UCCI; State v. John Scott (August 21, 1858), Box 35, Case 3122, UCCI; State v. Samuel Howell (August 21, 1858), Box 35, Case 3128, UCCI; State v. Samuel Summer, James M. Askew, John Scott (August 21, 1858), Box 35, Case 3131, UCCI; State v. James M. Askew (August 21, 1858), Box 35, Case 3328, UCCI.

20. State v. William Faucett and Thomas Jackson (September 6, 1858), Box 35, Case 3106, UCCI; State v. Thomas Jackson (June 18, 1856), Box 34, Case 3159, UCCI.

21. State v. John C. Powell (February 10, 1869), Box 36, Case 3966, UCCI; State v. Jackson Powell (June 14, 1869), Box 36, Case 3883, UCCI; State v. William Faucett (September 7, 1872), Box 36, Case 3173, UCCI.

22. State v. H. T. Hughes (July 10, 1869), Box 36, Case 3871, UCCI; State v. Benjamin Hawkins (July 22, 1869), Box 36, Case 4026, UCCI; State v John W. Sanders (July 22, 1869), Box 36, Case 4038, UCCI; State v. H. T. Hughes (August 11, 1871), Box 36, Case 4129, UCCI.

23. Jeff Forret, *Race Relations at the Margins: Slaves and Poor Whites in the Antebellum Southern Countryside* (Baton Rouge: Louisiana State University Press, 2006), 159–62, 183.

24. State v. William D. Gault (September 3, 1855), Box 34, Case 2862, UCCI; State v. Leonard Fowler and Wade Fowler (September 3, 1855), Box 34, Case 2910, UCCI.

25. State v. William W. James (April 20, 1856), Box 34, Case 2841, UCCI; State v. Isaac Faucett (April 18, 1856), Box 34, Case 2959, UCCI.

26. State v. William Faucett and William W. James (October 6, 1856), Box 34, Case 3013, UCCI. The governor later commuted half of Faucett's prison time.

27. State v. William Faucett, Samuel Sumner, and Charles T. Bogan (February 12, 1858), Box 34, Case 3068, UCCI.

28. Forret, *Race Relations at the Margins,* 53–61; State v. Benjamin Whitehead (September 6, 1854), Box 34, Case 2803, UCCI; State v. James M. Littlefield (August 2, 1857), Box 34, Case 3035, UCCI.

29. State v. William Faucett, Isaac Faucett, Fleet Smith, and Thomas Blassingame (April 1, 1858), Box 34, Case 3061, UCCI.

30. State v. Samuel Faucett and Aquilla Bentley (August 6, 1863), Box 35, Case 3536, UCCI; State v. Samuel Faucett (August 10, 1863), Box 35, Case 3544, UCCI; Bruce E. Baker, *This Mob Will Surely Take My Life: Lynchings in the Carolinas, 1871–1947* (London: Continuum, 2008), 22–23.

31. State v. Nancy White (April 17, 1867), Box 35, Case 3118, UCCI.

32. State v. Monroe Sumner (August 29, 1857), Box 34, Case 3016, UCCI; State v. John Turner, Nancy Turner, and Emiline Willard (May 21, 1858), Box 35, Case 3153, UCCI; State v. Elizabeth Willard (May 21, 1858), Box 35, Case 3112, UCCI; Victoria E. Bynum, *Unruly Women: The Politics of Social and Sexual Control in the Old South* (Chapel Hill: University of North Carolina Press, 1992), 89.

33. State v. Marshall Crenshaw (December 19, 1860), Box 37, Case 4589, UCCI; State v. William Faucett, John Garrett, and Rice Faucett (July 24, 1861), Box 35, Case 3434, UCCI; State v. Elizabeth Willard (July 27, 1861), Box 35, Case 3465, UCCI.

34. 1860 U.S. Census, Union County, S.C., NAMS M-653, reel 1227, p. 249.

35. Bynum, *Unruly Women,* 93; Forret, *Race Relations at the Margins,* 202–3.

36. State v. Sarah Vanderford (May 1, 1854), Box 34, Case 2762, UCCI. While Sarah Vanderford was a close neighbor of William W. Faucett, Lemuel McDaniel was a close neighbor of Pinkney William Faucett. Wesley Chapel was located about halfway between Pinkney and Unionville. Pinkney appears to have been where the Vanderford family had its roots (State v. James Fowler and Sarah Vanderford [February 20, 1857], Box 34, Case 2974, UCCI; State v. James Fowler and Sarah Vanderford [n.d.], Box 35, Case 3084, UCCI).

37. State v. Jackson Powell (August 27, 1859), Box 35, Case 3219; State v. Sarah Vanderford (September 5, 1859), Box 35, Case 3216, UCCI.

38. State v. Emily Jeter (June 5, 1871), Box 36, Case 4088, UCCI; State v. Jiner Palmer (December 9, 1872), Box 37, Case 4783, UCCI.

39. State v. Thomas Ivy (August 7, 1876), Box 40, Case 6149, UCCI.

40. A. P. Caraher to Bvt. Maj. H. Heide, February 17, 1868, Unionville, S.C., Subassistant Commissioner of Unionville, Letters Sent, South Carolina, vol. 278, roll 106, target 5, ser. 3360, no. 46, Bureau of Refugees, Freedmen, and Abandoned Lands, National Archives; State v. Thomas Hughes (February 15, 1868), Box 37, Case 4530, UCCI.

41. State v. Jackson Powell (August 21, 1864), Box 35, Case 3559, UCCI [incomplete paperwork]; State v. Hampton Nethers (January 10, 1869), Box 36, Case 3882, UCCI.

42. State v. Lizzy Willard (February 10, 1862), Box 35, Case 3481, UCCI; State v. Mary Ann Willard (March 11, 1897), Box 36, Case 3640, UCCI; State v. William Young (p.c.) (February 3, 1868), Box 38, Case 4994, UCCI; State v. William S. Dupree (October 18, 1872), Box 37, Case 4393, UCCI.

43. State v. William Young (p.c.); 1870 U.S. Census, Union County, S.C., NAMS M-593, reel 1510, p. 547A; *State v. Mary Ann Willard* (March 11, 1867) has incomplete paperwork, is unnumbered, and is filed behind *State v. William Faucett* (December 12, 1868), Box 36, Case 3640, UCCI. The filing system is chaotic: sometimes chronological, sometimes alphabetical, or with logically related cases together and consecutively numbered even when they span a period of time. The cases appear to have been numbered in batches, maybe each year, rather than as they arrived in the courthouse. Sometimes, as in this case, it appears that a clerk (or a sloppy later researcher, though these case files appear not to have been used much, if at all) pulled an already-numbered file or found an unnumbered loose paper relating to a case, then refiled it with other cases they were also looking at in relation to it. In this case, it appears that someone, likely in 1873, took several cases, including Faucett's, which had been numbered then pulled, and a number of unnumbered loose papers, including the 1867 Elizabeth Willard/Mary Ann Willard peace warrant, and placed them in with the most recent cases.

44. Testimony of J. Rice Rogers, in State v. John W. Sanders (July 22, 1869), Box 36, Case 4038, UCCI. This may be more complicated a claim than it seems. Sheriff Rice Rogers appears to have been drinking at the bar when the fight occurred rather than called to the scene, when he evoked his status as sheriff and attempted to arrest the combatant. The combatant in question was T. J. Greer, who did in fact occasionally hold positions of authority in the town.

45. State v. William Steen, H. G. Thompson, and J. Rice Rogers (January 17, 1870), Box 36, Case 3969, UCCI.

46. State v. Adam Thomson, Freedman (November 5, 1866), Box 36, Case 3846, UCCI; State v. W. W. Faucett (July 18, 1868), Box 37, Case 4581, UCCI; State v. John Minter (March 1, 1870), Box 36, Case 4036, UCCI; State v. William Faucett (July 3, 1871), Box 36, Case 4065, UCCI; State v. William Faucett (June 12, 1869), Box 36, Case 3862, UCCI. We cannot know Nix's race, perhaps because he had wisely left the area before the 1870 census, but from the fact that that he was represented by Ellison Scott, we can assume he was black.

47. State v. William Faucett (June 12, 1869).

48. "Commissioners of Election," *Yorkville (S.C.) Enquirer*, October 15, 1868, 2.

49. State v. William Faucett (October 28, 1868), Box 36, Case 3674, UCCI; State v. Amy Mobley (December 12, 1868), Box 36, Case 3721, UCCI.

50. 1870 U.S. Census, Union County, S.C., NAMS M-593, reel 1510, p. 537B; "Trial Justices,"

Daily Phoenix (Columbia, S.C.), May 3, 1870, 2; "School Elections in Union," *Yorkville Enquirer*, May 19, 1870, 2; "Maj. General C. L. Anderson, U.S.A.," *Daily Phoenix*, January 21, 1871, 2.

51. State v. William Faucett (July 1, 1870), Box 36, Case 4018, UCCI.

52. State v. Thomas L. Hughes (November 23, 1870), Box 38, Case 5100, UCCI.

53. Testimony of Simon Farr, in papers of the case of A. S. Wallace v. W. D. Simpson (February 28, 1869), *Miscellaneous Documents of the House of Representatives of the First Session of the Forty-First Congress* (Washington, D.C.: U.S. Government Printing Office, 1869), 49.

54. Testimony of J. A. Walker, in papers of the case of *A. S. Wallace v. W. D. Simpson* (March 10, 1870), Fourth Congressional District, South Carolina, 41st Cong., 2nd sess., Misc. Doc. 17, Additional Papers (Washington, D.C.: U.S. Government Printing Office, 1870), 30.

55. *Daily Phoenix*, reprinted in "Astounding Development," *Sumter (S.C.) Watchman*, September 21, 1870, 2.

56. Drury D. Going to Governor Scott, November 11, 1870, Box 13, Folder 6, Governor Scott Papers, South Carolina Department of Archives and History, Columbia; Inquest for Alfred B. Owens (November 8, 1870), Box 38, Case 5243, UCCI.

57. "Affairs in Union," *Daily Phoenix*, November 17, 1870, 1; 1870 U.S. Census, Union County, S.C., NAMS M-593, reel 1510, p. 487A.

58. *State v. Henry Cannon, Taylor Palmer, Fred. Green* (no date [January 1, 1871]), Box 37, Case 4123, UCCI.

59. *State v. Henry Cannon, Taylor Palmer, Fred. Green* (no date [January 1, 1871]), Box 37, Case 4123, UCCI.

60. *Daily Phoenix*, February 17, 1871, 3. This account of the Klan attacks in Union is more fully explored and defended in Elaine Frantz Parsons, *Ku-Klux: The Birth of the Klan during Reconstruction* (Chapel Hill: University of North Carolina Press, 2016), 238–62.

61. State v. William Faucett (June 12, 1869), Box 36, Case 3862, UCCI; State v. Joe Vanlew (October 29, 1870), Box 38, Case 4954, UCCI.

62. Testimony of James Steadman, *Report of the Joint Select Committee to Inquire into the Condition of Affairs in the Late Insurrectionary States*, vol. 4 [South Carolina, vol. 2] (Washington, D.C.: U.S. Government Printing Office, 1872), 1013.

63. State v. Chess Lancaster (January 6, 1874), Box 37, Case 4673, UCCI; State v. William Faucett (January 6, 1874), Box 37, Case 4428, UCCI.

64. State v. George Fowler (January 6, 1874), Box 37, Case 4430, UCCI.

65. "State News," *Orangeburg (S.C.) News*, February 7, 1874, 3; "State News," *Orangeburg News*, February 14, 1874, 5.

66. State v. George Fowler.

67. State v. Daniel McNeace and John Faucett (May 3, 1873), Box 37, Case 4700, UCCI [incomplete file]; 1850 U.S. Census, Union County, S.C., NAMS M-432, reel 859, p. 58A.

68. *State v. John Foscett* (December 30, 1874), Box 38, Case 5537, UCCI.

69. "A Riot and Stabbing Affray," *Yorkville Enquirer*, September 18, 1873.

Eureka!

LAW AND ORDER FOR SALE IN
GILDED AGE APPALACHIA

T. R. C. HUTTON

T rue equality before the law in a society of greatly unequal men is impossible," wrote Douglas Hay in 1975, but that "truth . . . is kept decently buried beneath a monument of legislation, judicial ingenuity and cant."[1] This was certainly true of late nineteenth-century Appalachia, where all white men had *de jure* access to due process and equal protection, but developments like the long-form deed and declines in the farm and forest economy put mountaineers at a *de facto* disadvantage against railroads and extractive industries.[2] But it was not always law in the courtrooms that opened the mountains to encroaching capitalists. Orderly market-driven societies require law enforcement, especially in a disorderly environment where legitimate jurisprudence was not always respected. Thus the birth of the short-lived career of the Gilded Age's "mountain detectives," rough men bred in the violent, depredated postbellum years who rejected yeomanry and regular wage labor in favor of a mercenary career. Under these unprecedented circumstances, mercenary work became an accepted form of law enforcement that harnessed the public good for private benefit.

The occupation of private detective is difficult to categorize within conventional understandings of separation of labor. It was not statutory law enforcement, although the historical record demonstrates that nineteenth-century private detectives were given essentially the same freedoms as policemen when it came to apprehending malefactors, minus the same degree of public oversight. It was a profession without the status that came almost naturally to nineteenth-century lawyers and physicians, both of whom were considered vital to civil society or to the immediate needs of any given community in the Western world. It could be called an early version of service economy, although its tasks were not menial, and it was a service only affordable to a select, relatively elite, group. Moreover, in the postbellum decades, it became, in some cases, a euphemism for domestic mercenary labor, especially around strike-prone workplaces defined by dangerous wage labor. Men on the margins of the economy could self-style as detectives to hide the fact that their skill set was scarcely greater than that of a particularly adept deer hunter. Gilded Age stresses on the economy made mercenary work all the more attractive for working-age men who found themselves lacking in property or employment, especially in places of great economic disruption like the factory cities of the Great Lakes states, the American Southwest (where the cowboys' droving economy was quickly giving way to mining and speculation), and central Appalachia. Just as these places nurtured mercenary labor due to human desperation, the labor disputes common to the regions supplied ample demand for its services. The occupation of private detective was irrevocably associated with human misery.

The "mountain detective" phenomenon was an outgrowth of the corporate demand for violence and surveillance in the wake of the Civil War, particularly in Appalachian Pennsylvania. Soon after the war, Pennsylvania capitalists recognized the importance of security in and around coal camps to stymie the organizing of unruly miners. Their "Pennsylvania Coal & Iron Police," a private security concern with connections to the famous Pinkerton Detective Agency, was essentially the first formal iteration of what would later be called the "mine guard system." Funded by a cabal of Pennsylvania industrialists, the Coal & Iron Police were on hand to put down the Molly Maguire conspiracy among Irish émigré miners. A few years later, they tried in vain to suppress local flare-ups of the Great Railroad Uprising of 1877.[3]

Industrialists from Pennsylvania and elsewhere in the Northeast began to take notice shortly after the Great Railroad Uprising of 1877 with the development of the Pocahontas and Flat-Top Coal Field in southern West Virginia and southwestern Virginia, and the resultant population boom in the area.[4] This created a new demand for law enforcement that neither state could provide, at least not to the satisfaction of industrialists like Jedediah Hotchkiss or Justus Collins. Even before Hotchkiss's Norfolk & Western Railroad could link the two commonwealths, and long before Collins's company towns were built, the area had to be "tamed."

Unlike in Pennsylvania, the Coal & Iron Police model had had little usage in Gilded Age West Virginia. By the 1880s, Pennsylvania had a bustling extractive and manufacturing economy sewn together by hundreds of miles of railroad track, whereas West Virginia was a sparsely populated woodland, especially in the south of the state where railroads were nonexistent until late in the 1880s. The Civil War had strengthened Pennsylvania, but it laid waste to southern West Virginia's agrarian economy and, in many places, the very cohesion of civil society. Law enforcement in the counties just north of the Virginia line was weak, but not due to labor unrest and rapid urbanization as in the states to the north. Rather, West Virginia and eastern Kentucky suffered from a combination of high fertility, outmigration, and devalued farmland, all adding up to a dispirited generation born around the time of the Civil War, who found their fortunes diminished. Although the mountains were not as violent as some observers claimed, the postwar availability of revolvers and repeating rifles exacerbated a tendency for male homosocial violence made worse by the increased production and consumption of whiskey.[5] And yet it was a relatively egalitarian society, at least among whites, without the same clear social boundary between Irish and Slavic labor, on one hand, and Anglo capital on the other, as seen in Pennsylvania. From an urban, northern perspective, central Appalachia was an unkempt wilderness, and one ripe for the plucking.

The influential but relatively brief career of Alfred W. Burnett, founder of the Eureka Detective Agency, demonstrates the quasi-colonial encroachment of northeastern capitalists into West Virginia, a theme familiar to students of Appalachian history. But it also reveals the important roles that surveillance, propaganda, and violence played in creating the Appalachian coal economy. Burnett was a college-educated Pennsylvania native from a middle-class family who moved to West Virginia a few years before the Pocahontas/Flat-Top bonanza. After trying school-teaching, bookkeeping, and mercantile work, Burnett got involved in various newspapers before hiring on as an agent of the U.S. Treasury Department in the late 1870s. In 1877, he founded Eureka Detectives, "the first agency of the kind South of Mason and Dixon's line," according to one biographer. The agency was incorporated three years later "for the purpose of detecting, arresting and bringing to justice persons charged with the commission of criminal offenses against the laws of any State, or of the United States, or those suspected to be guilty of crime."[6]

For the next decade, Burnett and his agents pursued thieves, murderers, and bootleggers, not always at the direct beck and call of the larger companies, but always with the express interest of "development and civilizing of the West Virginia coal region" and with the maximum degree of press exposure.[7] The public record portrays Burnett as a man of action ready to venture out into unfamiliar territory to capture even the most desperate mountain criminals. In 1880, numerous West Virginia newspapers reported his death at the hands of "a band of outlaws" after he had "gone below" to sparsely populated Fayette County. His safe arrival back in Charleston was reported the following month.[8] A few years later, Burnett was beaten within an inch of his life by two "roughs" while investigating a murder in southern Ohio.[9] Between his own criminal and civil cases, Burnett was sometimes enlisted by federal marshals or local law enforcement to assist in apprehending fugitives or transporting defendants in various cases, most involving theft (although, in 1885, one newspaper mentioned that Burnett was "occupied most of his time doing detective work for insurance companies").[10] After that, his comings and goings, including ventures as banal as a relaxing quail-hunting expedition, were mentioned in newspapers all over West Virginia and Ohio.[11] Like his better-known predecessor, Allan Pinkerton, Burnett understood that public relations were as important to his fortunes as was successful crime-solving. In most cases, the press was happy to oblige. "Capt. Burnett does not advertise himself or his profession in his contact with the public," wrote one Ohio reporter, "and one would not imagine that the smooth spoken, affable gentleman, with his quiet, dignified manners, is a terror to the worst class of criminals, and that one so mild and polished in social converse, is a fearless, iron-nerved official, whose duty it is to face the most reckless and depraved, and who constantly 'carries his life in his own hand.'"[12]

Unlike Pinkerton, Burnett did not establish his reputation as an ardent foe of organized labor, although he vaguely "faced dynamite" during the Hocking Valley, Ohio, coal strike.[13] He was also instrumental in putting down an attempted rail workers' strike in 1885, when, after a delayed payday, "fifteen foreign negroes" (probably recently arrived from Virginia) threatened to stop work on a rail line under construction east of Charleston. Burnett and others arrested most of the men, all of whom were tried by a local justice of the peace under the recently passed "red men's act"—an anticonspiracy state law passed with the explicit purpose of strike prevention—and jailed.[14] Even during normal working conditions, Eureka agents frequently arrested workers and transients for arson or for sabotaging railroads and other industrial properties, often to conceal company negligence and corner-cutting.[15] Suspect motives, like those of the man taken up by a Eureka agent in 1884 for burning stables belonging to a coal company, were rarely mentioned in the press.[16] Essentially, the Eureka agency was a tool of capital, but not an object of blunt force.

Politically, Burnett himself identified as a member of the Greenback Party and, early in his career, had worked at the Greenback organ *League and State*, published in Charleston. He also supported West Virginia's Knights of Labor locals during the close presidential election of 1884 and had directed his party to favor a "combination ticket"—but not fusion, he insisted to a Wheeling reporter—with the Republican Party. Greenbackers, he reasoned, shared the Republicans' protariff plank.[17] That fall, Burnett reportedly made a bet with a Charleston Democrat that, if Republican presidential candidate James G. Blaine did not win by a higher margin than James Garfield's modest victory over his Democratic challenger in 1880, the detective would swim the Kanawha River bank to bank for three hours. (The Democrat, who ended up winning the wager, was to have ridden a blind mule through the Charleston streets for the same number of hours had he lost.)[18] It is unknown if Burnett kept up his end of the bet, but it is clear that Burnett compartmentalized his politics from his profession. Shortly before his death, he ran for sheriff of a northern West Virginia county on the Republican ticket.[19]

Burnett employed a roving band of operatives, many of whom only worked for Eureka contractually, as needed, probably for cash wages. In the early 1880s, a Wheeling newspaper praised one of his agents, W. H. Triplet, as "a catcher of timber thieves and a terror to lawbreakers generally."[20] Eureka agent William Crowe was killed by a "black desperado" named Harry Christian near the Virginia border while transporting a prisoner.[21] William Baldwin, a Virginian who began working for Burnett around mid-decade, drew praise from his employer as "all nerves, full of grit, and one of the quickest men [Burnett] ever saw."[22] In 1888, Burnett reorganized his agency as a publicly traded corporation with Baldwin as one of the first five shareholders.[23] The next year Burnett dispatched Baldwin to southern West Virginia to hunt down an interracial ("mostly negroes," Burnett insisted) troupe of whiskey smugglers numbering more than one hundred men. "The people, particularly the businessmen got tired of this moonshine liquor traffic and retained us to work it up. We have succeeded beyond their expectation and ours," the boss detective boasted to a Wheeling, West Virginia, newspaper. He cited a recent letter from Baldwin that claimed nearly forty arrests.[24] A newspaper closer to the action doubted the veracity of Burnett's "Eureka canard," however, claiming that the agency only sought "notoriety or fame" by spreading "sensational lies about our people."[25]

Like other bounty hunters, many Eureka agents straddled the boundaries between law enforcement and criminality and were often accused of crimes every bit as heinous as those of their quarry. Burnett seemed to prefer operatives who lived incautious, violence-prone lives with access to the Appalachian underworld. In 1887, Dan Cunningham, a deputy federal marshal and former Eureka Detective Agency agent, was implicated in the robbery and murder of a minister in Roane County, West Virginia, and in a series of other violent crimes in the surrounding area.[26] Less than two years later a Eureka detective was apprehended by one of his fellows after being indicted for burning down a machine shop in Ronceverte, West Virginia.[27] Eureka agent H. B. Olliver shot a coal company clerk aboard a passenger train after noticing that the latter man was taking up two seats.[28] In 1891, "a colored barber" employed by Eureka disappeared from Charleston "after having committed an outrageous crime"— probably a rape or sexual assault—against his sister-in-law.[29] Later that year an accused check forger produced a Eureka badge upon his arrest in Pittsburgh.[30] Burnett managed to avoid such personal embarrassments despite his former or extant employees' misdeeds. His business was based on unveiling mysteries and hunting desperate men in an environment that was growing more desperate as the 1880s progressed.

The decade was a crucible for race relations in central Appalachia since many black southerners were just then migrating to the Kentucky and West Virginia coal fields. Burnett recognized that black suspects meant quicker convictions—and, therefore, surer bounty payoffs—in a white supremacist environment.[31] In late 1881, an intruder murdered three white youths in an Ashland, Kentucky, household. Over the next few years, a number of suspects, both black and white, were captured but then either dismissed or acquitted, with some of them almost falling victim to lynch law.[32] Burnett became convinced that the assailant was black and accused or arrested a series of black men in a campaign to exonerate one of the initial three white suspects from nearby Charleston.[33] "Alf. Burnett, the West Virginia detective, still adheres to the opinion that the Gibbons children were murdered by negroes and claims to have testimony that will establish his opinion," a Kentucky newspaper noted in the spring of 1883. Less than two months later, it reported, "Another Negro Arrested [by Burnett] for the Ashland Murders."[34] But, as another paper averred, it was believed in various northeastern Kentucky towns that "the whole matter has been engineered to save the necks of the miserable [white] rascals [who] so richly deserve the death fixed for their crimes."[35] "Some of the colored people," read another, "declare they knew all along the Ashland murder would be 'laid on a nigger,'" and rumors swirled that black citizens of Ashland would attempt to free Burnett's captives.[36] Burnett's partner "retired from the case" and publicly called Burnett's evidence "without foundation." After another acquittal of a black suspect, at least one Kentucky paper called for Burnett's tarring and feathering.[37] Within days a black man who had been Burnett's operative was shot in the leg after being attacked by a mob, and Burnett admitted his mistake (although he recanted his admission early the following year).[38] The white West Virginian whom Burnett was trying to protect signed a statement of innocence, allegedly in his own blood, but he was apparently executed. The case nevertheless continued to roil public opinion.[39] As one newspaper said: "More than three years have gone by and no circumstance has been developed throwing any light on the subject. It is true that detective Burnett arrested some negroes on the charge but the effort was an inglorious failure."[40]

The Ashland murders were probably Burnett's greatest disappointment, but his greatest claim to fame was his agency's role in a series of events the media dubbed the "Hatfield-McCoy feud." As Altina Waller demonstrated in her seminal social history, the pacification of the Hatfields was a tremendous public relations feat for West Virginia industry and an indication that mountaineers would finally become a stable working class, while also a verification of the innate violence of the mountain population. After a series of murders and at least one arson, the U.S. Supreme Court settled an extradition dispute between West Virginia and Kentucky, thus opening up legal manhunts motivated by bounties issued by both sides. In the summer of 1888, Burnett and some of his agents traveled to Kentucky to procure a man named Dave Stratton, who played a minor role in the "feud."[41] Over the next few months, Burnett kept track of affairs in Logan County and discussed them laconically with reporters while his operatives tried to capture men wanted by both states.[42] Nancy McCoy Hatfield, a woman living in Kentucky, kept Burnett abreast of various figures' key movements just across the state line.[43] In an effort to delegitimize Burnett's manhunt, members of the Hatfield family filed warrants for Burnett and his agent William Baldwin on a charge of "conspiracy."[44] Baldwin tangled with members of the Hatfield gang years later after he had started his own agency, but the warrants, which apparently never resulted in arrests or jail time for either detective, served as an odd anticlimax for Burnett's involvement in the matter.

Around the time of his fortieth birthday, Alfred Burnett seemed to tire of active detective work. In 1890, he retained an unnamed Pennsylvania oil company as a client.[45] He left Charleston and moved to a small Ohio River town on the Pennsylvania border near where his wife was raised.[46] Shortly after his aforementioned campaign for sheriff, he died in 1892 at age forty-two, probably from a lung ailment.[47] As a brand, the Eureka Detective Agency essentially died with him, although his protégé William Baldwin carried on his legacy and magnified it. Soon after Burnett died, Baldwin chartered the West Virginia Coal and Iron Police, no doubt inspired by Pennsylvania's similarly named organization.[48] The Pinkerton model of private detection was premised on the permanent imminence of class warfare initiated by labor against capital rather than the dangers posed by rural outlaws. Southwestern Pennsylvania's violent Homestead Strike played out a few months before Burnett's death, and strikes and rumors of strikes were becoming more and more common in West Virginia, especially in 1895. Baldwin probably recognized West Virginia's growing resemblance to its heavily industrialized neighbor to the north, and many of his own early recorded adventures dealt with his disciplining and punishing blacks from the South and Hungarian emigrants from the North.[49] He became the chief detective for the Norfolk & Western Railroad and moved his headquarters from Charleston to the boomtown of Roanoke, Virginia. At a 1905 law enforcement convention, Baldwin was dubbed "the Pinkerton of the south."[50]

A few years later, Baldwin made his own protégé, Thomas Felts, a business partner in the Baldwin-Felts Detective Agency. By the end of 1910, eight railroads employed its services.[51] The Baldwin-Felts Detective Agency went on to become the most notorious antagonist in the West Virginia "Mine wars" while also being involved in southern Colorado's Ludlow Massacre in 1914.[52] It used arguably the most extreme form of what was called the "mine guard system," the application of carceral tactics to the industrial workplace. With dozens, perhaps hundreds, of employees in multiple states, Baldwin-Felts was a far cry from Eureka in the sense that it provided businesses with a service based more around naked violence than arrest and investigation.

For this reason, Alfred Burnett's personal role in the development of Appalachia is not without ambiguity. Burnett was more opportunist than exploiter, a member of the Northeast's ever-shrinking middle class who probably initially saw a move south of the Mason-Dixon Line as a route to survival as much as prosperity. His interest in labor-related politics, coupled with a willingness to exploit racial prejudice for profit, was regressive and repugnant but consistent with white men of his generation. His affiliation with West Virginia's Greenback Party might have been based as much on cynical calculation as were his attempts to find black defendants for the sake of saving a condemned white man. Baldwin was neither a traditionalist nor a visionary innovator. He was an American of decent means who saw economic change and adjusted to it. For all his failings, he was a dealer in information more often than he was a dealer in death. Burnett's practice as a detective went beyond euphemism. He was not just the head of an organization that professionalized violence, as Baldwin later became. Burnett was an actual investigator, a seeker of hidden knowledge like Eugène François Vidocq, the original private detective, a half century before him. For that matter, most of Burnett's more celebrated cases (262 felony convictions out of about 1,200 "general arrests," according to one account) served the public good more than they did the interests of big business.[53] Yet, at the same time, accounts of his arrests and adventures told newspaper readers in the mountains and beyond that residents of the future coal fields were not just, as the *Appalachian Trade Journal* called them in 1899, "stolid hill dwellers" but also a criminal population that required pacification before the law.[54]

And this was what made Alfred Burnett's role in Appalachian history so insidious, if not exceptional: Burnett established law enforcement in southern West Virginia and the riverfront towns of Ohio and Kentucky as a for-profit pursuit. In many ways his detective work was a natural extension of his prior newspaper work. "He observed from his experience that 'if knowledge is power' it is as potent for evil as for good," said a biographical sketch written soon after his death, "that latter day crime is educated to scientific work, and hence abler to act nefariously and escape detection by the ancient system of officials."[55] The "ancient system of officials" referred to the unskilled sheriffs and town constables of the Mountaineer State and neighboring areas who answered to the public but, in an age of concealed revolvers and lynch mobs, often had little to show for it in terms of success. Burnett replaced their constitutionally managed bungling with the sort of expertise that only a college-educated professional (and a northerner to boot) could provide. "By the 1890s many Appalachians themselves had been convinced of the inadequacy of their own culture, and industrialization proceeded with little opposition," Altina Waller concluded in her social history of the Hatfield and McCoy affair.[56] Just as they were finding their culture inadequate, so, too, were they finding their public institutions ineffective and in need of replacement by men like Burnett. It was the beginning of the Progressive era's "search for order," and no one provided order better than experts with guns.

A half century of Appalachian historiography has illustrated the means through which industrialists supplanted yeomen, especially in the verdant hardwoods and coal fields of West Virginia and eastern Kentucky. But, if central Appalachia was truly an "internal colony," it required a *comprador* class that acted as mediator between capitalists and their future employees. It was a class that included lawyers, merchants, newspapermen, and lawmen, most of whom took the part of capital over labor during the Appalachian Gilded Age, but it also included the more restless offspring of the Victorian middle class, like Alf Burnett. The opportunistic dandy probably did not foresee being the forefather of an oppressive labor suppression system, nor did he likely see himself as a tool of capitalism. But Burnett's life and career demonstrate that the eventual struggle over Appalachia was not a stark binary between workers and owners but rather a combination of factors reflecting a deceptively complex society.

Notes

1. Douglas Hay, "Poaching and the Game Laws on Cannock Chase," in *Albion's Fatal Tree: Crime and Society in Eighteenth-Century England* (New York: Pantheon, 1975), 189.

2. The disadvantage of native mountaineers in the early industrial era is a common theme in Appalachian historiography. Among the more important contributions to this theme are Ronald D. Eller, *Miners, Millhands, and Mountaineers: Industrialization and the Appalachian South,*

1880–1930 (Knoxville: University of Tennessee Press, 1982); Wilma Dunaway, *The First American Frontier: Transition to Capitalism in Southern Appalachia, 1700–1860* (Chapel Hill: University of North Carolina Press, 1996); Paul Salstrom, *Appalachia's Path to Dependency: Rethinking a Region's Economic History, 1730–1940* (Lexington: University Press of Kentucky, 1997); and Ronald L. Lewis, *Transforming the Appalachian Countryside: Railroads, Deforestation, and Social Change in West Virginia, 1880–1920* (Chapel Hill: University of North Carolina Press, 1998).

3. Kevin Kenny, *Making Sense of the Molly Maguires* (New York: Oxford University Press, 1998), 107–9; Stephen H. Norwood, *Strikebreaking and Intimidation: Mercenaries and Masculinity in Twentieth-Century America* (Chapel Hill: University of North Carolina Press, 2002), 4, 120–27; Spencer J. Sadler, *Pennsylvania's Coal and Iron Police* (Charleston, S.C.: Arcadia, 2009); Stephanie Hoover, *The Kelayres Massacre: Politics and Murder in Pennsylvania's Anthracite Coal Country* (Charleston, S.C.: History Press, 2014), 19–21; Andrew B. Arnold, *Fueling the Gilded Age: Railroads, Miners, and Disorder in Pennsylvania Coal Country* (New York: New York University Press, 2014), 69; S. Paul O'Hara, *Inventing the Pinkertons; or, Spies, Sleuths, Mercenaries, and Thugs: Being a Story of the Nation's Most Famous (and Infamous) Detective Agency* (Baltimore: Johns Hopkins University Press, 2016), 58, 62–64, 73, 147–48.

4. Bill to *Wytheville (Va.) Dispatch,* Norfolk & Western Financial Documents (1882–1954), box 1, folder 4, Special Collections, Newman Library, Virginia Polytechnic Institute and State University, Blacksburg, Va.; John A. Williams, *West Virginia: A History* (New York: Norton, 1976), 52–54; Jerry B. Thomas, "Jedediah Hotchkiss, Gilded-Age Propagandist of Industrialism," *Virginia Magazine of History and Biography* 84, no. 2 (April 1976): 189–202; Eller, *Miners, Millhands, and Mountaineers,* 48–53, 71–75; Kenneth R. Bailey and Nell Irvin Painter, "A Judicious Mixture: Negroes and Immigrants in the West Virginia Mines, 1880–1917," in *Blacks in Appalachia,* ed. William H. Turner and Edward J. Cabbell (Lexington: University Press of Kentucky, 1985), 117–32; Ronald L. Lewis, *Black Coal Miners in America: Race, Class, and Community Conflict, 1780–1980* (Lexington: University Press of Kentucky, 1987), 129–31; Joe William Trotter, Jr., *Coal, Class, and Color: Blacks in Southern West Virginia* (Urbana: University of Illinois Press, 1990), 9–13, 17–21; Salstrom, *Appalachia's Path to Dependency,* 32, 74–77; Roger Fagge, *Power, Culture and Conflict in the Coalfields: West Virginia and South Wales, 1900–1922* (New York: Manchester University Press, 1996), 17; Sean Patrick Adams, *Old Dominion, Industrialized Commonwealth: Coal, Politics, and Economy in Antebellum America* (Baltimore: Johns Hopkins University Press, 2004), 210–40; Tim Konhaus, "'I Thought Things Would Be Different There': Lynching and the Black Community in Southern West Virginia, 1880–1933," *West Virginia History* 1 (Fall 2007): 25–43; Rand Dotson, *Roanoke, Virginia, 1882–1912: Magic City of the New South* (Knoxville: University of Tennessee Press, 2007), 1–30; Steven Stoll, *Ramp Hollow: The Ordeal of Appalachia* (New York: Hill and Wang, 2017), 166–69.

5. Altina Waller, *Feud: Hatfields, McCoys, and Social Change in Appalachia, 1860–1900* (Chapel Hill: University of North Carolina Press, 1988), 95–97; T. R. C. Hutton, *Bloody Breathitt: Politics and Violence in the Appalachian South* (Lexington: University Press of Kentucky, 2013), 133–38.

6. *Wheeling (W.V.) Daily Intelligencer,* December 4, 1879, and May 15, 1880; *Gallipolis (Ohio) Journal,* May 27, 1880; Point Pleasant (W.V.), *Weekly Register,* November 17, 1880; *Acts of the Legislature of West Virginia* (Wheeling: W. J. Johnston, 1881), 463–64; advertisement, *The Virginias: A*

Mining, Industrial and Scientific Journal, Devoted to the Development of Virginia and West Virginia 4, no. 11 (November 1883): ii; George Wesley Atkinson and Alvaro Franklin Gibbens, *Prominent Men of West Virginia: Biographical Sketches, the Growth and Advancement of the State, a Compendium of Returns of Every Election, a Record of Every State Officer* (Wheeling: Office of the Daily Intelligencer, 1890), 915–18 (quotation 915).

7. *Roanoke (Va.) Times*, January 3, 1893, p. 4.

8. *Weekly Register*, November 17, 1880 (quotations); *Charleston Journal*, quoted in *Gallipolis Journal*, December 16, 1880.

9. *Wheeling Daily Intelligencer*, August 16, 1884; *Belmont Chronicle* (St. Clair, Ohio), August 28, 1884; *Wheeling Daily Intelligencer*, August 18, 1884.

10. *Wheeling Daily Intelligencer*, June 5, 1884; *Wheeling (W.V) Register*, June 25, 1885; *Wheeling Register*, August 31, 1885.

11. *Wheeling Sunday Register*, September 28, 1884; *Hocking Sentinel* (Logan, Ohio), October 29, 1885; *Wheeling Sunday Register*, January 25, 1885.

12. *Hocking Sentinel*, October 8, 1885.

13. Atkinson and Gibbens, *Prominent Men of West Virginia*, 917.

14. *Wheeling Register*, July 24, 1885. The Red Men's Act would become far more well-known during the early twentieth century's West Virginia "Mine wars." Burnett's arrest of the dozen or so black workers in 1885 may have been the first arrest ever initiated in its name.

15. R. Scott Huffard, "Perilous Connections: Railroads, Capitalism and Mythmaking in the New South" (Ph.D. diss., University of Florida, 2013), 182–229.

16. *Wheeling Daily Intelligencer*, May 30, 1884.

17. *Wheeling Daily Intelligencer*, May 30, 1884; *Wheeling Daily Intelligencer*, October 22, 1884; *Weekly Register*, November 8, 1892.

18. *Indiana State Sentinel* (Indianapolis), November 12, 1884.

19. *Weekly Register*, July 26, 1892.

20. *Wheeling Daily Intelligencer*, August 7, 1883.

21. *Wheeling Daily Intelligencer*, July 18, 1891.

22. *Wheeling Daily Intelligencer*, April 4, 1889.

23. *Wheeling Daily Intelligencer*, July 9, 1888.

24. *Wheeling Daily Intelligencer*, April 4, 1889. Baldwin also had a side job investigating "illegal Republican voting" in a southern West Virginia town, but Burnett refused to comment on that since "that was not [Burnett's] side in politics."

25. *Braxton (W.V.) Democrat*, quoted in *Weekly Register*, April 17, 1889.

26. *Wheeling Register*, October 20, 1887; *Shepherdstown (W.V.) Register*, October 21, 1887; *Shepherdstown Register*, October 28, 1887; *Wheeling Intelligencer*, November 1, 1887; *Wheeling Register*, November 17, 1887; *Wheeling Intelligencer*, November 25, 1887; *Evening Star* (Washington, D.C.), October 21, 1887.

27. *Staunton (Va.) Spectator*, February 6, 1889.

28. *Roanoke Times*, October 9, 1890.

29. *Wheeling Daily Intelligencer*, February 7, 1891; *Shepherdstown Register*, February 13, 1891.

30. *Wheeling Daily Intelligencer,* July 18, 1891.

31. Williams, *West Virginia,* 52–54; Bailey and Painter, "Judicious Mixture," 117–32; Trotter, *Coal, Class, and Color,* 9–13, 17–21; Konhaus, "I Thought Things Would Be Different There," 25–43; Karida L. Brown, *Gone Home: Race & Roots through Appalachia* (Chapel Hill: University of North Carolina Press, 2018).

32. *South Kentuckian* (Hopkinsville), January 10, 1882.

33. *Hazel Green (Ky.) Herald,* April 1, 1885.

34. *Daily Evening Bulletin* (Maysville, Ky.), April 27, 1883; *Daily Evening Bulletin,* June 13, 1883; *Daily Evening Bulletin,* June 14, 1883; *Bourbon News* (Millersburg, Ky.), June 15, 1883; *Daily Evening Bulletin,* June 16, 1883.

35. *Semi-Weekly Interior Journal* (Stanford, Ky.), June 15, 1883.

36. *Daily Evening Bulletin,* June 15, 1883.

37. *Daily Evening Bulletin,* June 18, 1883; *Semi-Weekly Interior Journal,* June 19, 1883.

38. *Daily Evening Bulletin,* June 20, 1883; *Daily Evening Bulletin,* June 21, 1883; *Bourbon News,* June 15, 1883; *Daily Evening Bulletin,* February 24, 1884.

39. *Daily Evening Bulletin,* March 27, 1885.

40. *Daily Evening Bulletin,* March 6, 1885.

41. Waller, *Feud,* 219–20.

42. *Wheeling Daily Intelligencer,* October 17, 1888.

43. "The Dramatic Story of a Mountain Feud," *Current Literature* 1, no. 5 (November 1888): 417.

44. *Evening Star,* January 21, 1889.

45. *Wheeling Daily Intelligencer,* May 9, 1890.

46. *Hocking Sentinel,* March 25, 1886.

47. *Weekly Register,* November 8, 1892; *Hocking Sentinel,* November 10, 1892; *Shepherdstown Register,* November 18, 1892; *Spirit of Jefferson* (Charlestown, W.V.), November 22, 1892; "Average Reports," *The Medical Brief: A Monthly Journal of Practical Medicine* 20, no. 9 (September 1892): 1138.

48. *Weekly Register,* November 8, 1892; *Acts Passed by the Legislature of West Virginia at its Twenty-Third Regular Session, Beginning January 3, 1897* (Charleston: Will E. Forsyth, 1897), 149.

49. "Manifesto and Platform: Local Richmond, Socialist Party" (undated), Socialist Party of America: State and Local, 1902–1981, box 9, folder Virginia, Printed Ephemera Collection on the Socialist Party (U.S.), Collection PE 032, Series II, Tamiment Library & Robert F. Wagner Labor Archives, New York University; "A Bloody Fight between Negroes, Hungarians and Detectives," *Roanoke Times,* July 8, 1890; "Riot on a Train," *Pittsburgh Dispatch,* July 11, 1890; *Evening Star,* July 11, 1890; *Evening Bulletin,* July 11, 1890; *Wheeling Intelligencer,* July 11, 1890; *Wheeling Intelligencer,* July 19, 1890; *Roanoke Times,* May 31, 1895; *Wheeling Register,* June 9, 1895; David Alan Corbin, *Life, Work, and Rebellion in the Coal Fields: The Southern West Virginia Miners, 1880–1922* (Urbana: University of Illinois Press, 1989), 25–46; David Brody, *In Labor's Cause: Main Themes on the History of the American Worker* (New York: Oxford University Press, 1993), 142–43; Kazuko Uchimura, "Coal Operators and Market Competition: The Case of West Virginia's Smokeless Coalfields and the Fairmont Field, 1853–1933," *West Virginia History* 4 (Fall 2010): 65–66.

50. *Richmond Dispatch,* November 26, 1898; *Evening Star,* May 24–25, 1905.

51. *Tazewell (Va.) Republican*, October 6, 1910; *Richmond Times-Dispatch*, February 18, 1911.

52. Graham Adams, Jr., *The Age of Industrial Violence, 1910–1915: The Activities and Findings of the U.S. Commission on Industrial Relations* (New York: Columbia University Press, 1966); Howard B. Lee, *Bloodletting in Appalachia: The Story of West Virginia's Four Major Mine Wars and Other Thrilling Incidents of Its Coal Fields* (Morgantown: West Virginia University Press, 1969), 17–47; George S. McGovern and Leonard F. Guttridge, *The Great Coalfield War* (Boston: Houghton Mifflin, 1972); John A. Williams, *West Virginia and the Captains of Industry* (Morgantown: West Virginia University Library, 1976), 251–52; Elliott J. Gorn, *Mother Jones: The Most Dangerous Woman in America* (New York: Hill and Wang, 2001), 173–94; Anthony DeStefanis, "Violence and the Colorado National Guard: Masculinity, Race, Class, and Identity in the 1913–1914 Southern Colorado Coal Strike," in *Mining Women: Gender in the Development of a Global Industry, 1670 to the Present,* ed. Laurie Mercier and Jaclyn Gier (New York: Palgrave Macmillan, 2010), 195–212; Thomas G. Andrews, *Killing for Coal: America's Deadliest Labor War* (Cambridge, Mass.: Harvard University Press, 2010), 233–86; Corbin, *Life, Work, and Rebellion*, 87–136; Trotter, *Coal, Class, and Color*, 17, 51–51; Robert Shogan, *The Battle of Blair Mountain: The Story of America's Largest Labor Uprising* (New York: Basic, 2004), 6–7, 41–42; Norwood, *Strikebreaking and Intimidation*, 133–40; Frederick A. Barkey, *Working Class Radicals: The Socialist Party in West Virginia, 1898–1220* (Morgantown: West Virginia University Press, 2012), 85–86.

53. Atkinson and Gibbens, *Prominent Men of West Virginia*, 917.

54. Thomas, "Jedediah Hotchkiss," 202.

55. Atkinson and Gibbens, *Prominent Men of West Virginia*, 915.

56. Waller, *Feud*, 234.

CONTRIBUTORS

BRUCE E. BAKER is Reader in American History at Newcastle University. He is the author or editor of a number of books on the history of the American South, including, with Barbara Hahn, *The Cotton Kings: Capitalism and Corruption in Turn-of-the-Century New York and New Orleans*, and, with Carole Emberton, *Remembering Reconstruction: Struggles over the Meaning of America's Most Tumultuous Era*.

JIMMY L. BRYAN, JR., is professor of history at Lamar University. He is author of *The American Elsewhere: Adventure and Manliness in the Age of Expansion* and *More Zeal Than Discretion: The Westward Adventures of Walter P. Lane*, and editor of *Inventing Destiny: Cultural Explorations of U.S. Expansion* and *The Martial Imagination: Cultural Aspects of American Warfare*.

ALEXANDRA J. FINLEY is assistant professor of history at the University of Pittsburgh. She is the author of *An Intimate Economy: Enslaved Women, Work, and America's Domestic Slave Trade*. Her article "'Cash to Corinna': Domestic Labor and Sexual Economy in the 'Fancy Trade'" appeared in the *Journal of American History*.

JEFF FORRET is professor of history and Distinguished Faculty Research Fellow at Lamar University. His books include *Williams' Gang: A Notorious Slave Trader and His Cargo of Black Convicts*; the Frederick Douglass Prize–winning *Slave against Slave: Plantation Violence in the Old South*; and *Race Relations at the Margins: Slaves and Poor Whites in the Antebellum Southern Countryside*.

ELAINE S. FRANTZ is professor of history at Kent State University. She is author of *Ku-Klux: The Rise of the Klan in the Reconstruction Era* and *Manhood Lost:*

Fallen Men and Redeeming Women in the Nineteenth-Century United States. She is currently working on two projects: a history of policing and life outside the law in nineteenth- and twentieth-century Pittsburgh, and a history of the 1874 Women's Temperance Crusades.

T. R. C. HUTTON teaches history and American studies at the University of Tennessee. He has published *Bloody Breathitt: Politics and Violence in the Appalachian South* and various essays in *Jacobin*, the *Tribune*, and the *U.S. Intellectual History* blog. He recently contributed an essay to the anthology *Appalachian Reckoning: A Region Responds to "Hillbilly Elegy"* and is currently completing a history of the University of Tennessee's Knoxville campus.

JOHN LINDBECK is chairman of the History Department at Norfolk Academy in Norfolk, Virginia. He earned his Ph.D. in history from the University of Mississippi. His dissertation is titled "Slavery's Holy Profits: Religion and Capitalism in the Antebellum Lower Mississippi Valley."

MARIA R. MONTALVO is assistant professor of history at Emory University. She completed her dissertation, "The Slavers' Archive: Enslaved People, Power, and the Production of the Past in the Antebellum Courtroom," at Rice University.

RODNEY J. STEWARD is associate professor of history at the University of South Carolina, Salkehatchie. He is author of *David Schenck and the Contours of Confederate Identity* and a forthcoming manuscript exploring Confederate sequestration in greater detail.

JEFF STRICKLAND is professor of history at Montclair State University. He is the author of *Unequal Freedoms: Race, Ethnicity, and White Supremacy in Civil War-Era Charleston* and the forthcoming *All for Liberty: The Charleston Workhouse Slave Rebellion of 1849*.

INDEX

Subentries enclosed in square brackets are names of enslaved people, who often lack surnames in the written records. The enslaver's name appears as the main entry.